More Praise for In Search of Kinship

"*In Search of Kinship* is a book aglow with soul and heart and love and truth—and a prose that sings and dances and paints pictures and takes photographs. What *Kinship* is is a masterpiece. ... Yes, the book is about loss of tradition and the search for new traditions, but the quintessence of *Kinship* is more than that. It is a book about seeing beneath things ... and that beneath everything human and earth-bound lies a network of kinships as wondrous as life itself."

—Dale L. Walker,
Rocky Mountain News columnist

"I love this book—it touches me deeply, as the land does. Seeming to speak from the Mother Earth herself, it also articulates the words in my heart. *In Search of Kinship* takes us where we need to go in our awakening to an ecology of the sacred—from our ancestors' voices to those of the children."

—Brooke Medicine Eagle,
author of *Buffalo Woman Comes Singing*

"This book holds the power and passion to touch the core of kinship in every one of us. ... [Page's] insight is born of love—for the land, for her family, and for the spiritual connection that holds all creation in a web of togetherness. *Kinship* doesn't leave the reader where it found her—or him. It lets the reader soar, with Page, on the wings of an eagle, see the land as it is, and share the commitment of its heritage. If you are looking for hope, take this book with you. It will guide your journey and light your way."

—Gaydell Collier,
author of *Basic Horsemanship*

In Search
of
Kinship

In honor of the land,

Page Lambert

In Search *of* Kinship

Modern Pioneering on the Western Landscape

PAGE LAMBERT

Fulcrum Publishing
Golden, Colorado

Cover illustration: oil on panel "Caribou Tracks," copyright © 1996 Judith Currelly/Diane Farris Gallery, Vancouver, B.C.

Book design by Deborah Rich

The author would like to thank the following for permission to reprint:

Excerpt from *Prayers of Smoke*, copyright © 1990 by Barbara Means Adams. Reprinted by permission of Celestial Arts, P.O. Box 7123, Berkeley, CA 94707.

Library of Congress Cataloging-in-Publication Data

Lambert, Page.
    In search of kinship : modern pioneering on the western landscape / Page Lambert.
        p.   cm.
    ISBN 1-55591-266-4 (hardcover)
    1. Lambert, Page.   2. Sundance Region (Wyo.)—Biography.   3. Ranch life—Wyoming—Sundance Region.   4. Ranchers—Wyoming—Sundance Region—Biography.   5. Wyoming—Social life and customs.   I. Title.
F769.S86L36   1996
978.7'13—dc20
[B]   96-4321
                                                                                      CIP

Printed in the United States of America

0 9 8 7 6 5 4 3 2 1

Fulcrum Publishing
350 Indiana Street, Suite 350
Golden, Colorado 80401-5093
(800) 992-2908

Portions of this book have appeared in the following publications: *Borderland; Bugle, Journal of Elk and the Hunt; Casper Star Tribune; The Christian Science Monitor; Country Magazine; Country Extra; Cow Country; Guideposts; Parabola: Magazine of Myth and Tradition; Reader's Digest; Tumblewords*, University of Nevada Press; *The Stories That Shape Us: Contemporary Women Write About the West*, W. W. Norton; *Westering; Wren*; and *Wyoming, Hub of the Wheel*. Excerpts from this book were awarded a Fellowship for Excellence in Literature by the Wyoming Arts Council.

Contents

Acknowledgments

My father, Loren Dunton, has always carried the lance of a warrior. I thank him for his courage. My mother, Jane Dunton, has taught me the secret of the willows. I thank her for her gentleness.

I am indebted to my circle of friends at Bearlodge Writers, especially Gaydell Collier and Jeanne Rogers, and to Mike and Kathy Gear for their loyal support and endless encouragement. My utmost appreciation goes to my editor, Carmel Huestis, and to Win Blevins, for his timely guidance. To my sister, Brooke, for the chance to spiral inward. To my beloved husband, Mark, and my children, Matt and Sarah—for without them, there would be no stories.

And finally, in a circle of thankfulness, to God, and to the land and all her relations, for sustenance.

The Dawning of Connection

*The old people came literally to love the soil. They sat on the ground
with the feeling of being close to a mothering power. It was good for
the skin to touch the earth, and the old people liked to remove their
moccasins and walk with their bare feet on the sacred earth.*

—Luther Standing Bear[1]

I AM A WOMAN—of French, Dutch, Scotch-Irish, English, and
a small amount of Cherokee ancestry. Born in the suburbs
of Denver, in the foothills of the Rockies, I now live on a small
ranch near Sundance, Wyoming, with my husband, Mark, and our
two children, Matt and Sarah. We have lived here since the mid-
1980s with a few sheep, cows, horses, many whitetail deer,
porcupines, coyotes, and an occasional curious red fox. Our home
sits at the base of the Bear Lodge Mountains, part of the Wyoming
Black Hills. The history that is part of this land has slowly been
permeating my spirit, molding it, awakening it.

Beginning with our migration north to Wyoming, these stories
are linked to the land—stories of Mark and our children, of aborted
foals and orphaned calves, of summer fawns in the meadow, and of
their fathers, the bucks, in the fall.

Rooted in the old and ancient, these stories are about loss
of tradition and the quest to find new traditions. The heritage
bequeathed to Mark by five generations of ranchers who
reared their families beneath the shadow of Colorado's Wildcat Mountain tie him firmly to the soil. I eagerly adopted his
traditions from the moment we began our courtship, from the first
time we kissed, lying in a field of sweet purple alfalfa blossoms.

And now, seventeen years later, my own traditions struggle to be born.

Kinship chronicles our new life on a small Wyoming ranch and our search for answers. While the Supreme Court debates the right-to-die issue, I watch Romie, the half-Arab mare I have ridden for twenty-five years, become gaunt and gray. While the houses of Congress do battle over day-care legislation, I dry Sarah's tears and reassure her that tomorrow is Saturday and Mommy won't have to work in town. Barn-marauding raccoons kill three kittens. Simon, our mother cat, moves the only surviving kitten from one hiding place to another. I envy Simon's empowered maternal instincts and become angry at my own impotence.

A fellow writer from New York once asked me, "How are you, out there in Wyoming, connected to the grid?" I pictured his "grid" as a tangle of computer signals, fiber optics, and floating faxes—mass communication supplying endless up-to-the-minute facts and figures that buzzed over my head in a relentless race from coast to coast. The image caused me to take a deep breath as the weight of the grid bore down.

What I wanted to say, but did not, was this: I find connection by keeping my feet firmly rooted to the earth, following the paths of the whitetail deer, not the Dow-Jones average. I escape through wooded oak clusters, brushing imaginary cobwebs from my hair. Sanctuary is not found within four walls but high on a ridge where, lying on my back, I take long breaths. Echoes of the five o'clock news fade. The sky trail of a jet airplane wisps away. Blue sky appears. The resonant call of a hawk echoes off the ridge top. He soars above the hay meadow where the burrows of prairie gophers ripple the land. The winter-brittle stalk of a sage plant pushes into my back. I tug at the seed of a hound's-tongue weed sticking to my jeans, Velcro® in the embryonic state. I begin to feel the dawning of connection—not to our fast-paced life of politics and economics, but to this high ridge and rusty sandstone soil. I am linked to the earth's skin through the ashes of my ancestors, a blood relative to the wind and woods.

Had this question been asked of me when I was a twenty-four-year-old office supervisor with a financial planning firm in downtown Denver, my answer would have been very different.

Mark's ties to the land tethered my restlessness and brought into focus what I had always felt but in twenty years of city living had never prioritized. Beneath three inches of concrete sidewalk lies the earth. Through this seemingly impenetrable barrier, the lonely soil beckons. Layered beneath my modern genes, generations of earth-linked ancestors, dark-skinned and light, whisper timeless pleas. *Reconnect with the animals. Reconnect with the earth. Reconnect with your creator.*

Long before Mark and I strolled through his great-grandfather's apple trees, the Ute Indians camped on a bluff near Wildcat Mountain. Long before the days of barbed wire, the Arapaho used the waters of Plum Creek to guard their hunting grounds from the fierce Ute. Long before we transplanted our roots into the sage-soils of Wyoming, the Cheyenne and Lakota kept sacred the Black Hills.

To understand this land, the land the Delaware Indians called *Wyoming*—"upon the great plains"—would take more than a lifetime, more than one or two generations. She has begun to teach me of her history, allowed me to feel the rhythm of her heartbeat. Her hills embrace me, her winds clear my mind, her landscapes leave me vulnerable.

A few miles east of Sundance is a sinkhole two hundred feet across and fifty feet deep. Used between 1500 and 1850 by the Plains Indians to trap buffalo (probably the Shoshoni, Arapaho, Crow, Kiowa, Kiowa-Apache, Lakota, and Cheyenne), the bones of twenty thousand animals are buried here, along with thousands of artifacts. It is one of the best-preserved bison-killing sites in North America.

One day, after I discussed the excavation site with a friend, we drove toward Sundance Mountain, a lofty mass of land with gentle eastern slopes and steep, rugged western cliffs.

"I want to show you something," Jeanne said, slowing the car down. "Look at the mountain—see the shape? See how it looks like a buffalo lying down? There's his head, sloping back to his haunches. See it?"

I did see. Like a timeless prehistoric creature, the mountain rose up from the prairie, the shadow of a buffalo silhouetted against the eastern sky. *Like the old buffalo bull back in Colorado when I was a child, the one who rested beneath the pine trees, a massive boulder rounded smooth by time. With huge horned head erect and dull eyes staring, he would rise, hind legs and undersized haunches first. He would unbuckle his front legs. The hide that covered the knee joints was rubbed hairless. I never tried to outstare him but left him to his dusty memories.*

But this buffalo had no legs. Massive shoulders, rubbed hairless, were darkened with pine trees. And deep within the once fiery igneous core, a heart atrophied.

The Makaha of the Oglala (a division of the Lakota) believe that, according to ancient prophecy, we are living in the last days of the Fourth World, when all the hair is gone from the hide of the buffalo and he stands on his last remaining leg.[2] Spirituality, which has been overwhelmed by the physical in each succeeding world (as the human race progresses through each age) is now almost totally hidden. The fourth age represents the final revolution of time before spirituality once again surfaces from the murky depths where modern man has forced it to dwell.

According to folklore, in the ancient days of the Lakota, First Buffalo spoke to an herb gatherer and said, "My tribe and I will come back to you in great numbers. Use us wisely, for one day we will go back into the mountains again. And when we have gone, the Indians will be no more."[3]

We must find a way to return First Buffalo to a state of wholeness. The heart of the people, *all* people, must awaken. For if the buffalo does indeed disappear into the mountain, he will also take with him the antelope and the deer, the great winged-ones of the sky and the crawling-ones of the soil. He will even take with him his cousins, the long-horned Texas cattle, the Scottish Angus, the holy white cows of India—yes, even the domesticated four-legged creatures of the white man—for deep within their atrophied hearts also stirs a wildness, a long-forgotten power.

Kinship's stories, about this Wyoming land and the animals with whom we share it, have been influenced by people who walked the deer paths and held the same ancient rocks in their bronzed hands centuries ago. When I stare at Sundance Mountain, I think of the Fourth World prophecies of the Lakota, not only of the sacred buffalo standing on one remaining leg, but also of White Buffalo Calf Woman who came more recently to the Oglala. She brought hope to the people and restored a sense of dignity, honor, and power to all women.

When I kneel and rub the leaf of a silver sage between my fingers, I think of her, and of the young girl who, long ago, wished to lay a gift at the altar of White Buffalo Calf Woman but was so poor that she had nothing to give but a bouquet of dried, brown weeds. I smell the pungent sage and am reminded that, according to the Oglala story, it was the girl's genuine, simple faith that turned the weeds to silver sage. I think, also, of my deaf grandmother, Effie, living as a young wife in the middle of the Mojave Desert, plucking a single stalk of sage to lay upon her pillow. And of my paternal grandmother, Helen, whose own trail of ancestral tears has marked my path, and the paths of my children, in ways I have yet to understand.

When I hike to the top of the ridge and lie on my back, sometimes I hold my breath so that not even the sound of my breathing is a distraction. The sage-scented wind floats around me, blowing through my hair, touching upon my bare cheek. I hear the gentle sound of breathing and know it is not my own. Whose then? The young Oglala holding her bouquet of weeds? My pioneering grandmother Effie, her long silken hair coiled wreath-like upon her head? Grandmother Helen—painful stories of Oklahoma buried beneath her slightly darker skin? Perhaps all three. Perhaps their breaths have become the wind, their shadows the shifting clouds that caress the red-topped buttes.

I listen for their whispers. They tell me to smell the sage, to hear the old stories, to see the hope ... .

Prologue

The Barn Inherited

R ED WYOMING DIRT, LIKE BITTERSWEET MEMORIES, clings to the stringy roots of the amaryllis bulb. I peel back translucent, slippery layers of skin, baring white flesh beneath. The strong odor of onion makes my mouth water.

These wild onions grow on the high places of our Wyoming ranch, reminding me of the wild Colorado mountain onions I ate as a child. We moved from our mountain home to the fringe of the city, where horse pastures and hay fields rubbed up against encroaching asphalt avenues. To the north of this home, spread like royal carpet, was a golf course. To the east, wild cottonwoods gathered along the banks of the South Platte River. To the south, the golf course ended and farmland began. Green, closely cropped fairways gave way to timothy and brome grasses. Golden fields of wheat arched gently in the summer breezes.

During hot, still days I meandered down to the river and sat for hours by a frog pond hidden in thick clusters of reeds and willows. I walked the sand-washed shores of the Platte in search of petrified wood, finding more often a reassuring solitude where my thoughts could swirl, uninterrupted, within the eddies of my mind.

Had I followed the river south ten miles, I would have come to Plum Creek. Plum Creek led to Indian Creek, and Indian Creek crossed the Lambert Ranch. This ranch, homesteaded in 1862 by my husband's great-great-grandfather, rested in the heart of Indian Creek Valley in the foothills of the Rocky Mountains.

In 1859, three years before Mark's ranch was homesteaded, a settler named John H. Craig staked a claim at the junction of East and West Plum Creeks, building a circular corral on an open expanse of prairie. This corral became a landmark, and its location subsequently was referred to as Round Corral. Ten years later this site would be renamed the Town of Plum, and in 1882 the name would be changed once again—this time to Sedalia.[1]

Local history, and family history, speaks of the Ute, the Arapaho, and the Cheyenne. Stonecalf, a Ute, and his wife, Echensa, Crying Bird, had often camped where John Craig built his round corral.[2] Continual racial tension between the Ute and the Plains Indians caused skirmish after skirmish, and smoke signals rising from Wildcat Mountain were often seen from as far as twenty-five miles away.[3]

By 1869, the Plains Indians were reservation-bound, and the warfare between the two factions subsided—it is believed that one of the last Ute battles took place in a neighbor's meadow adjacent to Mark's family ranch.

The Ute, now able to come and go as they pleased, camped for several summers (during the mid-1870s) on a bluff near the Lambert Ranch. Chief Colorow once teased Mark's grandmother's uncle, wishing to trade ponies, beads, and masks for his fair-haired baby boy. But to the family, it was no joking matter. "I remember pulling on Mother's skirts," wrote an older sister, "and begging her not to make the trade."[4]

Had I walked upriver from the frog pond by the river where I spent my childhood, I would have arrived at Indian Creek. I would have seen Mark, with his dark hair cut close and his brown eyes brooding, picking apples from the orchard below the barn or riding bareback on his horse, Quickflower. His 4-H calf, the one he raised from his first cow, would be drinking the cool creek water. Or Mark might have been hunting for arrow points out in the horse pasture. Or perhaps he leaned against the old barn, out of the wind and on the sunny side—gently chewing on a piece of hay. Perhaps his father stood beside him, digging small holes in the dirt with his boot, looking for the glimmer of his lost wedding ring.

A small frame house, erected on the same spot where the original log cabin used to be, stood next to an imposing brick ranch house. Mark's great-grandfather, the son of a stonecutter, built the brick house back in 1909 but chose to live out his last few years in the old log cabin—the same cabin Mark lived in as a boy, the same cabin in which his great-great-grandfather homesteaded.

Nearby is the thirty-foot-tall stone applehouse, built from stones handpicked and carried from the fields. Here the family processed cider and vinegar. Twenty-eight thousand apple trees, planted in 1894 by Mark's great-grandfather, provided the fruit. An ingenious gravity-fed irrigation system carried water to each tree. Hereford cattle grazed the surrounding pastures, and alfalfa fields blossomed purple each summer.

The death of Mark's grandfather ended these special years. While I spent summer days vacillating between the frog pond on the river's edge and the golf course, Mark's life changed dramatically. With the death of the patriarch in 1957 and the encroachment of Denver, life on the ranch turned bitter. Siblings fought with siblings, cousins fought with cousins. Like divorced parents fighting over custody, the heirs pulled at the seams of the ranch, finally tearing asunder the carefully quilted life of their ancestors. The man-made boundaries of the ranch would not yield to the needs of the many heirs.

Much later, during the early years of our marriage, partitioning proved impossible, and even the courts could not find an equitable way to split the land. Valuable water rights on Indian Creek were impossible to divide. Denver reached greedy fingers toward the flesh of the ranch while the heart of the ranch, already broken, began to atrophy. The land would be sold.

In 1965, spring runoff and June rains filled the mountain creeks to overflowing. Swollen, fast-moving Indian Creek fed her waters into Plum Creek; Plum Creek raced downhill, spewing tons of rainwater into the Platte. Stranded ranchers paced up and down washed-out roads. Mark stood and watched the debris pile up, huge cottonwoods cast about like pieces of driftwood. He felt cast aside himself, adrift in the cold war waged by the heirs of the ranch.

Downstream, the Platte River left her banks, spreading destruction over the land. A twenty-five-foot wall of water raced toward our home on the golf course, depositing three feet of mud and live fish in our living room. The house, pushed off its foundation, was no longer worth the mortgage.

Snow fell on the wild onions of childhood and lay heavy upon the sagging roof of a grandfather's barn. It melted and flowed downhill into streams leading to creeks crossing fertile ranchland. Dirt from the high country mingled with the river bed. White amaryllis seeds washed downstream coming to rest amid layers of city-bound topsoil. Buffalo bones were unearthed and lay naked, unrecognized, among the bones of Hereford cows and spotted ponies. A wild onion sprouted upward through the eye socket of a parched skull.

Mark and I stood miles apart on the threshold, unaware. The barn, built on high ground, was safe but orphaned, the uprooted dreams of his grandfather floating just beyond reach.

The river returned to her bed and a temporary calmness emerged from chaos. Reaching into the denim pocket of his Wranglers, Mark caressed the smooth stone of a Ute arrow point, feeling as helpless to turn the tide as Chief Colorow must have felt when collecting his humbling government rations.

I walked the flood-washed shores, tracing the whirling grain of a piece of petrified cottonwood, looking for signs of life, not yet beginning to spiral inward, not yet in bloom, only just beginning to look to the earth, and to the sky, for answers.

In Search
of
Kinship

1

The Migration

*I will here try to write a bigofery of the blood that flows in my vaines.
Fire has caused all records to be destroyed so I have to trust to my
memory that I have been told and what has transpired under my own
observation. My name is William Thompson Lambert, borned
September 18th, 1850 … .*

THE HANDWRITTEN AUTOBIOGRAPHY that my husband
Mark's great-grandfather wrote on his eighty-eighth
birthday uses up only fourteen small pieces of note-sized
stationery—a page for every six years lived, give or take a few
months. Even Lakota winter-counts, the annual paintings done by the
tribe's historian, would have told a larger story.

The only written record I have of my maternal grandmother
Effie's life begins in 1910 when, as a young wife, she and her
husband homesteaded 160 acres in the middle of the Mojave Desert
(home to the Mohave Indians and later the site of Edwards Air
Force Base).

If I retrace Mark's heritage and mine, our children Matt and Sarah
actually have sixteen great-great-grandparents who lived most of their
lives on American soil. Assuming that each grandparent lived an
average of sixty or seventy years, together their lives would span more
than ten centuries. The two sparse but cherished autobiographies that
exist barely reflect a few breaths of life, let alone a thousand years of
living. And they reveal nothing of true hardship—they mention no
deafness or suicide, no hidden mixed-breed blood.

"It was a happy life and the hardest ten years of my life from
the standpoint of work," writes my grandmother Effie. "But youth
knows no limit … . I have been one of the fortunate to have had that

experience of pioneering. Starting out at scratch." I admire her optimism.

But I wish she had also written of her father's death (my great-grandfather) when she was ten, and of my great-grandmother's suicide less than a year later. I wish she had written about what it was like to find yourself suddenly orphaned, separated forever from your brother and sister, and then sent a thousand miles away to a strange childless aunt living in California. I wish she had written of the anguish she felt when, as a maturing young girl, she stayed in bed for three days, secretly bleeding, thinking she was dying some horrible death because no one had told her about menstruation. I wish she had written about becoming deaf at the age of eighteen, about a world suddenly silent.

There is one line in her journal, however, with a resonant undercurrent that reveals far more about her life in the Mojave than any of the others. "I knew when I saw dust in the distance," she writes, "that it was someone coming to our place, for there was no place else to go. ..."

When Mark's great-great-grandfather died in March 1887, the obituary that appeared in the *Denver News* was written in that era's usual flowery and extravagant manner:

> Death of Joseph Lambert. After a prolonged illness of some four months, another Colorado pioneer passed away at high noon Sunday. His illness gave warning of its fatal nature from its first inception, and the long hours endured by him of patient watching for the note of its ending gave constant evidence of his unfaltering faith, that death was but a birth to a most glorious and unending life—an eternity of extended usefulness and joy.
>
> Mr. Lambert leaves a wife who, with his only son, have been his tireless watchers, ministering to his every want—for his illness has confined him to a chair—to recline was impossible.
>
> He was a native of the State of Maine; a Quaker by birth—a disciple of William Penn. He was a man of iron will and determination, of great force of character, exalted sense of right, a man of sterling integrity, unflinching in the discharge of every trust and duty from

which no influence could swerve him. So long as he conceived in it to be right, he was as immovable as rock.

As immovable as rock—words written about a man who was a stonecutter by trade and later a rancher by necessity and choice—a man who, in 1856, left the civilized streets of Maine to take his Quaker wife and asthmatic son to the healing high-country atmosphere of Colorado. He did not go west to conquer or to kill, despite the dictates of the policy of Manifest Destiny in the nineteenth century or the condemnation of politically correct thinking in the twentieth. Thus sprouted my husband's, and therefore my children's, Rocky Mountain roots, thus began their ancestor's pioneering journey.

I picture Cynthia, Mark's great-great-grandmother, seated on their new Baine Thimbleskane wagon, a few remaining possessions along with a year's worth of edibles loaded behind. She clutches her Bible in one hand and her young son in the other, hoping that Colorado's rarefied air will bring an end to young William's bleeding lung attacks. She smiles bravely at Joseph, her husband the stonecutter, as she tightens the ribbons on her bonnet. He pulls the wide brim of his hat securely down, shading his dark eyes, and moves closer to the yoked animals. Lifting a long leather bullwhip high into the dawn, he calls out to the two teams, urging them onward, urging them westward. The loud crack of the whip's tail splits the air, leaving an invisible welt in the sky. Cynthia's blood races, her eyes open wide, and the wagon begins to move slowly into tomorrow.

One hundred thirty years later Mark and I left Colorado and journeyed four hundred miles north. Instead of two yoke of cattle we had two vehicles: an old green 1974 Ford pickup truck pulling a horse trailer, and a faded red 1976 LTD. Mark led the way, driving the pickup with three-year-old Matthew buckled in next to him. Hondo, our black Lab, and Chinook, an abandoned Great Pyrenees, rode in the trailer. I followed behind, listening to the quiet murmurings of our six-week-old daughter Sarah, who slept strapped in the infant seat next to me.

Our ancestors probably had better sense than to travel across the plains of Wyoming in the hard months of winter. No doubt the

Lakota and Northern Cheyenne knew to stay in their winter camps during the Moon of Frost in the Tipi. Yet Mark and I pushed on, challenging the twenty-four-degrees-*below*-zero weather, scraping the ice from the windows, stopping every two hours when Sarah's hungry whimpers caused my milk to flow.

Were we crazy? To move to a strange place in search of a small ranch that might not even exist? In the dead of winter? Jobless? Dreamless? *Ah, no.* There's the difference. We were full of dreams, and full of fear—fear that our dream was a dream of the past, incapable of surviving in these modern times of "range reform," when ranchland is priced according to its future subdivision potential. The bulldozers had already cut deep swaths into the prairie grasslands beneath Wildcat Mountain. The deer had already retreated farther into the foothills, and the coyotes had begun giving birth to mongrel pups.

Sarah whimpered, pushing against the restraining straps of the car seat, then settled back into an innocent sleep. Dusk had fallen, obscuring the thickening snow clouds that hung ominously overhead. The taillights of the horse trailer glowed red, beckoning me onward. I thought of Mark up ahead and of the fragile roots we hoped to transplant into new soil, new terrain, hoping that the path we traveled wasn't an anachronism, hoping that *we* weren't anachronisms.

I thought of when I first met Mark, eight years before, taking no credit for the impulse that led me one night to a barn dance in a small town south of Denver. I had ridden along on fate's wings, carried by a gracious God with a forgiving nature—and an insistent girlfriend who didn't want to go by herself to meet her date. When Mark, with dark wavy hair, long sideburns, and a broad-brimmed black cowboy hat, approached me, I was caught off balance.

"Wanta dance?" he asked in an easy, rural voice. His brown eyes, flecked with a touch of good-natured orneriness, reminded me of those of Romie, my half-Arab mare.

"No, thank you," I said as I turned away, used to the quick come-ons of the nightclub scene and to men who told tacky jokes, wore three-piece suits, and had one-track minds. I watched Mark out of the corner of my eye. He started away, then pivoted on the heel of his polished cowboy boot and strode purposefully back.

"We're dancing." He took my hand, gently but firmly, and led me onto the middle of the sawdust-covered floor. He was sure of himself. I wanted to know why.

I did not know how to swing-dance country-style. The disco scene was a solitary gyration—partner-dancing rarely occurred. I confessed my ineptitude. Mark was a gracious instructor, smooth despite being slightly intoxicated. We twirled and two-stepped, my waist-long blonde hair flying behind me while my feet hurried to keep time with Mark's. Then the band took a break and everyone went outside to cool off.

The band began the last set. Mark and I twirled to the rhythm of the country music, and the more he spun me around him, the more entranced I became. He held my hand in the air and I pivoted beneath like a moth circling a flame.

We said good-night back outside. He did not try to kiss me but asked, instead, for my phone number.

"I don't usually give out my number on a first date. Besides," I said, "it's a small town. We'll see each other again." My girlfriend's date also knew Mark.

"Denver a small town?" Mark looked slightly taken aback, a little less self-assured. But he recovered quickly, the bit of playfulness in his voice edged with seriousness. "Well," he paused, "I only ask once."

"Then I guess you'll only get one answer," I replied cockily, knowing that he could ferret out my number if he really wanted to. And I hoped he did.

Two weeks later my girlfriend and I again ventured away from the city and stopped in a bar and lounge close to Mark's stomping grounds. A country-western band was about to play the last number of the evening. Our eyes adjusted to the smoky dimness as we walked toward the back of the room. I trailed behind, less courageous. Half-empty tables began to take shape in the subdued lighting.

The lead singer announced last call and couples filtered off the dance floor. Across the room a lone figure sat. I could see Wrangler-clad legs and western riding boots. A dark cowboy hat tipped forward, hiding the eyes. A mustache covered the somber mouth. I slipped along the back wall until I stood behind the seated cowboy and the unmistakable profile. I tapped him on the shoulder.

"I told you it was a small town."

Mark looked up at me. He smiled. "Let's dance."

Once again, he led me onto the dance floor. Only this time it was the last song, and it was a slow song. He pulled his hat down tightly and we began gliding over the floor, floating along to the old Hank Williams tune, "I'm So Lonesome I Could Cry."

I rested my head on Mark's shoulder. Our bodies touched, close one minute, then separating, then close again. We slid across the dance floor in a synchronized rhythm, our arms around each other. The lead singer continued his Hank Williams drawl, singing about nights that never ended, about a loneliness worse than dying.

I didn't know then, of course, about the death of the ranch, about the withering roots and the broken dreams. But even so, I didn't want the song to end, didn't want the lights to come on.

Mark squeezed my hand. His muscles were strong from hard work, his step sure. I breathed in his scent, clean with a faint hint of aftershave. His western shirt had pearl snaps down the front and his large silver belt buckle brushed against my ribs. The singer crooned the last line of the song and I wondered, as the song ended, if Mark knew loneliness as intimately as Hank Williams seemed to.

Mark walked me to the car. This time he asked if he could kiss me without waiting for the answer.

"Aren't you going to ask me for my phone number?" I teased, half afraid that he had been serious when he said he only asked once.

"I've already got it," was his quick reply.

In a few days he called the Denver high-rise office building where I was an office supervisor and spoke to the receptionist.

"Howdy, Ma'am. Is Page there?"

His rural voice and country manners seemed out of place among the perfectly groomed men who walked up and down the halls. But as his forthright manner and old-fashioned charm softened my citified shell, I began to realize that it was I who was out of place.

Our courtship lasted eleven months. Mark drove sixty miles round-trip for each date. The restaurants we ate in were not often fancy, nor were dirty jokes bandied about. His friends tipped their hats and offered me their chairs. We drank coffee in small cafes amidst talk of horses and cattle. The subject of breeding was commonplace and discussed nonchalantly. "How many covers did it take on that mare? She was still open, huh, after all that? ... Scrotal measurement sure is better on those Angus bulls—that's all those damn buyers seem to care about, semen count and scrotal size. Now if you ask me, it's the performance records you got to look at. ... Heard Riley's bull got in with the neighbor's heifers— they're gonna have to pull every one of them calves come spring. Last year it was prolapsed uteruses, this year's gonna be hundred-pound calves. ..."

The cowboys were unaware of how their talk affected me. Country women were used to it, many did the pulling and measuring themselves. Every word had a graphic connotation, a literal sensual meaning—no snide insinuations were made, just basic meaning. Raw and vital.

The city's grip weakened, the weight of the grid lightened. My mare, Romie, my one continual tie to the country, became a regular part of my weekends again. Mark and I rode together through the sage and yucca pastures. We tied our horses to the lanky limbs of the ponderosa pines and hugged standing beneath frost-covered boughs. I blushed when he kissed me.

Late winter turned to early spring. We trailered Romie twenty miles to where a stallion waited impatiently. Romie whinnied and raised her tail brazenly, prancing back and forth in the pen. The stallion was all business and wasted no time. Romie's eagerness embarrassed me. I turned into the north wind, hoping to chill the rising color from my cheeks.

Our courtship continued. One April day Mark took me to his family's ranch. We stood together beneath the apple trees planted by his great-grandfather, and slowly, little by little, he told me the story of the ranch, a story full of sacrifice and heartbreak. Then, on the same night that he told me the story of his father's death beneath those same apple trees, Mark asked me to marry him.

I knew he would only ask once.

2

The Forked Path

WE ENDED UP TEMPORARILY in Belle Fourche, South Dakota, a modest rural town less than fifteen miles from Wyoming's northeast corner and on the northern edge of the Black Hills, where ridges of sandstone and limestone rise from the plains in dark pine green uplifts. A weathered billboard proudly proclaims the town to be the geographical "Center of the Nation and Wool-Shipping Capital." Belle Fourche is French for "beautiful fork," so named because two tributaries of the Belle Fourche River join there. The Belle Fourche flows eastward into the Cheyenne River, whose waters finally join the Great Muddy—the Missouri River.

I knew little of the history and mythology of this area's earlier inhabitants—the American Indians and the pioneering Americans. The land has since demanded, in her own subtle way, that I educate myself. To the southeast, pushing up from the mixed-grass prairie is Bear Butte, as sacred a place to the Cheyenne and Lakota people as was Mt. Sinai to Moses. The Makaha (of the Lakota) believe this ancient volcano to be the source of all souls.

Near here, also, is the highest point east of the Rocky Mountains, Harney Peak (a name abhorred by some of the Lakota, whose ancestors in 1855 were slaughtered by Colonel William S. Harney at Ash Hollow, near the forks of the Platte).[1] It was here that the Oglala medicine man, Black Elk, asked to be taken before he died. From the top of the mountain he cried out to the Great Spirit, "I recall the great vision you sent me. It may be that some little root of the sacred tree still lives. Nourish it then, that it may leaf and bloom and fill with singing birds."[2]

This was for us a testing place, a place of choices. Like the fork in the river, here our lives would choose which path to take. The mettle of our conviction had already been tested when we loaded our belongings and left Colorado. Now the four of us gathered as a family and, no longer near our other familial support systems, would have to learn to lean on one another.

We moved into a small two-story farmhouse on the outskirts of town, the only place available where Hondo and Chinook would have room to run. Cornfields and white Charolais cattle surrounded the farmhouse. Roadside asparagus grew up and down the irrigation ditches, and sturdy hibiscus flanked the fence that separated the yard from the corn. Mark began working for different ranchers: lambing, calving, and putting up hay. During the fall run, he worked late-nights at the livestock sale yards, where cattle were auctioned by the thousands.

I spent hours sitting in the rocking chair nursing Sarah and looking at real estate brochures while waiting for Mark to come home. I hesitated to decorate this temporary home, then succumbed to the nesting instinct and chose pastel pinks, greens, and blues for Sarah's nursery. Matt's upstairs room boasted bright primary colors—reds, yellows, and royal blues.

"Mom?" Matt would ask for the umpteenth time while pointing at a framed woven horse blanket I had hung on the cracked adobe wall. "Why is there a horse blanket on the wall?"

"Because it's special," I would answer.

"Why?" he would ask.

"Because it was Romie's."

"Where is Romie?"

"Back in Colorado with the other horses."

"Why?"

"Because we have nowhere else to keep her yet."

"Why?"

And so the conversation would continue. I did not tell him that perhaps, by the time we found a small ranch of our own, Romie would be too old to make the journey north. Nor did I tell him that the horse blanket, which had rested on Romie's back for more than twenty years, was not just a memento, a tangible piece of the past, but also a link to the future.

Nor did Matt understand the panic in my reprimanding voice when he straddled the large century-old apple cider crock with the words "Lambert Apple Orchard" painted on the side and, kicking, yelled, "Yee hah!" Of the hundreds that were made, it was Mark's only keepsake.

In the spring we picked the wild asparagus from the roadside and meandered through the green fields of corn, feeling the hot Dakota wind on our faces, remembering the cool Colorado breeze that wafted from the mountains down to the foothills, thinking of our families scattered across a thousand miles of country. Hondo, lucky to be only a dog, chased happily after sticks and balls while Chinook slowed him down by hanging on to his tail, enjoying her own version of the game.

In the fall we lit the fire in the woodburning stove with brochures of ranches for sale whose land taxes were so high that only the rich could afford them. We shook our heads to trailer-housed acreages and broken-down homesteads, seeing the ghost of Mark's old ranch in all the skeletal barns and dilapidated sheds. Mark's ranch was not the only victim—hundreds died each year. The causes of death were as varied as were the families forced to move to town: skyrocketing taxes, poor market prices, poor grass (sometimes from overgrazing, more often from drought), or petty quarrels turned to family feuds. Those ranches that survived, cared for by families who had nurtured the land for generations, were not for sale.

I experienced a dawning in Belle Fourche, a centering. The whirlwind that had cast my life about spiraled down into a focused, pivotal purpose. The rivers flowed on, the South Platte of my childhood, and the Belle Fourche of our new life. Their strong currents cut deep banks, and for the first time I began to wonder about the other human beings who had once lived near their shores, forded their waters, and skirted their quicksand. I began to wonder about the Cheyenne and Lakota, and the Crow and Kiowa before them.

In the middle of the night, when I reached across the well-worn sheets for Mark, I knew that he dreamt of the ranch back home, of the sound of the cottonwood leaves and the smell of purple alfalfa blossoms, of the hand-carried stones in the walls of the abandoned applehouse.

It was tempting to give it all up, to take our children back and succumb to city life—buy a nice house in a nice neighborhood near a nice, secure job. But Mark's words, spoken the night he asked me to marry him, left no room for doubt. "Before you say yes," he had said, "I want you to know something—really *know* it." He stared at me, his dark eyes unblinking, unwavering. I listened.

"I will never, and I mean *never*, live in the city."

In 1857, Mark's great-great-grandparents left Maine and headed for Colorado, but they, too, were forced to take up temporary residence partway along the journey—near the home of the Thompsons, relatives living near Muscatine, Iowa, on the shores of the Mississippi River. In his biography, young William mentions a neighbor of the Thompsons, a Mrs. Beebe, who had recently been widowed and therefore was in need of a ranch hand.

"Her place must have been some twenty miles north," William remembered. "We got in a bobsled with a wagonbed and side-boards, the bottom filled with hay, a buffalo robe over us and soapstones heated at our feet. Father sat with the driver. I enjoyed that ride greatly. ..."

"I'd be beholden to you, Mr. Lambert," Mrs. Beebe had asked William's father, "if you'd stay and run my place for me."

"I know nothing about farming," answered Joseph, "for I am a stonecutter, more used to native granite and marble than to cattle or crops."

"All I want is an honest man," Mrs. Beebe answered simply.

And so Joseph began his apprenticeship, learning skills that would be passed on to William, and to William, Jr., and to William, Jr.'s children, to his son, Joseph M., and to Joseph M.'s children, Mark and Keith and Kendra, and then to Mark's children, and to their cousins.

While apprenticing for Mrs. Beebe, Joseph met a Mr. Wilson Kirk, a noted bee man, who hoped to harvest honey on Mrs. Beebe's land. "Father introduced him to Mrs. Beebe," writes William, "and said he believed Mr. Kirk to be an honest man. In a year's time, Wilson Kirk had sold much honey and turned the money over to Mrs. Beebe."

"How much have you left for yourself?" she asked him.

"Not one cent. I love to work, attending those little fellows, they're so industrious."

"Mr. Joseph Lambert has been a great help to me since he first landed in Muscatine and if he had not given you a good word, I do not think I would have found you. The bee raising is very profitable in the sale of strained honey. It is a very healthy food. Mr. and Mrs. Lambert will go west with their son. Be as liberal with him as possible."

The bee money was shared with Joseph, and he then had enough money to continue the journey westward. But three years had passed, it was now 1860, and Joseph feared the way west might no longer be safe for his family, for the Pikes Peak gold rush had hit in 1859. Desperate men, hot with gold fever, were said to roam the hills.

"Thousands of men were on the move, going and coming," wrote Robert Perkin in *The First Hundred Years*. "Draft oxen bawled their discomfort. Wagon wheels strained and creaked, and the long bull whips cracked. Over the whole turmoil, a tumult of shouting, much of it profane."[3] Needless to say, the Plains Indians were not pleased.

"The white men were trespassing again, and their noisy coming frightened away the game. The soldiers had promised that this country where the Rockies rise from the high plains would remain forever a hunting preserve for the Arapahoes and Cheyennes. There had been a pipe and presents to seal the bargain, and the chiefs had pledged their braves to good behavior ... yet now the country swarmed with white men who had come so swiftly and in such great numbers that protest was impossible ... a sweeping flood of men and animals that darkened the prairie."[4]

So Joseph set out by himself for Denver, ending up in Georgetown, Colorado, where he worked cutting stone with large steel hammers. He did not succumb to the gold fever but worked hard saving money, working toward the day when he would be able to bring his wife and asthmatic son to the healing high-country air.

A year later, in 1861, he returned to Iowa for his family, and, together once again, they continued their journey westward, traveling this time in a Baine Thimbleskane wagon. William mentions little about the trip in his autobiography: no marauding Indians, no blizzards.

It would take Joseph, Cynthia, and young William five years from when they left Maine to finally arrive in Colorado. Not only had insufficient finances delayed the journey, but Joseph had probably waited, as well, until the Cheyenne and Arapaho had been "persuaded" to give up their claim to the Pikes Peak region (a disputed claim, according to the Ute). If he and Cynthia ever found tempting the idea of returning to their quieter life in Maine, the needs of their son surely spurred them onward.

"At Omaha, Nebraska I had my last bleeding lung attack," William writes. "Before we reached Denver, I was a pretty rugged boy."

William was eleven years old by then. In the mid-1800s, most boys that age probably were pretty rugged. And it was a good thing, for he was left alone with his mother while Joseph returned to Georgetown, where he had again found temporary work as a stonecutter.

> My father selected a place up towards Golden City where there was water and grass and a scattering of dry oak brush to build a fire in the camp stove, leaving us with eatables and blankets to keep warm. Rover my dog enjoyed the outdoor life.
>
> Denver at that time had a bad set of men. Life to them was "to get money, no matter how." Father was worried and discussed the matter with his employers and they advised him to move us to a place off the main road to Colorado City. So one afternoon Father came— we packed up and started south. We crossed the south fork of the Platte River and finally landed on Indian Creek near a mountain that afterwards I learned was called Wildcat Mountain. There was plenty of good grass and water nearby. We took the bed of the Baine Thimbleskane wagon, put it on the ground and banked it up with dirt. ...

There is a certain irony in the fact that the need to escape city crime was what led Mark's ancestors to Wildcat Mountain. Does nothing, really, ever change?

Our actual search took us more than five years also, though our stay in Belle Fourche lasted a little less than two years. We visited real estate offices, drove down miles of rutted roads, read through piles of brochures on land for sale not only in South Dakota and Wyoming, but Montana, Idaho, Nebraska, and Utah as well. A series of coincidences culminating in a phone call finally led us to the right place.

"A friend of ours from church suggested we give you a call," said Mark to a banker in Sundance, Wyoming, forty-five minutes away. "He thought you might know of a ranch for sale out your way."

"As a matter of fact, I do know of one about four miles from town. Let me give you the realtor's name."

The town was built at the base of the Bear Lodge Mountains, which form the western edge of the Black Hills. We met the realtor in town, drove three miles on paved highway, then turned west onto a county dirt road.

"See over there," the realtor pointed, "where the pine trees start, past the red washouts—that's where the boundary on the deeded land begins."

Hills rose up from the prairie, and great red eroded gullies cut deep caverns into the land. Clusters of oak brush and hawthorn bushes lined the dry creekbed that paralleled the county road. Occasional sage plants were replaced by juvenile ponderosa pine trees, which thickened and matured as we approached the high ridge overlooking the buildings. At an S-curve in the road, two-hundred-year-old oak trees appeared. An old homesteader's cabin rested among plum bushes, chokecherries, and more hawthorns. Below the old cabin stood a wooden barn, thirty-five feet high at the apex of its metal roof. Pigeons perched on the utility poles and a pair of bluebirds nested in a knothole. Old splintered wooden fences surrounded the barn on two sides, forming five different corrals. Two granary buildings, fifteen by twenty-five feet, completed the permanent structures. One was located across the dry creekbed, at the east end of the large hay meadow. The other sat to the west of the barn, amid more oak trees.

"Whose house trailer is that?" Mark asked.

"Belongs to the brand inspector. He kinda takes care of things over here for the owners. But when he moves he'll be taking the trailer with him."

The property had telephone lines, electricity, three developed springs, and a marginal hand-dug well. There were corrals, storage buildings, good shelter, and an old barn. It had hay ground and pasture land, evergreens and even deciduous trees. But there was no house. There *was* good soil, dark and moist beneath the oaks, fertile and loose—just right for the tender roots of an old family tree.

I touched the weathered side of the barn and felt the heat of the sun. A breeze blew across the hay meadow, where three whitetail deer grazed, and I heard the wind blow through the tops of the ponderosas. The high-altitude cry of a hawk echoed off the ridge.

"I should warn you," the realtor said, "this is snow country. Gets deep in here."

It is not the storms that frighten me, but searching for the future in the shadows of the past.

I walked over to where Mark stood alone with his hands pushed into the pockets of his Wranglers. His black hat shaded his dark hair and dark eyes. He searched the horizon, silent and pensive. He turned and watched Matt and Sarah, who were climbing on the corral.

Then, very quietly, he said to me, "We'll have to build a home. Maybe over there, facing south, where the oak trees meet the draw." His voice trailed off.

I took a deep breath and pictured a modest home nestled beneath the trees. I pictured Mark shoveling out the orphaned barn, sweeping away the old, moldy hay until the wooden floor lay bare. Just the soul of the barn would remain. From this sweeping we would begin the rebuilding of our lives. Mark would journey south and gather up the rest of our scattered possessions, bringing them back to this barn, swept free and bare. The old Heiser saddles would rest on the manger, Romie's bridle could hang on the wall by the door. We would have to find a place for the blankets, the rest of the tack, the salves and medicines. Fresh hay would be stacked neatly, up high in the loft.

Slowly, little by little, the wooden floor would be covered again with pieces of hay—our hay, cut and baled for our horses and cattle to feed on when the ground turned hard and white, *when the storms came.*

3

Planting Roots, Raising Logs

ARK AND I STOOD BY THE BARN and surveyed the land, searching for the right building site, imagining the brand inspector's trailer finally gone and the place all to ourselves. We watched the sun rise in the east, toward town, and set in the west, beyond the high ridge. We sat overlooking the snow-filled draw and imagined a bay-window view. We lay down on our backs, side by side, and imagined a candlelit bedroom. Yes, we would build the house beneath the oaks, overlooking the creek.

I began working full-time at the local bank, and Mark got a seasonal range technician job with the U.S. Forest Service. The reality of finances meant we would have to work in town, and no home yet on the ranch meant we had to live there as well. A rancher for whom Mark worked part-time had an elderly father living in the basement apartment of a small house in town. He needed someone to live in the upstairs apartment who would be willing to do his father's cleaning and cooking in exchange for rent. We thought it over (I had to do more thinking than Mark did), and finally said yes.

The preliminary stages of building went achingly slow. I bored the women at work with drawings and floor plans. We researched construction options and decided on a log home kit. Architects formalized our sketches and placed an order for windows and logs cut to our specifications. We economized on floor coverings but splurged and spent extra dollars on a bay window and two half-circle windows—windows that would welcome the landscape indoors. The main room would have an open vaulted ceiling combining kitchen, dining area, and living room. The actual construction of the house would have to wait at least a year. In the meantime, Matt was ready to start kindergarten next week.

In my anxiousness with the chores of motherhood, I knew that I had hurried him along, and with the knowing came the guilt. Had our parents done the same? Had Mark's father, with the growing of each season's hay, rushed to harrow and irrigate, to await the rain impatiently? Did he hold immature seed in his hands and look ahead to the days when the alfalfa would blossom and the pollen turn to powder? Did he look upon the neatly stacked bales with a sense of relief, yet still feel a touch of melancholy at the ending of summer? Would I repeat the error and hurry Sarah along, as I had hurried Matt?

I tried to slow down, to realize that I couldn't time their needs to the ticking of my clock. I took them for hikes out at the ranch, walking side by side, listening to the Wyoming wind sweep across the hay meadow. The wind ruffled their baby-fine hair, just as it ruffled the fading spots on the coats of the fawns who grazed alongside their mothers in the field.

"You cold?" I had asked one day, holding their chilled hands in mine. Sarah, only three, nodded yes.

"No!" said Matt, a six-year-old proud of being able to voice his own opinion—excited about school, only a week away.

We continued our walk through the oak trees that bordered the meadow. Autumn leaves cloaked the ground, hiding the summer grasses that had grown brittle beneath the hot breath of August. I lifted Sarah to my hip and felt her legs wrap themselves around my waist. I pulled the hood of Matt's jacket up, surprised when he did not object.

"Mom," he asked, "how long is it until next week?"

"Three more days," I answered, thinking back to the day before, when I had taken him to school for a language-skills screening test.

The teacher had met with each child individually. I took time off from work and went with Matt, sharing his anxiety as we approached the substantial brick building. He held my hand as we walked down the sidewalk and up to the large double doors. He held my hand as we walked down the wide, long carpeted halls to the door of his kindergarten room. I waited in the hall while his teacher told him a story and asked him questions. Then the screening was over and it was time to go. Matt started to reach up for my hand as we left, then, changing his mind, he dropped his hand to his side and swung it freely in time with the other.

This sudden act of independence took my breath away and stilled my steps as I watched him break stride and skip down the hall. Was he growing up too quickly for *our* dreams? Would he become so used to living in town that he would find it more enticing than walks in the woods? Would he someday reject the inheritance we wished to give him? I had imagined him to be a tender young sapling, *rooted to our soil.* Must I now admit that he was more like a fledgling, eager to fly far from the nest?

How *does* one pass on tradition? What magic formula exists? Or are traditions like most other things, not valued until they are taken away? Is our generation the only generation to place more importance on the future than the past? When did grandparents cease to be important? Were Mark and I fools to build our dreams upon the dreams of our forebears?

When Black Elk stood on Harney Peak and cried out to the Six Grandfathers, he linked yesterday with tomorrow, one century to the next. But the final few chapters of *Black Elk Speaks* show that even this great medicine man suffered doubts.

The last chapter, "The End of the Dream," refers to the time following the massacre of Big Foot's people at Wounded Knee. Black Elk had seen the bloodshed: the dead women and children. He had fought the soldiers. A feeling of despair and hopelessness permeates the writing as he looks back.

"And I, to whom so great a vision was given in my youth—you see me now a pitiful old man who has nothing, for the nation's hoop is broken and scattered. There is no center any longer, and the sacred tree is dead."[1]

Yet only a few days later, when he stood on Harney Peak, he expressed a faith in the future, a belief that the sacred tree might not be dead after all.

"I recall the great vision you sent me. It may be that some little root of the sacred tree still lives. Nourish it then, that it may leaf and bloom and fill with singing birds. ..."

Had Black Elk always known that the new growth of the sacred tree depended upon the old roots? And what message was in it for me? What, if anything, did it have to do with Mark and me? Would Matt and Sarah someday witness the flowering of this tree?

"I had had a great vision," Black Elk tells us, "and I should have depended only upon that to guide me to the good. But I followed the lesser visions. ... It is hard to follow one great vision in this world of darkness and of many changing shadows. Among those shadows men get lost."[2]

Winter brought a new face to the land. The gnarled trunks of the barren oak trees stood deep in stark white snow. Pine trees serrated the pale blue sky, cutting the world in half. On weekends we bundled the kids up and went out to the ranch. Hondo, free from his town pen, rode in the back of the pickup. Chinook had disappeared in Belle Fourche months ago, possibly drowned in the river or shot by a rancher protecting his flock from a vagrant dog who would not stay home. Hondo had finally resigned himself to her absence. Once at the ranch he held his head high and his tail erect, waiting for the wooded scents to reach him. He leapt from the truck and ran circles in the snow, stopping to sniff at every deer trail, at every squirrel track. Matt and Sarah threw sticks for him and Hondo floundered after them, thrusting his massive Labrador chest in the snow to cool.

Spring came. The brand inspector moved his trailer and we had the place to ourselves. Weather, which dictates all plans in Wyoming, at last allowed Mark to bring our horses to their new home. The day Mark was supposed to arrive back from Colorado, I checked the water in the stock tank at least five times.

"When's he gonna be here?" Sarah asked impatiently, missing her father but too young to remember the horses.

"Soon," I answered, pacing nervously back and forth in front of the barn. "Soon."

I felt my throat tighten as I watched Mark come down the county road and pull into the driveway with the wood-slatted stock trailer behind him. I gave him a quick hug and then swung open the hinged gate.

Romie, now an old mare of twenty-six, backed out of the trailer. I led her away, holding one hand near her nostrils and speaking intimately to her, saying things I didn't want anyone else to hear. She raised her head and took in the scent of this new land, then lowered her muzzle and sniffed my hand. I rubbed her nose and she nickered softly to me, pressing her head against my chest. I put my cheek on her neck and felt how small it had become. Her muscular prime was long since gone.

I had brought her here to die. I did not know when, or how, but I knew that someday her bones would lie among the sage, or in a red dirt crevice where the sun would bleach them white. Perhaps, though, we would be graced with a few more years—time enough for Matt and Sarah to climb upon her bent back and feel her move gently beneath them—time enough for her to learn where the tender grasses grow. Time enough for us to take one last ride together.

It was the third year of a bad drought. Late June brought with it the beginning of the fire season. Skeptics thought the land would stay hot and dry, that the drought would never end. Then a brief rain greened the pastures back up and new growth thickened the hay field. Skeptics said we would not find water if we drilled a new well. We drilled anyway—after we had it witched by an old-time trapper named Charlie.

In his eighties, Charlie had lived in this country for over sixty years but still called himself a newcomer. He knew our property back when the old county road crossed in front of the homestead cabin. He had located water on it before and knew where old wells had been.

For twenty dollars we listened to two hours of history and geology, talk of recharge areas, chalky gypsum, and the Minnelusa water table. Charlie used to witch with wood but now used brass or copper rods.

"I'm getting too old for wood, it's too dang hard to hold on to. These here brass curtain rods are easier." Charlie walked across the road at the west end of the hay field.

"This is the recharge area I was talkin' bout. See, up there," he pointed behind him, to where the Bear Lodge Mountains met the new county road. "That's where the runoff gathers. Right about here. Open that gate, would ya, Mark. Right about here there's an underground stream."

The rods started quivering, and Charlie clamped his jaws shut. The bent ends gravitated toward the earth. Charlie walked forward, then stopped.

"Yep, right there it is. Let's see how wide it is."

He made a ninety-degree turn. The rods pulled downward as he walked ten feet, then the tension abruptly ceased. "About ten feet, that's what I figured. Let's go back and see where it picks up again down in the trees."

The underground stream seemed to be about ten feet wide and, according to Charlie, less than fifty feet down. Among the oak trees, close to one of the granaries, the rods again bent downward.

"Drill right there and you'll have yourself a good little well. Now it's gonna be hard water, full of minerals, but still good. You'd have to go way down to get into soft water. Drill right there, and you'll do fine."

As Charlie drove away in his old green 1940s Jeep pickup, we wondered if we were nuts. Maybe we should spend a few hundred bucks and hire a geologist, a professional. Instead, we asked another old-timer, a neighbor, to witch it for us again. We didn't tell him what Charlie had found.

J. W. and his wife, Lois, owned a ranch up the road. When J. W. came over he carried willow branches. He walked along in the oak trees. When he came to the spot Charlie had said to drill on (with no coaching from us), the willow branches pulled down so forcefully that J. W.'s face turned red as he tried to keep his grip. The force of the pull ripped the bark from the branch. We could see why Charlie had switched to brass.

Asking someone to witch water is a bit like asking him to pray for you. It takes a lot out of a person. It is a gift, this ability to witch. It is also an exchange of faith.

We drilled in that exact spot. We did not hire a geologist. At thirty-seven feet the drillers hit water, but the well hole's plastic casing wouldn't hold, so the drillers took a break and went to get steel casing. The steel casing held. At forty feet and eleven gallons per minute, the drillers quit. But we couldn't celebrate quite yet. Lab testing would have to confirm the water's potability.

Time at the ranch was limited. We had no house, just the barn and corrals and granaries. We had no cows of our own, and instead took in cattle from other ranchers. We would sell our first hay crop to them as well, for their cattle to feed upon when winter came.

The summer remained dry. Each community had fire crews on call to fight the continual blazes that flared in the wake of lightning storms. Thunder cracked off the peaks of the Bear Lodge and high ridges of our ranch.

The bank where I worked, like the town's coffee shop, was an information center for local news. One of the ranch women who came in often brought word of rabid skunks.

"A skunk attacked two of our cows out in the corral this morning," she said, wiping the sweat from her dusty brow. "Bit the nose of one cow and hung on like a bulldog till the cow finally shook her off—tossed her head so hard the skunk flew through the air and landed in the next pen. Then the danged thing grabbed on to the nose of another cow. Finally disappeared into the barn. Shot the thing just as it was going for one of the calves."

"What'd the vet say?" we asked.

"Said we'd better shoot the wild barn cats, tame ones too. Damn skunks."

Recurring reports of rabies over a large area indicated a bad cycle. We warned Matt and Sarah, walking the fine line between education and fear—a scary thing, a rabid animal.

Mark spent long hours at work fighting forest fires. I kept his supper warm, then, giving up, finally refrigerated the leftovers. He came home at midnight one Sunday and the smell of the acrid smoke in the bedroom awakened me. Missing him after his seventeen hours on duty, I was glad to "smell" him home.

He showered, rinsing away the smell of the forest and fire, before crawling into bed next to me. I wished that he had not showered so that I could have fallen asleep with the smell of his smoke and labor in the room, encouraging dreams of him and his life outside of mine.

Completion of the paperwork for the mortgage company took entire days. The Department of Agriculture's report on the water sample from our well came back. In black and white, it boldly stated, "Water unsafe to drink due to coliform bacteria contamination." The words panicked me. We disinfected the well, used sterile plastic gloves obtained from the local extension office, and retested. The contamination possibly came from the testing itself, and not the water. We mailed the new sample to the state lab and waited. Again, bad news. Four more times we retested until, finally, the sample was approved. Now the mortgage company could finish processing the loan.

My grandmother Effie, in the distilled diary of her life, writes briefly about building her first home in the Mojave. She mentions no Department of Agriculture, no mortgage company.

Clifford and his brother Ralph first went out and drilled a domestic well, nineteen feet, and installed a hand pump. Then hurriedly built a one room board and bat shack, using sheets to partition off two bedrooms, to live in while they were building a three bedroom home. [She must have been referring to a "board and batten" shack, batten being small strips of wood used to cover joints between boards.]

We, the family of two children, left Los Angeles in April with a wagon and team, a cow, two dozen chickens, three pair of pigeons, an Irish Setter dog, and the most needed household things. Other goods were sent by freight (put off at your own risk).

We moved into the new home before the interior was finished again using sheets for partitions. After the home was finished we drilled another well by the side of the dining room porch where it would be more convenient, and installed a 1-1/2 horse power engine and a small storage tank. Cold running water, in the house!

By this time, I, too, would have been thrilled with cold running water. But despite the more stringent requirements of the 1990s, work on our house progressed. The foundation and blocks for the basement went up. My father and stepmother flew out from San Francisco and stood in the exposed basement.

"This is gonna be my bedroom, Grandpa, right here!" Matt stood at an imaginary door. "And there's Sarah's, through there," he pointed. Sarah stood on tiptoe, pretending to look out her window down into the creekbed.

"You mean you're going to have bedrooms?" Dad kidded, "I thought they were going to make you sleep in the barn."

Dad never expressed dismay at my lifestyle, never said that he wished I still worked in the city for a financial planning firm, following in *his* footsteps. He spoke openly to me about his respect for Mark. Still, I wondered sometimes if he didn't feel an occasional twinge when he saw well-dressed women seated in the boardrooms of San Francisco's financial institutions. He still lived life in the fast lane despite his seventy-plus years, and his twice-annual visits never lasted more than three or four days—just long enough for him to unwind but not long enough for the restlessness to take hold.

Mark was not the only member of his family to feel the urge to go north when the old ranch sold. His brother Keith, though reluctant to leave, brought his wife, Cindy, and three children to Sundance. Family! We rejoiced, fully aware that with the proximity of family came the risk of rivalry. It was, after all, family feuding among the heirs that finally led to the demise of their ranch. But we held on to the belief that had their father not died, his sisters would not have made life so difficult for their widowed sister-in-law. Upon us, the next generation, fell the responsibility of peace-keeping.

Keith had long ago learned the carpenter trade, and we grate-fully hired him to become the brains (and brawn) behind the construction of our home. Mark worked with him on weekends and evenings, and the subfloor was soon built. A truck and semitrailer arrived from Montana loaded with pre-cut and num-bered logs. Old school friends of Mark's who lived two hours away in South Dakota drove their cherry-picker rig over and helped us unload the huge plastic-covered bundles of wood. I brought out thermoses of hot chocolate and hot chili. We sat on the subfloor and shared our first meal.

Fall departed subtly as winter approached. We raised several "courses" of logs, and the walls began to take shape. I helped put the insulation between each log, trying not to laugh when Mark and Keith accidentally placed a cumbersome log backward—in which case an occasional slightly vulgar word would shoot into the nearby trees like a pellet of dung.

The weather, a constant threat, became a relentless taskmaster. Mark spent all his free time working on the house. I bundled the kids up whenever I could and went out to help, brushing the snow off the logs and sweeping the subfloor bare. I hauled what logs I could carry, matching the numbers written on the end of the logs with the appropriate piles. We struggled to get the walls up and the roof on before hard winter set in. A squirrel scolded us constantly from her perch in a tree that grew by the dining-room corner of the house. She did not like the fact that her peace and quiet had been disturbed. We named her Sassy.

She lined the nest of her oak home with wood shavings and dried leaves. We filled the spaces between our lodgepole logs with caulk and foam. She ran up and down the limbs of her tree, in and out of the knotholes and tunnels. We oiled the split graining of the wooden logs with preservative and nailed shingles on the high-pitched roof trusses. Sassy readied herself for another winter; we prepared ourselves for a new life—carved from the memories of an old one.

4

Inside Out

OPPORTUNITY HAD CHRISTENED THE NEW YEAR like drops of rain falling on parched fields, and we prided ourselves on continuing to focus, undeterred, on our goals. But the pressures of parenting, moving, working, and building the house left little time for being husband and wife. Romantic feelings surfaced, then were pushed under by responsibility. I stared at the Valentine's Day card I had bought and began to write "Dear Mark," then lifted the pen, unsure of what to say.

Did romantic thoughts still find time to seep into Mark's consciousness? Was he able to make the transition, when looking at me across a table covered in blueprints and loan papers, from business partner to lover? The mortgage company outlined strict building codes to which we had to adhere: the foundation must be just so, the subfloor squared to the quarter-inch, the logs foamed and caulked and bolted. But no one had supplied us with a blueprint for our marriage. No one gauged *our* foundation and judged it worthy of lasting a lifetime. No one inspected it for hairline cracks that could, if left untended, expand into gaping chasms too wide to bridge.

What I felt for Mark remained, too often, inside. I took a deep breath and, touching pen to card, began again.

"Dear Mark, I long to turn myself inside out for you, to soften up a little—not all at once, like a rush of hot air, but more like a gentle warm breeze hinting of better days—like the Chinook that will surely come. ..."

Faith. The raft on which to weather all storms. Still, I wondered, *who was in charge of weighing the ballast?*

After work Friday, instead of going straight to the house in town I grabbed the kids and headed out to the ranch. The high-fifties spring weather was exhilarating. Rapidly melting snow caused the ditches to overflow and fill the dams and reservoirs. Winter's grip at last loosened. I slowed the car as we approached the ranch. Water ran everywhere. A pond appeared overnight in the small hay field, enveloping the stock tank until only the round-rimmed top showed. The dam, dry just yesterday, now shimmered like a looking glass mirroring the blue sky and clouds. Once at the house, I went inside quickly and found Mark, who stood looking out the unfinished bay window to the draw below.

"Not a dry creekbed today, is it?" he said, putting his arm around my waist. Water rushed powerfully by, racing down the small winding ravine like a silvery serpent finally set free.

"How long do you think it will last?" I asked.

"No longer than the snow," he answered.

But, as it turned out, that was long enough. The brief exhilaration swelled our sails and allowed us to ride the relentless waves a little longer. Only one more month and the house would be livable. One more month.

The snow runoff was not the only messenger of spring's arrival on the ranch, nor were the ambitious scouts of tender grass poking their spears through the dirt. The prairie gopher also brought news of winter's retreat.

Sooner even than the buds on the trees, prompter than the migrating birds, the prairie gopher announced the end of winter—churning beneath the earth's surface, raising furrows of moist soil that stretched, snakelike, across the hay fields. These furrows wound down the borrow ditches and up the sides of washouts. The skin of the land turned inside out, exposing dark, nutritious flesh, and I envied the earth her gophers.

These trails were proof the killing freeze had withdrawn its lingering breath from the earth's thick hide and from the rich soil bed where the gnarled roots of the old oaks slept.

Gophers. Tunneling beneath our ambitions, finding purpose in the dark recesses where roots and rodents re-create. So much unseen, so much unheard—at night, when we sleep. Honeycombed civilizations till the earth, oblivious to our surface struggles. Fall's cultivation becomes spring's promise.

From the barren ridge southwest of the house I am able to see across the tops of the pine trees, beyond their tips to the deep purple shadows of the Black Hills. The pines suck in the moisture of the morning dew and I find myself envying the dew's vital role; so quickly the dew becomes the tree. My osmosis does not happen as quickly, the process is more arduous. To truly find kinship in these woods, among her forest creatures and the spirits of the past, I must peel back more than one layer of the distant mountains.

While these ponderosa pines serrate the Wyoming horizon, my father looks across San Francisco's bay. The prison on Alcatraz Island stands silhouetted against the California sky, and I wonder if he ever thinks about the American Indian activists who, in 1969, seized the island in testament of the fact that it had once belonged to them. I wonder if he ever feels connected to their plight because of his own Cherokee ancestry.

The vague memories of my grandparents call out to me from as far as a thousand miles away and as near as the closest ridge. My mother stares at the high peaks of Colorado's Continental Divide, and my only sister gazes across the Pacific Ocean, across the tops of Hawaii's coconut-laden palm trees. Mark's mother, still in Colorado, drives past the dirt road that leads to the old ranch where she reared her children. She looks back but does not turn around. A bulldozer cuts more deep swaths into the prairie, guided by wooden stakes marking the boundaries of the next subdivision.

Like scattered wisps of a single cloud, we drift apart, caught in the fast-moving currents of the time.

Sassy the squirrel scolded us loudly as we carried furniture and boxes past her tree, up the stairs to the deck, and into the kitchen. Her tail, fluffed up to twice its normal size, madly twitched back and forth. Hondo sat beneath her tree, head cocked, eyes looking upward.

I hung Romie's framed horse blanket on the log wall by the bay window. Mark gingerly carried in the large apple cider crock and placed it on the carpet, tucking it safely in a corner.

In our third week in our new home the neighboring ranchers surprised us with a housewarming party. Seven different families drove down the driveway and parked their outfits beneath the oak trees.

"Hi, Page," said Lois, carrying in a container full of sandwiches. "You don't have any plans for supper, do you?"

"Well, no," I said, looking out the window at Pat as she stepped onto the deck, arms loaded with plates and cups.

"Pat, what are you guys up to?" I questioned, a smile dawning on my face.

"We're having a shivaree. We can't let you folks move into the neighborhood without a proper shivaree!" She scurried about the kitchen and I watched helplessly as more women filed in the door and bustled about arranging salads and sandwiches, setting platters of cookies next to thermoses of hot coffee and pitchers of cold lemonade.

"What's going on, Mom?" asked Matt and Sarah.

"We're being shivareed!" I laughed. "Go outside and watch for Daddy to come home."

I glanced through the half-circle windows and saw Mark's old green pickup pull down the driveway. Pat's husband, Robert, walked to the truck and handed Mark a frosty beer. Mark stepped down, took the beer, passed it from one hand to the other, then wiped his palm on his jeans and shook Robert's hand. Together they wandered over to a group of men who were busy pounding horseshoe stakes into the ground and setting up folding chairs and picnic tables.

I glanced back at Pat. The sides of her tanned face turned up in a smile as she scooped chunks of ice into plastic glasses. But her eyes were strained, and I knew that this day, this shivaree, was not easy for her.

This land had once been Pat's and her husband's, the vital northern section of their own ranch. Not very long ago it had given birth to their dreams and cradled their hopes. But hard times, a poor market, and ill health had forced them to sell off a portion. The warm welcome they gave us did not come cheap.

"Page," Mark said, coming into the kitchen, "did you know about this?"

"Not a thing. I would have put on my good jeans if I'd known!"

"Hold that door open, would ya?" Pat asked, turning to watch Mark's brother Keith and another neighbor struggle with a large rectangular cardboard box. They eased the heavy load through the door, setting it down in the middle of the living room near the woodburning stove. Pat stuck her head out the door and hollered.

"Hey, everyone, come on inside for a minute."

J. W. sauntered into the room and gave Mark a hearty slap on the back. Lois winked at me. Matt and Sarah eyed the huge present, mouths half open.

"Mark and Page, stand over there by that present and let us take your picture while you open it. You kids get over there too."

Charlotte and Lee, our nearest neighbors, handed us a card while their son, Wade, resisted the impulse to tear at the package.

"Congratulations to all of you," the card read. Written below were the signatures of twenty-nine of our neighbors, a few of whom we had only met for the first time that day.

"Well, aren't you going to open it?" someone wheedled impatiently. "Don't just stand there, open the dang thing!"

Matt and Sarah tore at the wrapping paper while Mark pulled out his pocket knife and ran the blade down the seams of the box. Inside was a brand-new propane barbecue with shiny black paint, redwood handles, and a fold-down wooden shelf.

"We expect to be invited back for steaks now," teased Robert.

"Yeah. All of us!" someone else piped up.

"Now you'll have no excuse for not being neighborly," Pat added. Then everyone began milling around, the formal ordeal over and the real partying about to begin.

"We got three who think they know how to play horseshoes. Anyone brave enough to be the fourth?"

"How'd you ever get anyone to partner up with you?"

"Partner? Who said anything about a partner? I aim to take you all on. ..."

Mark and I stood amidst the chaos, watching our new neighbors enjoy themselves, letting our homesick souls succumb to their good-natured friendliness. If there were quarrels among the neighbors, none were evident that day. No one argued about fences that needed mending or cows that needed tending. The troops had rallied, and a truce had been called. It was time to put up the hoes and let the saddle horses rest. It was time to shivaree!

After everyone left, Sassy, who had retreated into her tree, came out and perched on a limb. The house grew quiet. The sun cast soft late-afternoon beams in through the south-facing windows. The log walls, oiled but unstained, glowed golden. Each had distinct markings—blue-tinted graining or small checks—signs of stress that split open the smooth wood surface. Small circles of growth marked the core of these lodgepole pines, brought from the Bitterroot Mountains of Montana. Lodgepoles were named so because the Plains Indians used the tall, straight trees to build their tipis. Eight to twenty buffalo skins would drape the poles of the lodge. During the Moon of Popping Trees, ashes from the lodge fire's smoke would stain the tips of the poles black.

Our logs would grow darker, too, from the smoke of our winter fires. The golden tones would deepen. Forest squirrels would no longer run up and down the length of their trunks. But the sounds of Matt's and Sarah's laughter would echo off the logs; the occasional sound of bickering would be absorbed within the knotholes.

This home said, "Stay, stay here. Plant young seedlings in the dirt. Wait for them to grow tall. Listen to the snow melt and run down the draw each spring, watch the hay grow tall and the deer grow fat. Sweep out the barn again, if you must, to make room for each season's crop. Heal old wounds, suffer new ones. But stay. For it is a good place to grow old."

Summer again brought forest fires. A blaze roared in the pine trees above J. W.'s and Lois's place, the flames igniting the treetops like a burning oil slick. Farther from home, Yellowstone burned, Idaho burned, California burned. Fires were everywhere.

"How would you feel if they sent me out of state to fight fires for a couple of weeks?" Mark asked.

"Two weeks?" It seemed like a long time.

"Could be less, could be more."

We had no stock of our own yet that required care, except the horses, and I knew I could tend to them.

"Two weeks isn't so long, I guess, to be gone fighting fires."

"You'll have to keep an eye on our place," he said, taking off his cowboy hat and running his fingers through his dark hair, "in case of fire."

"I know," I said, thinking about different flames already burning close to home, *the ones too long ignored because they were harder to see.* I thought about the promise I had written on Mark's Valentine's Day card, to turn myself inside out a little, allow the softness to show. But I let the flames burn unnoticed, let Mark go on not noticing.

Perhaps the heat of the fires will bring the Chinook.

5

Old Shadows, New Stories

MARK IS MANY THINGS. He is the great-great-grandson of a stonecutter who brought his family west in a Baine Thimbleskane wagon 130 years ago. He is a son with memories of a father dead a quarter of a century. For seventeen years he has been my partner, sharing family deaths and family divorces.

He was there when the labor nurse ran from the hospital room yelling, "Fetal distress! We have a fetal distress emergency in here!" He was there to roll the bed down the hall into the operating room. He was there when the doctor cut open my abdomen, reaching inside to pull Matt from my womb.

Later, while still lost in the numbness of anesthesia and barely able to lift my groggy head, I heard his soothing voice as he held our son to my swollen breast. So began our parenting, so continues our partnering.

These are intimate stories. They make up the flesh and blood of our relationship. But what of Mark's heart and soul? And what of mine? What of the stories I really want to tell?

Mark belongs to an endangered species: He is a cowboy. And I am the wife of a cowboy. He does not cowboy all day, every day—not since his grandfather's hired man used to take him along, not since long before the old ranch was sold. What is a grieving boy to do? Dust the cobwebs from his father's saddle, cinch tight his own girth?

A displaced spirit, he dreams. He builds a new life, hardening his heart against those who say his life is only a myth to be dispelled, those who would remythologize the West. He rides when he can, helps work the neighbor's cattle. He reaches inside the neighbor's heifer, feeling for front feet. He speaks in a soothing voice and pulls in rhythm to the silent heaves of the young cow. A calf is born. He breaks the membrane that still clings to the wet nostrils, then steps back to let the new mother smell her offspring. He returns to his new home, to his own barn. The Heiser saddle he rode in as a boy, the same saddle his father rode in as a boy, rests on the manger. He does not need to dust it now. The saddle is used often, when Matt rides with him. The latigos are oiled, the rigging rings polished.

Mark does not wear jinglebobs on his spurs to announce his coming. He is a private person. Even I, in daring to tell his stories, tread on hallowed ground.

Most ranchers are like that—private. And perhaps that very privacy has more to do with the West's elusive nature than we care to admit. For you won't hear the neighbors bragging about the five hundred dollars they spent to erect a windmill in their reservoir, the hours of labor to build the pontoon structure on which the windmill sits. And all this to aerate the water so the fish will survive the frigid winter. Most won't tell you, either, about the bales of hay added each year to that old nesting structure built down by the dam, where the pair of wild geese nest each spring. It is time, now, to tell these stories.

It is fashionable of late to deride the rancher, to deny the current life of the cowboy. Many writers and journalists are unable to resist the trendy temptation to gnaw away with biting words at *all* ranchers. They—either from ignorance or laziness—insist on wedding the family rancher to the corporate cattle conglomerate. Thus, the sins of the boardroom moguls, most of whom have never birthed a calf or rested a field, are being visited upon us all.

While I was reading a literary magazine, a particular essay grabbed my attention. The author spoke, with tongue in cheek, of sleeping out-of-doors, and I found myself, unarmed and off guard, smiling at her imagery. Then I felt my gut twist as, with the flick of a pen, she revealed her hidden agenda. She referred to the outdoor job of cowboys as "a job that Americans understand: Keeping track of property." Her tone, in that brief confrontation, was derogatory and all-knowing. *Property?* The word had the smell of political rhetoric about it. By property did she mean our neighbor's old 4-H cow, the one brushed and curried each fall, the one all the kids won ribbons on, the one who kept a calf by her side for nine years?

Another essay comes to mind, not literary but written in the thrifty language of the working cowboy. The author described his outdoor job a little differently: "The snow was knee-deep on a horse. It was damn cold. But that's a cowboy's life. Save the livestock."

The author who referred to a cowboy's job as "keeping track of property" must not have been listening last night when the neighbor talked about all seven of those goslings taking flight and heading south, keeping right on the tails of the goose and gander. What a sight it was. Last year only two babies survived, and the year before that, none.

She does not tell Mark's story, or mine, or our neighbor's. I am angry, but mainly I am sad. Americans understand much more than keeping track of property. Her cutting remark is not harmless. It is like a powerful slow poison, working deep into the system until finally it reaches the heart.

Perhaps she does not understand it is Mark's heart that atrophies. Oh, to be able to sit with her on the ridge overlooking our barn. At dawn. We would sit quietly, breathing in the cold early morning air, waiting. And then they would appear. The sun and the sky. Soft light would fill the valley, turning the frozen whiskers on Romie's muzzle to silver. If we were lucky, we might even hear the call of wild geese.

Maybe then she would listen. Maybe then he would talk.

Endangered species. There are many that need our protection. Thousands of species have come and gone since the beginning, all in nature's own good time.

But when man, a servant of nature, pushes forward too quickly, he runs the risk of sabotaging his own good intentions. The Industrial Revolution changed man's concept of time. And it changed man's concept of family. Fathers left their farms and ranches and went to town to work. Staying behind were the mothers, and the daughters and sons. Robert Bly talks of male grief, grief that began when the men left home. "In ancient times you were always with your father. He taught you how to do things, he taught you how to farm, he taught you whatever it was he did. You learned from him."[1]

Mark learned from his father and his grandfather. He learned by running on short legs behind long ones, by reaching for a capable hand and always finding it there. In good time, keeping to nature's seasons, the cycle will repeat itself. Mark now walks hand in hand down to the barn with Matt and Sarah. Oftentimes we *all* walk hand in hand down to the barn. True, the barn is not his grandfather's. But our footsteps carry with them generations of history.

The Makaha Indians are members of one of the seven bands of the Oglala. The Oglala are one of the tribes of the Seven Campfires. We call them by the derogatory Chippewa word *Sioux*, meaning "treacherous snake"; they would prefer to be known as *Lakota*. Pushed westward by the Chippewa, their migration into the Black Hills began during the latter part of the eighteenth century. In 1776, the Cheyenne battled the Oglala near Hot Springs (South Dakota) but were unable to retain their upland hunting grounds. The Lakota's presence in the Black Hills soon forced the Crow Indians to move west, and the Kiowa to move south.[2] By 1856, the year Mark's great-great-grandparents began their migration west with their asthmatic son, the Lakota numbered in the thousands and dominated the plains north to the British possessions, south to the Platte River, and west to the Rocky Mountains. And the United States had already put into effect the Indian Extermination Policy.

Barbara Means Adams, from the tribe of Black Elk, speaks eloquently about the Makaha Indians in *Prayers of Smoke*. She speaks of living in cycles of seven—of our lives completing a different phase every seven years. The first seven years of life, a Makaha child is treated very specially, having just come from the spirit world. During this time the grandparents teach about service, respect, sharing, pride, and achievement. The child is taught to "honor peace and wisdom and to walk the spiritual path."[3]

During the next seven years, boys and girls learn about their separate roles. Makaha girls learn much from their mothers and grandmothers. Toward the end of this cycle, as their bodies change, they are taken by their elders to visit the moon hut. They do not lie in bed believing that they are dying a terrible death, as did my grandmother. They are told, instead, that their monthly blood is a lifelong gift to the tribe, likened to a warrior's sacrifice when he pierces himself during the sacred Sun Dance. They are not made to feel ashamed of their bodies but are taught that the ability to bear children gives them great, sacred power. The boys learn to hunt and track, to become proficient with bow and arrow, and they feel a traditional pride in their ability to provide meat for their family and hides for shelter and clothing.

Did Mark learn these things during his first fourteen years? Did I? For me, the rituals were missing, the sense of continuity and belonging. My grandparents lived a thousand miles away, and the drops of Cherokee blood that flowed in my grandmother Helen's veins were anathema, her Cherokee heritage a hidden shame. She told me no stories of Oklahoma, shared no traditions from the old life. I did not realize until adulthood that there had been an "old" life.

She did tell me stories of the Washington logging camps where she and my grandfather spent their summers, stories of cooking flapjacks for twenty men, of huge logging trucks careening down narrow mountain roads. "A mountain lion," she once told me, "leapt out of the trees and jumped straight over the truck. Damn thing barely cleared our heads, then ran down the other side of the mountain!"

My Uncle Howard tells me she was known for three things: being a great cook, a crack shot with a rifle, and a damn good fisherman. "She would stick the barrel of her .22 out the window of her cook tent," he would say, laughing, "shoot the head off a blue grouse from fifty yards away, then throw it in the stew pot!" She also, he later confided in me, sometimes drank too much. "And I hated that," he said, "hated to see her that way ... because everyone loved her so much."

But I remember her best standing behind the jewelry counter at the Sea Captain's Chest on Fisherman's Wharf in San Francisco, souvenir-seeking tourists nearly hiding her short, stout figure from view.

"Her sales boss once told me," my father related, "that Helen was the only clerk he had who managed to sell an overstocked order of black-beaded necklaces. 'How'd you do it?' I asked your grandmother. 'I gave the beads a name,' she said simply, 'called them Caviar Beads.' "

Mark's memories are more vivid and detailed—framed with the day-to-day interactions upon which a relationship is built. His grandfather taught him much in their first four years together, the time when a Makaha grandparent would be responsible for his grandchild.

By the third cycle of life a Makaha child has absorbed the beliefs of her people. She enters adulthood with an understanding of her purpose. Life's energy, which had begun to wane, waxes with renewed vigor. By the time I was fourteen my address had changed nine times without getting nearer to any of my grandparents. I entered the third cycle of my life already grown, worldly realities heavy upon my shoulders.

And what of Matt and Sarah? Were they learning to "honor peace and wisdom and walk the spiritual path"? Where were the old people now? Who would teach Matt and Sarah what one can only learn after generations of living?

I like to think that wisdom is not bounded by geography, that a grandparent's love can transcend both time and distance. I like to think that we walk in the shadow of our ancestors' love.

6

Simon

In medicine stories as in medicine life, it is always difficult to discern where the mundane merges with the arcane. Their boundaries are not sharp and distinct but barely discernible and, for long stretches, invisible, like faint trails in the grass and forests left by small creatures.

—Paula Gunn Allen[1]

SIMON, RAISED HERE ON THE RANCH, came with the place. We took to her beautiful Siamese markings, vivid blue eyes, and litter of kittens immediately. We kept them all confined to the barn for the first week so that Simon could adjust to us. The kittens—two black and two gray—leapt and bounced after imaginary mouse tails, enthralled with their world in the hay. Simon stood guard, not trusting the large black dog who had invaded her territory.

Temporarily exiled from the barn and forced to stand outside the open barn door, Hondo quivered and whined. Simon and the kittens strutted just inside, flaunting their privileged status. Simon, not sure about the permanence of Hondo's exile, arched her back like a mountain lion and made ferocious hissing noises whenever he ventured an inch too near.

I patted Hondo's black head and talked into his sad, gentle brown eyes, reassuring him that he wasn't being scolded. Soon, he would be able to go back into the barn.

One morning we walked down to the barn and opened the door to find Simon and all four kittens were gone. Had we disturbed them too often? Did Simon need a quieter atmosphere in which to rear her young? Matt, Sarah, and I searched, calling her name as we walked along. We looked in both outdoor granary buildings, we searched the old homestead cabin, we even walked to an old abandoned shed across the draw, calling all the while, "Simon, Simon, Simon?"

But there was no sign of her or the kittens. After ten days we gave up hope. Then, two weeks after her disappearance, Mark and the kids were in the truck headed to town, and there, by a culvert close to the road, sat Simon and one of the little black kittens.

"Matt, isn't that Simon over there?" Mark slowed the truck down and pulled over onto the soft shoulder.

"It is, Dad, it is!" Sarah strained against the seat belt and pressed her nose to the glass.

"Where are the rest of the kittens, Dad?"

"I don't know, Matt," Mark answered, "I only see one."

Patient coaxing finally cajoled Simon and her kitten out of the culvert, but there was no sign of the other three. Matt and Sarah gathered Simon and the kitten into the truck, oblivious to the hawk-winged shadow that darkened the roadside field in narrowing predatory circles. Mark turned the truck around and headed in the direction of home.

We increased our daily trips to the barn, carrying with us savory snacks not usually fed to barn cats. This time, I decided, I would resort to bribery. Simon warmed up to us right away, but the black kitten, turned feral in his two weeks away, would not come near. Then one morning he disappeared altogether. Two days later, Simon too was gone.

A week later a flash of black fur ran in front of us before disappearing into the tall stands of redtop grass near the granary. The black kitten! The next day Simon reappeared in the barn, and soon we saw regular glimpses of the black kitten as he darted from hiding place to hiding place, becoming all the while less feral and more daring in his proximity. We continued the bribery. Simon stayed and the black kitten began to appear in the barn at feeding time, venturing near the food once we were well out of the way.

"The kitten has no name," Sarah observed one day, looking at me accusingly.

"A kitten ought to have a name." She repeated the thought, peering at me with intense brown eyes. "You have a name, Mom."

No arguing that fact. I heard my "name" spoken imploringly dozens of times each day; it had become an intrinsic part of my identity. But I was already beginning to understand what many a pioneer woman had known: Naming an animal creates a commitment and an attachment. Effie, my maternal grandmother, probably would have preferred not to know the name of my mother's tame bunny when, during the Depression, she had been forced to cook the rabbit. My mother, despite the hunger gnawing at her belly, did not eat the stew.

"Let's name him Black Jack," Matt piped up, "after Dad's old mule."

"Black Jack," Sarah repeated, testing the feel of the words. "That sounds good."

The kitten was officially christened, and once named, was more tame. Before long he greeted us at the barn with meows and purrs and cattish rubs about the legs. Simon, now trusting of Hondo's gentle disposition, no longer felt the need to hiss. The transformation became complete when, sitting in the bay window one late afternoon, I watched Mark come back to the house after doing chores. Hondo, as always, followed him faithfully, and scampering behind, prancing playfully in Hondo's long shadow, were Black Jack and Simon.

Black Jack, grown long and lanky with a silken sleekness to his ebony coat, became Sarah's constant companion. He cuddled rag-like in her arms, all four feet flopping in the air as she carried him from place to place, and would remain in that vulnerable position for hours. Sarah whispered his name often in a little girl's voice that hinted of a woman's heart.

Simon became pregnant again. Her belly swelled, hanging low with heaviness. The female in me sympathized with her awkwardness, especially so soon after nursing Black Jack's litter. Within a few weeks Simon's shape returned to its Siamese litheness, and we knew she had a new litter of kittens hidden somewhere. I picked her up and gently turned her on her back. Her nipples were swollen a tender pink, the fur around each moist and matted down in tiny suckling circles.

"Simon moved her kittens into the barn last night," Mark said one morning, wiping his boots on the mudroom rug after returning to the house. "She's got 'em in the manger."

Matt, Sarah, and I hurried out to the barn, zipping our jackets as we walked. Hondo and Black Jack led the way. When we got to the barn I called Hondo back, taking his dark head with its graying muzzle in my hands.

"Buddy," I said in a hushed voice, "you can't come in this time. You're gonna have to stay out of the barn again for a while until Simon's kittens grow a little, just for a while." He quivered, his muscled body tense with anticipation. Then he grew still, his eyes sad with comprehension.

"That's right, buddy," I repeated, wrapping my arms around his thick black neck, "you've gotta stay out."

The three of us peered inside the dark manger. Simon greeted us, then went straight for the food dish with Black Jack. As our eyes adjusted to the dimness, small shapes nestled together began to take form.

"Oh, Mom, they're so tiny," Sarah whispered.

Our voices and the sound of Simon's meows woke the kittens, who rose, staggering and swaying like five little drunken mice— two black ones, two gray striped ones, and a creamy gray one.

"Can we pick them up, please, Mom?" Matt and Sarah pleaded in unison.

"No," I explained, "they're too young to be touched. Not for a long time, until they're much, much bigger." I resisted the urge to pick them up myself, wishing I had seen Simon carry them into the barn, one by one, placing them deep into the wooden manger, which smelled of chewed oats and dusty hay.

The next day we heard faint meows from at least two more kittens, coming not from the manger but from beneath the floor-boards near the old John Deere wagon. I silently took count. Seven kittens. Simon had at least seven kittens, maybe more. Did she split the kittens up because these weren't healthy, or did she share her mothering equally between the two litters? I wanted her to retrieve the kittens who meowed so persistently beneath the floor. I stood helplessly over them, needing to trust Simon's own instincts.

The meowing continued. I carried Simon over to the floor, the cries filtering through the porous floorboards. She heard them, of course, but I viewed her lack of response as indifference. Each day the meows grew more feeble until, on the fourth day, they ceased altogether.

"What's happened to the kittens, Mom? Are they there? We can't hear them, Mom."

"I know. I can't hear them either. Maybe Simon moved them, or maybe they were sick and Simon didn't want to get the other kittens sick too." My conjectures eluded the real issue floating above us like the shadow of the hawk circling the field.

The other five kittens explored more of their manger each day, enlarging their territory one brave flick of the tail at a time. The timid creamy gray kitten preferred the safety of the manger's dark corner but followed her siblings nonetheless.

One day we entered the barn and found the kittens, having escaped the confines of the manger, chasing one another in circles with wispy pigeon feathers stuck to their mouths—giddy with freedom. I inspected the manger and found where the boards had split apart, leaving a crack large enough for a kitten to escape.

The next day Simon hid three of the kittens outside under the granary by the house, and two kittens remained in the barn. The following afternoon the three kittens were gone from under the granary; the other two were still loose in the barn. I worried about their fate, wishing Simon would reunite them. The kittens, barely five weeks old, were not yet ready for the perils of the world. Not listening to my own instincts, I put the two back in the manger and scrounged around until I found a wedge-shaped piece of wood with which to block the crack. I forced it into the opening securely enough that it wouldn't be dislodged by two curious kittens.

Outside, Matt yelled at Hondo as a high-pitched yowl came from the wood pile. Hondo stood holding the creamy gray kitten in his large Labrador mouth.

"No, Hondo. Drop her, Hondo." I used my sternest voice. The kitten was wet but unharmed by Hondo's gentle grip; he only wanted to affectionately nuzzle her on the nape of the neck. I carried the kitten back to the barn and carefully placed her in the manger with the other two kittens.

Seven. Simon had had at least seven kittens, and now we were down to three. And of the first litter, only Black Jack had survived.

Monday morning—a work day and school day lay ahead. I hurried to get Matt and Sarah fed and dressed, feeling my pulse shift out of Sunday slow-gear into Monday fast-gear. Mark came up from the barn and closed the door slowly behind him. Something was wrong.

"An animal got in the barn last night and killed the kittens—mutilated them."

"Mutilated them? All of them?" I asked in disbelief, feeling my stomach lurch.

"Well, I heard one meowing but couldn't find it."

My mind skipped quickly over all the possibilities. *Mutilated. Dead.* All but one, lying alone and injured.

Certain things are more important, even, than Monday mornings. I tugged on my jeans, shoved my bare feet into my cowboy boots, pulled a sweatshirt over my head, and went to the barn.

The flashlight lit up the scene in the manger too well. Two kittens lay in the hay, one missing a head and the other his hindquarters. Exposed entrails hung from torn-open stomachs. A feather clung to bloody fur. I called out to the remaining kitten. Answering me with a frightened squeak, she huddled at the far end of the manger—where I had wedged the wood the day before.

They had been trapped. The realization hit me instantly. Drawing in my breath, I exhaled slowly, daring to think about the hand I had played in the fate of the kittens. I picked up the only survivor and drew her out of the shadowy manger into the light. The timid creamy gray kitten—rescued by Hondo the day before—shivered in my hands.

Why had I meddled? Why couldn't I have left well-enough alone? Leaning against a wooden beam in the cold privacy of the barn, I cried. I cried not only for the dead kittens but for Mark as well. I cried because he still had no cows of his own, and because we both missed Colorado. I cried for the ranchers who no longer took the time to properly care for their animals and the land on which they lived, and I cried for the ranchers who cared intimately for the land and about the land, but who were being forced to leave because of politics and economics.

I wept, too, because the Chinook for which I patiently waited had yet to thaw the thin layers of ice that had accumulated, year after year, on the heart of my marriage. But I wept the hardest because I knew that the true Chinook would have to come from within, not without.

Simon rubbed against my legs, meowing plaintively, telling me perhaps about the night's ordeal. I knelt down and ran my fingers along her spine, then petted her soft belly, feeling her swollen nipples through the thick tawny fur. Placing the gray kitten next to her on the floor, I reached into the manger and jerked the wedge-shaped board loose, exposing the open crack. Then I turned to go, leaving Simon to her kitten.

So much milk for one kitten.

I walked slowly back to the house—slowly back to Monday morning.

7

Eagle Feathers
and Wounded Spirits

JERKED UP THE COVERS on our bed while Matt, now seven, followed on my heels, vainly trying to visit. I gave up making the bed; it was almost time to leave for work—there was no chance to smooth the wrinkled covers, no time for listening.

"Sarah," I called impatiently, "get over here so that I can fix your hair."

The brush moved quickly up and down through the long, tangled hair. "Ouch, Mommy, you're hurting me!"

My heart ached. I wanted to slow down, to gently brush Sarah's hair, to answer Matt's questions—but there just wasn't time. I rebelled against the unfairness. This familiar agony ripped at my insides, little by little, working day by working day. My children were missing out on irretrievable moments of mothering, and the guilt for me was overwhelming.

"Mommy," Sarah pleaded with tear-filled eyes, "when can we just stay home together? I just want to stay home with you." The unfairness tugged not only her hair but her heartstrings as well. To a four-year-old, the stretch between Monday and Saturday is an eternity. Her need for me, for stillness shared, for a gradual lengthening of the cord between us, was inborn. Pushing away my strong desire to nurture and protect Matt and Sarah did not help.

My job allowed me six personal days off a year (excluding vacation time, which had to be taken consecutively, and personal sick leave). These days were to be reserved for dental appointments, eye-care appointments, sick children, and funerals. Assuming I scheduled all appointments after 4:00 P.M. on work days (and assuming no one died), I could save the six days for times when

Matt and Sarah were home ill: an average of three days per child each year. Mark's part-time job (which lacked permanent status) didn't allow him much more flexibility, and our jobs had more leniency than many. I lived in dread of the mornings when I would awaken to the sound of a deep cough or the touch of a fevered cheek. God forbid epidemics.

Sarah winced as the bristles of the brush found their way through her long light brown hair. I was tempted, for a moment, to reach for the scissors, to cut the tangles and snarls from our life. But as I held the strands of her hair in my hand, I remembered there are other cultures that believe that to cut a person's hair is to rob her of an intrinsic, intimate power; long-haired cultures where, in the privacy of his lodge, a husband could be found tenderly pulling a porcupine-quill hairbrush through his wife's night-colored hair, weaving the strands into braids of tradition. I softened.

"Come here, honey." Putting the brush down, I took Sarah in my arms and led her to the rocking chair. *Damn the rush.* Her wounded spirit, our wounded spirits, needed time to heal.

This is my job too—keeping her spirit whole and strong, equipping her for the future. But too many work-day mornings were filled with brief hugs and hurried kisses—mere tokens, wispy apologies fleeting enough to fit into my busy and bossy schedule. Sarah, not fooled, knew she was being shortchanged. A four-year-old knows these things.

A government study costing hundreds of thousands of dollars is not necessary to prove the innate wrongness of this. Ask any mother to grab hold of her deep-down gut feelings. Ask any four-year-old. The answer will be obvious.

Modern opportunities may expand my horizons, but without time to sift the fertile earth through my fingers, horizons become meaningless. Don't steal my motherhood from me; don't snatch the childhood from my child.

What can I, a white woman of the liberal 1990s, learn from other cultures? In which direction shall I turn to seek a better way? To whom can I go?

There is a Makaha ceremony for girls called *Ishna*. Described by Barbara Adams in *Prayers of Smoke*, Ishna is a preparation for marriage and children. A young girl, when her parents decide she is ready, is led by a woman elder into a tipi. She is dressed in new clothes that have been purified in the smoke of sage and sweet grass.

> The old woman paints the girl's face red, symbolizing rebirth and the earth. Women represent the earth, which makes everything grow.
>
> Four men bring a bear robe, and they carry the girl on it to the center of the ceremonial grounds.[1]

The girl's ancestors are discussed and revered, her family history spoken of eloquently by elders. People speak highly of the girl and are given gifts by the girl's family. A specially chosen elder speaks to *Wakan Tanka* on her behalf, and sage and sweet grass are again burned. She is given stalks of corn, which symbolize the making of relatives. Finally, a white breast feather from a spotted eagle is given to the girl.

> The eagle plume is attached to a circle made out of porcupine quills. It is confirmation that the girl has committed herself to the service of the people. It symbolizes her intention to practice the virtues of kindness, generosity, and truthfulness. The eagle plume is the only feather a virgin is allowed to wear.[2]

An honor song, especially created for this girl, is then sung. It will be sung one final time when she is buried. After the smoking of the ceremonial pipe, the girl leads the people on a circular dance, following the path of the sun. Her parents and grandparents dance by her side, her relatives and friends follow behind. A sweat-lodge ceremony completes the celebration, and then there is great feasting and the giving of presents.

Boys, too, have a coming-of-age ritual. But the eagle feather the boy receives he has obtained himself, from the breast of a golden eagle. He captured the eaglet, fed the young bird, cared for him, and when the time was right, "the boy would put the sacred braided rope around the eagle's neck and slowly choke it."[3] The eagle's life is memorialized by a staff upon which the head of the eagle is placed, and it will belong to the boy until he dies. The wing bones and eagle claws will be used in other sacred ceremonies. The smoke of sweet grass and sage will be fanned by the eagle wings. These things will be passed on from generation to generation.

From generation to generation? Do the wing bones and eagle plumes, then, belong not only to the past, but to the future as well? Do the answers I seek reside not only with my grandmothers, but also with their grandchildren—with Matt and Sarah? Perhaps it is through their eyes, through the eyes of the next generation, that my own culture gains significance.

Though we were well settled into our new home, a few boxes remained unpacked. Tackling a box of books, I picked up a copy of Sheila Burnford's *The Incredible Journey* and opened the faded red cover. My father's handwriting, scrawled across the endpaper, read: "To Page, age ten and a half, a good student and an animal lover—who is going to take some interesting journey herself if I'm any judge! Love, Daddy. Christmas, 1962."

I held far more than a faded book in my hands: I held the memories of a young girl—the daughter I was then, and still am now. Carefully placing the book on the stairs, I reached into the box and took out another piece of my childhood, a book of poetry by Helen Lowrie Marshall, *Hold to Your Dream*, given to me by my mother when I was sixteen. I laid it gingerly on top of the first book, as if it might break after so many years of being packed away.

There is a sadness in having to pack things away that is different from the lightness one feels in giving something away. Before we moved from Colorado, I gave many things away. We hauled boxes and boxes of books to the library, but these special books were coupled too closely to the pains and joys of growing up to be given away. A few I kept not just because of the words and stories within them, but also because of the water stains and muddy discolorations on the outside, remnants of the Platte River flood. Others, classics, I kept to someday share with Matt and Sarah.

Reaching into the box again, I pulled out a collection of children's stories, each bound in a maroon cover with gold lettering: *Black Beauty, Treasure Island, Heidi, Alice in Wonderland,*

Robinson Crusoe, King Arthur, The Arabian Nights, and *Robin Hood.* Oh, the adventures that awaited Matt and Sarah, the travels to foreign lands and foreign times—Fred Gipson's *Old Yeller* and *Lad: A Dog* by Albert Payson Terhune. Next I took out two books by Walter Farley, *The Black Stallion and Satan* and *The Black Stallion Returns.* These I placed on the stairs next to the growing pile of memories: the brief times I spent curled up with my father as he stretched out in his favorite yellow-leather armchair—leaning into strong arms and a broad, masculine chest. I thought of Mark and the moments he spends listening to Matt and Sarah, the way he lies down on top of their covers at bedtime, saying prayers, waiting for worries to surface.

I took out five different Nancy Drew mysteries and watched myself mature; then *Peony* by Pearl S. Buck, *Travels with Charlie* by John Steinbeck, and his poignant *The Grapes of Wrath.* The next several books I had not read in their entirety: a selection of stories and poems by Rudyard Kipling; *The Song of Songs Which Is Solomon's,* created by Solomon, inspired by the Creator, a true classic; *The Odyssey* of Homer; the story of *Beowulf.* So overwhelming—these works of art, each uniquely inspired, each addressing mankind's universal quests.

The box was almost empty, save for two large volumes—the *Outline of History* by H. G. Wells. An unfathomable endeavor, this outline of history. I struggle with the history of my own meager life, my own family, my own limited experience.

I stood up and stretched, then lifted the empty box to carry it to the door. A small volume slid from beneath a cardboard flap—Willa Cather's *O Pioneers!* I sat back down and flipped through the pages, stopping when I came to this highlighted text:

> She had never known before how much the country meant to her. The chirping of the insects down in the long grass had been like the sweetest music. She had felt as if her heart were hiding down there, somewhere, with the quail and the plover and all the little wild things that crooned or buzzed in the sun. Under the long shaggy ridges, she felt the future stirring.[4]

The future stirring? How is it that moments of serendipitous destiny make one feel both grand and insignificant at the same time? I took a deep breath, then sighed, placing the unobtrusive book on top of the precariously tall pile.

These pages of the past, home at last, will stand upright on shelves where they will be dusted and cared for once again, read and reread, and finally passed on.

The sound of the ringing phone startled me, and I dashed upstairs. "Hello?"

"Hi, Pagie, it's Dad."

"Hi, Dad." I smiled. No one else called me Pagie. "What're you doing?"

"I'm at the Denver airport, en route to San Francisco after a business trip. I'm standing in a phone booth."

"You must've known I was reminiscing. I just unpacked a box full of old books. Remember giving me a copy of *The Incredible Journey?*"

"Yeah, I do."

"Hold on, I'll read you what you wrote." I ran downstairs, retrieved the book, and brought it quickly back up.

"How'd you know I'd be calling from the airport?" he asked.

"I didn't. Just hoping you'd call, I guess. Here's what you said. ..."

There was a silence on the other end of the phone when I finished reading the inscription. The noises of the traveling crowd in the background filtered through, but Dad said nothing. An invisible chord had been struck, a bond that transcended distance and time. I listened for a moment to this quiet harmony, this father and daughter symphony.

"Dad?"

"I'm here, honey, just kinda choked up. That was twenty-eight years ago."

"I know, Dad, I know."

I hung up the phone and walked over to the bookshelves, already crowded with books Mark and I had acquired over the years. I slid the faded red book between an old copy of *The Virginian* and a new copy of A. B. Guthrie's *The Big Sky*. On the shelf above rested a paperback edition of Dee Brown's *Bury My Heart at Wounded Knee.* My dog-eared copy of *Black Elk Speaks* stood beside a borrowed volume of John Ehle's *Trail of Tears: The Rise and Fall of the Cherokee Nation.*

For me, each page I turned of *The Trail of Tears* had been a search for signs of ancestral bonds, yet during the entire search I had felt like an interloper, a modern fraud among authentic caretakers of the past. Had I actually expected to sniff out blood relatives whose tracks, whose very names, were lost to me?

The tracks of my maternal grandmother, Effie, were more easily followed yet still led to frustrating dead ends. In my most vivid childhood image of her, we are in her bedroom; I am kneeling on a braided rug at her feet, and she is seated at her vanity. I watch while she gracefully pulls a filigreed boar-bristle hairbrush through waist-length silver hair—hair that, during the daytime, crowned her head in a swirling coil of white.

Sarah will never share a similar memory. Mark's mother wears her hair short and practical, a style that suits her. My own mother's hair, ravaged by the holocaust of chemotherapy, is just now beginning to push hesitant tips through a tender scalp.

Nor will Sarah ever experience the Makaha ceremony, Ishna. The feathers she playfully wears in her hair more often than not belong to a barn pigeon or a blue jay. But perhaps there *are* ceremonies we can pass on, eagle feathers of a different sort— ceremonies born anew. But first I must find the time to smooth the wrinkled covers, to listen to the voices of my children, to sift the cool earth between my fingers and feel the future stirring. ...

8

If Trees Could Talk

MARK AND I HAVE COME TO ACCEPT our transplanted status, and so, also, has the land—the acorn-mulched earth and sage-strewn prairie has embraced us, forgiving us the transgressions of those who came before. Not all are so quick to forgive. The taproot of Mark's family tree pushes downward and the soil opens and softens, giving freely of her nutritious moisture. I feel this forgiveness when I burrow through the scrub oaks or walk the high ridges, and I feel the embrace in each gust of cold air or warm whisper, knowing all the while that the earth's ability to forgive cannot last forever.

Beneath the earth, beyond view but not beyond vision, are mirror images of the eighty-foot-tall bur oaks that encircle our log home. Taproots resembling inverted trunks push downward, their central shafts branching out with hairy root tips that grip the soil, mirroring the limbs above and the slick deep green leaves that reach toward the sky.

These oaks too have had to acclimate, for they would be more at home in a temperate eastern climate than here in the arid West. Yet the Audubon handbook on grasslands lists them as "the most characteristic tree of the prairies, bordering and invading the grassland, individual trees often surviving in isolated splendor."[1] They especially seem to be at home in the Black Hills.

My sister once told me (as partial explanation for why she lives in Hawaii) that she believes people to be like trees—in search of the climate to which they are best suited. If that is true, then she is like the graceful Hawaiian pandanus, whose trunk is scarred with gentle spirals, each circle marking where a leaf once grew. The elements have not roughened her edges but softened her nature.

To traditional American Indians, all trees are sacred. The old Lakota used to refer to trees as the "Standing People," and the cottonwood was the most sacred of all. During the Second World of Lakota mythology (when plants and animals began populating the earth), it was the cottonwood who whispered to the Little People and showed them how to fold leaves into cone-shaped tipis. It is the trunk of the cottonwood around which the sun-gazers still tether themselves during the ceremonial Sun Dance.

By 1862, when Mark's great-great-grandparents arrived in Colorado and laid the wooden bed of their wagon upon the prairie beneath Wildcat Mountain, the Civil War was already placing great demands on the timber resources of the country. Eastward pressure on the Teton Lakota mounted. That same year, the Santee appeared in the camps of the Oglala on the upper Missouri River. They brought with them white women and children captured during their raids in Minnesota.

Further south, the Arapaho, Cheyenne, and Ute waged war against one another and counted coup on the settlers while camped on the Platte bottoms. Many whites living in or near Denver began "spoiling for a muss" with the Indians, fearing that sporadic raiding would soon culminate in all-out warfare. The Plains Indians knew by then that "they were being hemmed in, driven, and harried toward extermination, and they were fighting back."[2]

By 1873, nine years after the massacre of a peaceful Cheyenne village at Sand Creek in Colorado, and six years before the Meeker massacre on Milk Creek, also in Colorado, by White River Ute,[3] the U.S. government passed the Timber Culture Act, which offered free land to settlers willing to plant trees on 40 acres of each 160-acre claim.

That same year, Mark's great-grandfather William T. Lambert fell in love with a young Missouri woman named Rachel. No longer a thin-limbed asthmatic boy, William was now a capable man of twenty-three, trained in civil engineering and already raising his own livestock. In the years that followed, "Rachel did all the cooking for the family and up to twenty-five hired men daily. She was the real director of the ranch. They would kill two hogs a week for meat and she could cut up and dress a hog and have it in the cooler within the hour. Never a meal was served that there was not fried pork on the table. Hand-churning was done every morning—so there was plenty of butter and milk."

It would be another twenty years, however, before William planted his renowned orchard of twenty-eight thousand apple trees, probably too late to take advantage of the government's Timber Culture Act. Then, in May 1905, William and Rachel's five-year-old son, Webster, died. The sweet-scented orchard brought only a brief reprieve from disaster. "The summer of 1905 was busy," Rachel wrote in her journal, "because the fruit trees did very well. A stone building was built to process the apples. Then the frame house burned in the fall of 1906. There was a disease that killed most of the horses and pigs. One fall ninety percent of the apples were frozen on the trees in mid-September. The following spring a late frost killed the blooms."

Perhaps the orchard was a foolish venture. Wallace Stegner would, no doubt, have chastised Mark's forebears for even attempting to grow fruit trees in the eastern foothills of the Rockies. In *The American West as Living Space*, Stegner says, in reference to large-scale irrigation agriculture (which the orchard actually was not), that, "We go on praising apples as if eating them were an injunction of the Ten Commandments."[4] He also makes reference to Mary Austin's "quiet but profound truth ... that the land will not be lived in except in its own fashion."[5]

The facts that Stegner assails us with in his book fall upon our consciences like hail from the sky—reminding us of the havoc bad politics have wreaked upon the rivers of the West. "I confess the facts make this Westerner yearn for the old days on the Milk and the Missouri when those rivers ran free, and we were trying to learn how to live with the country, and the country seemed both hard and simple, and the world and I were young, when irrigation had not yet grown beyond its legitimate bounds and the West provided for its thin population a hard living but a wonderful life."[6]

Stegner's summation in the center section of the book does not bode well for the future: "... the West is no more the Eden that I once thought it, than the Garden of the World that the boosters and engineers tried to make it; and neither nostalgia nor boosterism can any longer make a case for it as the geography of hope."[7]

Hope. And vision. If these do not exist here in the West, then where?

Even though I am unable to see the taproots of the giant oaks, I will not lose faith in their existence. Mark and I will not plant an orchard among the sage, nor will we plow up the native grasslands. We will grieve the loss of the wild herds of bison whose great hooves used to stomp the brittle prairie into fruitfulness.

But we will also marvel at their domesticated cousins, the cattle who now roam the plains—descendants of the aurochs, which in turn are descended from the extinct European bison.[8] We will patiently explain to the uninformed why the prairie will die if hooved ruminants are removed. We will hold grazed grass in our fingertips and know that, because of the cattle, the rays of sun are able to reach the plant's growth points. And when necessary, we will rest our pastures, understanding that too much rest leads to atrophy.

We will do these things because of our ancestors, and because of our children. We will endure, sending anchoring taproots twenty feet into the soil so that our own mirror images may reach their outstretched limbs one hundred hopeful feet into the western sky.

9

Deerstalking

... as a Lakota male I had passed through one of the first stages of becoming a responsible person on the way to acquiring tribal cultural ideals ... to kill for food is a reality of life and is necessary if others are to live ... as my first kill, it was a significant moment which needed to be impressed upon my mind.

—Arthur Amiotte[1]

FOUR STRANDS OF WIRE, barbed, ran in tight horizontal lines next to the highway. Four hoofed legs hung limply, earthbound, the struggle gone from them now as the last breath was gone from the buck. He lay draped over the top wire, suspended between his world and ours.

The deer have grown fat and courageous, browsing in the meadow, sleeping in the thickets of oak brush, wandering across the roads. This deer had seen several hunting seasons already, bounded across many highways, vaulted easily over many fences. But this time he misjudged the distance, confused perhaps by the unnatural speed of an oncoming car. Such a waste, a loss. I cursed the highway silently, the ribbon of death, this by-product of progress.

We've watched the deer all summer, seen the fawns grow taller as they stood next to their mothers in the meadow, counted the muddy hoofprints left behind them at the spring. The young bucks band together and cruise the countryside, sensing change. On weekends, I follow Hondo down the deer paths, walking in single file through the woods with Matt and Sarah, our eyes searching the ground and trees around us. With each sign, droppings on the path or a patch on the limb of an aspen rubbed antler-smooth, we feel one step closer to their world. We get one quick magic glimpse of forest life.

Our first hunting season on the ranch approached. The Bear Lodge Mountains in which we live are part of northeastern Wyoming. Our small town, Sundance, is known as the whitetail deer capital of the world. Enthusiasts come here eagerly each fall to hunt the public forests and private ranchland.

Many are responsible, hard-working men and women who look forward to being in the hills and outdoors. They, like Chris, a local friend of ours, marvel at the quickness of the whitetail and give thanks if they are skilled and lucky enough to bring meat home to their families.

But hunts do not always work out as expected. Last year, Chris, a wildlife expert, came across a badly wounded buck in the woods. He faced a difficult choice: fill his license by shooting the suffering animal, whose meat by now was ruined; shoot the animal but leave him untagged and continue hunting, which would have been illegal; let the animal die a slow death and move on in search of a healthy buck who could provide meat for the table—a legal though immoral choice. He reluctantly chose the first, meatless option.

There are those hunters who would not have fretted over Chris's dilemma. They bring no honor with them and leave no honor behind when they are gone. I have heard them boast of their prowess while eating locally raised chicken-fried steak at the corner cafe. And I have seen the ungutted deer riding their tailgates, heads slumped with the weight of heavy, useless antlers—imposing trophies to be hung above mantels—testimonials to tall tales. Their peers may not know that the flesh of the deer rots by the roadside, but the hunter knows. Such people are less than hunters, and to call them hunters is a betrayal to men and women like Chris. They have been unfaithful to an age-old trust and have broken the link that joins them to life's cycle.

Matt is keenly aware of the ambiguity of the situation; his questions are to the point. All summer we have shared the land with the deer, felt privileged to see them. Then hunting season approaches and he knows his father will hunt. Matt looks forward to the chance to hike the woods and walk the deer and cattle paths, but he feels an inner conflict even at his young age. He anxiously awaits this chance to be alone with Mark, man-to-man. But at night, when I am tucking him into bed and we are alone, he speaks in questions.

"Remember the fawn we saw this summer, Mom, the one out in the horse pasture where Dad was fixing fence?" And then I remember, too, the newborn fawn hidden in the deep grass that first hot day of summer. Panting from dehydration when we found him, he was much smaller than normal—a twin perhaps. Hondo towered over him, delicately licking the fawn's drooping ears while the kids and Mark hurried to the house for warm milk. They returned too late.

"Remember him, Mom? He was so cute. He had those little spots all over him and he wasn't any bigger than Simon. How come his mom just left him there? Do you think we scared her away?" We could have, I knew. But I wondered why she had chosen a spot so close to the barn to give birth. Were we less of a threat than the coyotes on the hill?

"I wouldn't want to shoot a doe, Mom, 'cause what if she had a baby? Do you think someone shot her mom?" No, I explained, it wasn't hunting season yet, not for another five months, and by then the fawns would know enough to raise their own tail-flags at the first sign of danger.

"I want to go with Dad to shoot a buck when I get older. How old will I have to be, Mom?" Then I remember a story my father told me, not about the first time he ever hunted, but about the last time. He and my mother were spending their honeymoon by Lake Tahoe, near Yosemite. As they walked together through the forest, my father spotted a five-point buck near a clearing in the trees. He knelt, lifting his rifle to take aim. My mother stepped quietly away, watching him. Their eyes met and he saw a sad, rueful expression upon her face. Across the clearing, the buck stood motionless, alert and wary, nostrils flared. Then my father saw the doe—standing a few yards away from the buck, staring straight at my dad. He looked from her wide, frozen eyes to my mother's, and then slowly he lowered the rifle and, taking her arm, walked away.

When you are grown, Matt, will you remember the fawn who died in the grass? Will you say a prayer for him, as well as for the deer who graces our dinner table?

"Mom, can I ask you something?" *Of course, but I may not have the answer.* I wait patiently for the question, and it seems to take a long time.

"Mom, how come I want to hunt so much but I get sad inside at the same time?" I see the beginning of a crystal tear in his eye and wonder if he has noticed the one in mine.

Ah, the double-edged sword. I should have all the answers, yet I have none. Mark respects life, he understands why I anguish over the buck draped across the barbed wire. What inner drive is it, then, that causes him to hoist the rifle onto his shoulders and traipse quietly across the draw and into the thickets of oak brush in the cold pre-dawn? Filling the freezer is part of it, but it is not the entire answer, not in this age of supermarket convenience that fools many people into thinking that meat naturally grows inside of plastic wrap. The answer goes deeper than that.

It is partly the challenge of the tracking, meeting the whitetail, alert and cautious, in his own territory, knowing all the while that the deer sees more, is deaf to nothing—an intuitive creature. But that still is only part of the explanation.

It is also the sensual and gratifying sound as one foot after another touches the earth, causing the dry leaves to mate with the dirt. It is stepping outside our door and breathing the same air that the deer breathe, seeing them graze on our meadow. This is no more our land, though, than is the sky above us our sky. Our ownership is fleeting, superficial, man-made. We *would* go to war over it, though—we would fight the subdividers and the "range reformers" to the death over its title, but that is precisely because *we do* realize that the land does not belong to us, but rather has been entrusted to our stewardship.

Part of the answer is looking up into the sky when the sentinel hawk takes flight and circles, knowing that somewhere nearby a buck watches the same hawk, hears the dry leaf. It is the memory deep within of a great-grandfather walking a similar path, seeing a similar hawk.

That is only the first, conscious layer of memory, however. If I peel back the layers, go centuries deep, draw the bowstring taut and chant a song of praise to the Great Provider, then I begin to sense the natural order of things. I begin to put the pieces together. My father's story was romantic and he did the right thing, for him, at that moment in the woods. But I know now that the antlers which will adorn our log walls will not be a trophy, but a key to an ancient past.

When Arthur Amiotte, a Lakota artist and writer, tells of the time he killed his first animal, he tells also of the rituals that accompanied this first kill. His grandmother invited many people, preparing a feast of celebration. All shared a cooked morsel of the tiny bird who had died so that a six-year-old boy might experience this rite of passage. All understood it as "a significant moment which needed to be impressed" upon a young boy's mind.

How do I put all this into words that *my* young son will understand? I talk to him about God, I read to myself from Deuteronomy, and I try to teach him about honor—esteem for all that lives, respect for all that dies. He learns these things from me, and from his father, but I envy Mr. Amiotte his traditions and wonder what our ranching neighbors would think if we invited them to taste a bite of baked blue jay or sautéed garter snake.

Some of them would understand, especially those who still take the time to deep-fry the oysters cut from the scrotums of the bull calves at branding time. These are not eaten for the nutrients they contain but rather for the vitality they symbolize—the actual seed of life. When Mark brings deer meat home for our table, I want Matt and Sarah to appreciate the hard winters that were endured, the fawns that were fathered.

The double-edged sword cuts deep, right to the quick.

On opening day of hunting season Mark did, indeed, bring a deer home. It was snowing lightly, the timid winter sun hung close to the earth. He headed out past the barn and across the draw, the dry snow crunching beneath his feet. He tracked the deer for two hours in the early morning, and then shot him clean—dropping him fast. He had to drag him a mile, up a steep-sided aspen gulch, through the tall brush, and then out of the woods and across the hay field. The well-developed buck almost outweighed Mark. When I first saw the deer, stripped of his tawny coat and hanging by the antlers in the granary, he was stretched taller than either of us. His muscles lay exposed, covered by transparent membranes. I touched a front hoof and it moved loosely in response, not yet stiff with death. That night I fried the tenderloins cut from his back for supper and saw his glassy eyes in the hot grease.

Eating wild meat was not new to me; back in Colorado we often had elk in the freezer. But this was my first time to experience it from beginning to end, from deer grazing in the meadow to meat frying in the pan. When Mark brought the heart and liver into the house and Matt and Sarah asked to see it, I was confronted by a moment of truth. To understand this thing, I needed to face it full on. So I reached inside the plastic bag and withdrew the heart. Matt and Sarah stood on each side of me, their expressions full of curious amazement.

"That's his heart," they said, needing no answer. It was warm in my hands, the pulsating memory still strong. I had never seen blood so red, not even my own. It clung to my hand and to the spaces between my fingers. For a moment I felt the civilized layers of memory peel away once again. Genetic impressions surfaced, revealing the beginnings of a nervous system no longer guided solely by instinct, but which had embraced tradition as well. The blood on my skin became, for a split second, familiar.

I slowly placed the heart back in the bag while Matt and Sarah "oohed and aahed." It was with reluctance that I washed the stubborn blood from my fingers, for I was glad that I had held this deer's heart in my hands, giving to him a proper farewell.

The questions Matt and Sarah ask force me to look inward, to examine my beliefs and actions. And sometimes this probing makes me uncomfortable, for it strips me of my cloak of rationalization. Hunting is not a tradition to be taken lightly. Traditions, like legacies, are passed on from one generation to the next and should have meaning and value. We should not be afraid, nor should we forget, to celebrate even the smallest of birds, the tiniest of kittens.

When Matt is grown and has a family of his own, he may also choose to hunt and fill his winter freezer. And if his children question him, as he questions me, I hope his answers do not come too easily. I hope that he will still shed that solitary tear.

10

Forced to Trade

*I seem to stand on the bank of a river. My wife and little girl are beside
me. In front the river is wide and impassable, and behind are
perpendicular cliffs. No man of my race ever stood there before.
There is no tradition to guide me.*

—Standing Bear of the Poncas, 1879[1]

ERCHED IN OUR OAK CHINA HUTCH next to my grandmother's
antique cocoa set is a picture of Mark and me taken on our
honeymoon in Jackson, Wyoming. The photo technique is
old-fashioned, popular in western tourist towns because of the
antique, intaglio-like effect. The image is photographed directly
onto the back of a piece of glass, like the old tintypes, and the glass,
painted in sepia tones, becomes the actual picture.

This is our wedding portrait, framed in antiqued gold wood
and matted with etched copper. I am not wearing a white satin
gown, however, but am dressed as an Indian maiden—wearing a
white, fringed doeskin tunic adorned with bands of porcupine quill
work. Around my neck is a beaded buffalo-bone choker that is too
large, more aptly suited to a man's muscular neck. At the time, I did
not recognize the embroidery as quill work nor the choker as bone.
My blonde waist-long hair—banded in two ponytails held together
by sunburst-beaded leather ties—drapes modestly across my leather-
covered breasts. The costume, all but the hair ties, belonged to the
studio.

Mark is wearing leather chaps over his faded Wranglers. The
triangular point of his neckerchief hangs down, covering the collar
on his western shirt. Both his shirt and leather vest have snap
closures, and his riding chaps are fringed. His cowboy hat is tipped
to the side, and his dark mustache curls slightly down at the corners.

His hair is dark; no flecks of gray yet appear. On one arm he carries a lever-action rifle, and strapped around his waist is a leather holster and six-shooter. Most of what Mark wears is his own, all but the firearms—these he did not bring on our Wyoming honeymoon.

We stand side by side in the portrait, our arms hooked together in a gesture that taunts history while pointing to the future. What would married life have been like back then for such a couple? An American Indian and an Anglo cowboy would not have had an easy time of things.

The young woman in the picture stands by her man's side with head held high, and unlike many traditional Indian brides with downcast eyes, she stares straight at the camera. Her expression is confident and proud. The youthful-looking cowboy does not appear trail-weary. Did he spruce himself up for the occasion perhaps—pay a couple of bits for a tub of hot water and a bar of lye soap? Had he grown tired of the long cattle drives and the solitary lifestyle? Did the two of them meet and, despite all odds, fall in love? Did the cowboy trade with a reservation-bound chief—fresh beef for a daughter's chance at a new life? Or maybe he had even traded his best horse?

Would Mark still, after all these years, trade his best horse for me? This question will appall many of my liberated friends. Yet, I wonder … *Would I still urge my father to accept the trade? Would I be worth the cowboy's best horse, even now?*

But I am not an Indian maiden. The small amount of Cherokee ancestry I have does not warrant my registration on the rolls. The cowboy in Mark, however, goes deep. And life is still not easy in these historic times. Good horses, like good partners, are hard to find.

The appearance of the horse liberated the Plains Indians, revolutionizing their hunting and warring cultures. The buffalo no longer had to be hunted on foot, nor did the camp dogs have to pack the people's belongings from one encampment to the next. Tipis became larger and more spacious because the horses, the *sacred dogs*, could pull large travois behind them. The warrior's work, and the woman's work, became much easier.

Some ranchers, both red and white, have replaced their horses with four-wheelers. "Wish they'd invented these things years ago. Hell, they don't buck, can't break a leg, and you won't founder 'em on green grass. Don't need to saddle the damn things neither!" Not all ranchers are so vocal about the loss of tradition: many park their four-wheelers *behind* the barn, out of sight. Yet for some, especially older ranchers with arthritic bones, the machines have been liberating—giving them back their mobility, allowing them a few more years of calving-out heifers and fixing fence.

Mark swings a saddle onto the back of a horse as if he were born doing it. I cannot imagine him *not* doing it. I cannot imagine burying him without laying a supple bridle alongside his prone body, a bridle that still smells of horse sweat and leather. I cannot imagine burying him without leaving him a set of well-worn reins around which to wrap his fingers. But if I do outlive him, I doubt I will have the courage to sacrifice his favorite war horse for him to ride upon in The Land of Many Lodges, as the Indian maiden in the portrait would have been willing to do. I hope they both will forgive me this cowardice, this feeble-hearted lack of faith.

When John (Fire) Lame Deer talks about Lakota culture in *Lame Deer: Seeker of Visions*, he talks about both the old culture and the new. Referring to the sacred Sun Dance, he says,

> It is good to see people hold onto their Indianness ... . There are some old-timers among us, pointing to the deep scars on their chests, scoffing at the dancers of today.
>
> "They don't go underneath the muscle," they say. "It's only the flesh ... the young men have gone soft."
>
> They complain that nobody hangs suspended anymore, or drags eight buffalo skulls after him till his flesh is stripped from his shoulder blades.[2]

But John (Fire) Lame Deer did not believe the young men had gone soft, for he knew that this era carries with it invisible sacrifices, sacrifices that tear not at the flesh, but at the spirit.

No, in many ways the dancers of today are braver than those of days gone by. They must fight not only the weariness, the thirst and the pain, but also the enemy within their own heart—the disbelief, the doubts, the temptation to leave for the city, to forget one's people. ...[3]

I risk angering the spirit of John (Fire) Lame Deer when I compare the plight of the cowboy and Indian and find it to be similar. Seventeen years ago, when I clothed myself in the quilled doeskin dress of an Indian maiden, I risked angering the spirit of the woman who once wore that dress, though the thought never occurred to me then. I risk her anger still. But I do not believe that our life experiences are so different that we have less in common than we share. Did she not, also, once stand proudly beside her husband? And did not her husband once stand proudly beside her?

Placing the antique-looking wedding portrait back in the china hutch, I stare out the bay window. Our two old mares, Cindy (whom Mark broke and trained) and Romie, graze in the thick grass that grows beneath the oak trees. The geldings graze nearby. Romie's roan-colored hairs are now tinged with gray, her taut muscles more flaccid with the passing of each cold winter; yet I remember her when she was *my* war horse, when we counted coups together.

Five generations of Lamberts planted their roots in the foothills of the Rockies, rearing their children and raising their crops and livestock. Had we been able to stay, Matt and Sarah would have been the sixth—and we did not choose to leave the ranch; that decision was not ours to make.

Denver has spread like an oil slick in the last one hundred years, swallowing up grasslands and ranches and wildlife habitat at an alarming rate. In all directions, north, south, east, and west, the city has spread. Crime and concrete have hardened the city; high taxes and high rises have changed its outer, and inner, profiles.

A decade after our honeymoon journey took us north, Mark and I again returned to Wyoming, trying to outrun the oil slick. The decision to leave our native Colorado was a hard and painful one to make, for we were leaving behind both good land and good people. But we were not the first to flee encroachment—nor were the American Indians. We all know that man has been encroaching on man since Cain slew Abel, in varying degrees of holocaust.

Mark and I face no genocide. We do not fear for the lives of our children. But we do fear the enemy within our own hearts—the disbelief, the doubts—and we fear this, the most recent battle, with the rural western way of life. We fear that decisions about grazing (on public and private lands) are being made by bureaucrats far removed from the land herself.

The land is much more than a series of artificially drawn boundaries—sections and townships, Bureau of Land Management parcels and forest service allotments. The land is marshes and meadows, deep draws and dry gulches, streams that flow from neighbor to neighbor, from high country to harrowed field.

Who will be the caretakers of the future if there is no one left to remember the land as she once was? Who better understands her than those who know intimately the dust of her parched soil during time of drought, the abundance of her wildflowers during time of plenty?

We also, like Standing Bear of the Poncas, feel as if we have been backed up against the sheer perpendicular walls of the cliffs of change. And we cannot help but wonder what tradition will guide *us* into the next century.

11

Elusive Prey

The spirit always finds a pathway. The Chanunpa, Sacred Pipe, finds a pathway. It's like a deer trail, it's going to lead you to medicines and waterholes and a shelter.

—Wallace Black Elk[1]

I DECIDED TO PURCHASE MY FIRST deer-hunting license less for the meat than for the camaraderie. I wanted to be alone with Mark in the woods, where we could forget our twentieth-century jobs and our twentieth-century mortgage. We arranged for a baby-sitter and waved good-bye to Matt and Sarah as they stood on the deck holding Black Jack and the surviving gray kitten, aptly named Tuffy.

Lightly falling ice-like snowflakes stung with a tiny prick as they hit my cheek. Layered for the weather, I wore long underwear, jeans, two pairs of socks, two sweaters, and a vest hidden beneath my insulated coveralls. A fluorescent-orange hunting vest provided the final layer. Our boots crunched in the snow as we walked down the path to the barn. Mark carried the rifle slung across his shoulder, the bullets stuffed in his down vest. Hondo, usually our constant companion, had to stay at the barn.

"Hey, buddy," Mark said, tousling the fur on Hondo's rugged black head, "you'd scare the deer away if we let you come." Dejected, Hondo sat on the wooden floor, then lowered his chest and placed his muzzle on his outstretched paws.

Mark, used to doing these things for himself, removed the bullets from his vest and loaded the 270 Winchester. Putting the safety on, he hoisted the rifle (which had no fancy scope) back onto his shoulder, and we headed away from the barn, across the draw and up the hill.

The timid sun hung close, a low-wattage frosted bulb in the winter sky. Mark struck a steady, even pace. I fought impatience before allowing his rhythm to prevail. We walked side by side, his ease and quiet ways drifting subtly around me like unstirred cream in black coffee. Our steps left gray imprints in the dusting of snow.

By all rights, *I* should have been carrying the weapon—should have been carrying on my grandmother Helen's tradition. I imagined her lifting her own gun, feeling the hardness of its wooden stock against her shoulder, feeling the power of the rifle's recoil as she pulled the trigger.

This, my first hunting experience, was a self-test of sorts, a "put your money where your mouth is" challenge to myself. Not to see if I could kill a buck, but to see if I could catch a whiff of the past, a sense of our human predator instinct—pure in its direction, aimed not at the corporate ladder nor at fellow man, but at food, sustenance. I was also testing my own predator instinct—which may have surfaced sooner had I been carrying the weapon.

Our eyes scanned the horizon for deer. Mark walked purposefully, poised. We headed straight up the steep side of a small butte, not the easy way but the most direct. I panted, small puffs of breath escaping my mouth, then I stopped after another fifty uphill yards—winded. Mark walked ten more yards to the top of the butte, then waited. I plodded on and finally joined him on the vantage point. To the north, the barn and house nestled among the trees; to the west, the big hay field bordered the high pine ridge; to the south and east (on the state-owned land we lease) were hills covered with pines and oak brush. Great red cuts of weather-eroded gullies gouged washouts into the rolling grassland.

"Pretty good view from up here," Mark said, sitting down on the top boulder of several that made up the crest of the butte.

Despite the opaque snow, we did have a good view. He lifted the binoculars that hung around his neck and peered into them, aiming down the draw. Then he slowly steered them around, pausing every few inches.

"See anything?" I asked, forcing my mind to focus on the hunt.

"No, nothing yet." He handed me the binoculars. "Here, take a look if you want."

I took them from him and looked at length around the ranch. The binoculars captured circular scenes and brought them close for my inspection. I saw no deer, no birds, no hunters on the state land. We seemed to be the only creatures foolish enough to sit on a rock on the top of a hill on a cold, snowy morning. I brought the binoculars around until Mark came in view. His dark, reddish mustache blurred at this close range, and his eyes filled the lenses. I handed the binoculars back.

"Think everything is holed up because of the snow?" I asked.

"Could be." He reached out and touched me, putting his gloved hand on the leg of my coveralls. It was the first time he had touched me all morning. I wondered if he knew how each small gesture such as this affected me. One of the secrets of being married to a man like Mark is noticing the small gestures, for they tell a private, silent story. So often with us our best talks make no noise.

On the high, exposed butte the subfreezing temperature penetrated even our many layers of clothing. Mark, in response, rose to go, and we headed down the other side, abreast of each other. No longer winded, I found that my little-used office muscles loosened with exertion. We walked for an hour but saw no wildlife. Even the squirrels stayed hidden in their beds of dried leaves.

"I've never seen it so quiet out here." Mark's low tone didn't disturb the silence. I remembered many walks by myself, in woods too quiet, when I wished just once to eavesdrop unnoticed, to be accepted as a fellow creature of the wild. But for me, the deer paths led nowhere—I did not recognize their signposts or their destinations.

We talked about simple things as we walked, not speaking at great length but in sentences half-finished. Partners and lovers speak this way, but then, so also do two strangers who have just met and do not wish to reveal vulnerable intimacies.

The snow continued. The morning grew long and the air warmed. The sun made a brief appearance, pushing the clouds aside just long enough to cast black shadows upon the whiteness. We crested a short hill and were confronted on the other side by three large Angus-cross bulls who greeted us sullenly. They had not yet been retrieved by our neighbors, who leased summer pasture from us for their cows and calves. Two of the bulls were lying down. The third, wary of humans not horseback, rose in obvious agitation and eyed us suspiciously.

Mark walked on, unconcerned, while I hurried to catch up, wondering if fluorescent orange had the same affect on bulls as did the color red. The standing bull lifted his head and, with eyes glaring, rotated it in our direction. We soon disappeared up the next hill and out of the bull's vision and range. How easy to become not the predator but the prey.

Circling behind the highest ridge, we found our first fresh sign—hoofprints cutting deeply into the shallow snow. We followed the tracks, winding in and out of the oak trees and brush on a steep, narrow path. The deer remained sure-footed; I slid often, leaving a telltale muddy slide mark.

"Do you think it's a buck?" I asked.

"Could be, or a heavy doe. Can't tell really."

We came upon fresh spoor—a group of small, warm, dark brown droppings left directly in the path—visible earthy residue of the elusive animal we followed. I was content being led on this slow-paced chase, the deer breaking the trail. He went up, then down, then circled, always close to bushes with low-hanging branches that forced us to walk doubled over.

In a small clearing another set of deer tracks joined the ones we followed. These smaller tracks made less of an indentation in the snow. Then a third set of tracks, made by a coyote, began circling the deer tracks. The stalking took a new twist. No longer the only predators, we now followed the bold coyote who stalked the deer as well. The even, well-spaced tracks of the deer indicated neither was injured. Perhaps the coyote planned for the future, preparing to scavenge if opportunity came his way. Maybe, only curious, he went the way of the crowd.

The larger set of deer tracks moved three feet off the path, where steam rose from a melted yellow hole in the snow. I took off my glove and reached toward the stained snow, feeling the warmth that had melted the snow down to bare ground.

"It's still warm. They can't be very far ahead. Do you think a buck marked this spot?" It occurred to me I should ask for the rifle.

"Probably so," Mark answered. "Have to wait and see."

The coyote's tracks stopped at the fresh urine, then went on another foot where he, too, left his scent on a low bush. It wouldn't have surprised me if Mark, trudging down the path, fought an urge to do the same. If it would help stop the "war on the West," the threat to private property rights, and the encroaching subdivisions, I would be willing to personally mark every inch of our territory. The act would, at least, lend a bit of levity to the situation.

There is a supernatural aura in the lingering presence of a creature who takes a journey just one step ahead of yours. We often journey through life that way, in pursuit of the invisible. There was a lesson to be learned from the deer's steady, unfaltering steps.

"Where are you going?" I asked Mark as he headed off the path and up a hill.

"Oh, thought we might stop up here and see if they don't cross over in front of us."

I followed him up the hill where he already sat, leaning against a tall ponderosa. He rested the rifle on his bent knees, the barrel pointing aimlessly across the steep draw below. I sat next to him and placed my hand on his thigh, relaxing my head onto his shoulder.

Only a month or so ago, on a hot fall day, I had come up here by myself, following a cattle trail and looking for turkey feathers. The wild turkeys often use the easy paths cut by the cattle. Led astray by a bluebird who flitted from tree to tree, I followed. Turning from the cow path, I climbed straight up, my hands finding balance on the steep ground until I finally reached the same spot where Mark and I now sat. I had given up the bluebird chase but arrived at the top hot and out of breath. Taking off my windbreaker and the shirt beneath, I basked in the luxury of that very private sunny clearing, the view of the distant mountains obscured by the thick pine needles.

Later, I told Mark about the walk and the sunbath, and of wishing that he had been by my side. So here we now sat, both thinking the same thing, layered in fluorescent clothing.

The soft sound of leaves crunching came from across the draw. Between two trees stepped a nut-brown doe. She paused and pointed her nose upwind toward us, stared in our direction, then moved on, disappearing into the pines. Behind her came a fawn, moving quickly to catch up. Then he too was gone.

These deer were not the ones we tracked. They had come from the opposite direction. I sat next to Mark, my hand still on his thigh, the rifle still resting on his knees. We watched the doe and fawn appear, then vanish, like apparitions. I felt I knew them intimately, yet not at all—not so unlike a husband and wife.

We rose from the cold ground and I thought of how good the hot sun on my skin had felt a month before, and of how much better it would have felt had Mark been with me. He stood next to me, waiting, his black neckerchief knotted around his neck. I hoped that next spring we would return to this place, just the two of us, not needing the rifle as an excuse. I wanted to watch the bluebird fly from tree to tree, to feel the sun warm our winter-chilled bones. I wanted to recapture that elusive prey, a vision of ourselves as man and woman.

12

Turkey Tracks

The way of the Cherokee is to know the past is gone. Though a golden thread still links us to it ... it no longer holds us captive.
—Joyce Sequichie Hifler[1]

YESTERDAY A NORTHWESTERLY WIND turned lightly falling snow into a blizzard. White covered the countryside, then the wind swept the ridges bare, piling drifts one upon the other. The deer, coyotes, and turkeys remained hidden, waiting for the storm to pass.

Then the blizzard was over. The wild turkeys wandered up and down the steep hill next to the county road where the pine trees shelter the ground. On the other side of the road, our side, snow still covers everything.

Inside our log home, sequestered in my own private world, I watch the glow of the embers from the woodburning stove. It is midafternoon, and Matt and Sarah are still napping. Opening the door to the stove slowly so smoke will not drift into the room, I bend low and blow onto the smoldering red-orange wood. The embers coax forth flames that caress the sides of the logs in a heated embrace.

Mark felled the tree from which these logs were cut. He split the large pieces of dead oak and stacked these wooden bones, layer upon layer, by the side of the house. I am grateful he wants to provide for me in this basic way, though I would be capable of doing these things. I could split the logs and fill the woodbox. It would take longer and not be done as well at first, but that is not the point.

Reaching into the woodbox, I carefully pick out a log, put it into the stove, and blow again on the embers. Warmth radiates from the flames. Outside, the tractor makes deep, grumbling metallic sounds as Mark pushes snow from the driveway, the loader scraping and moving the snow to a pile that grows larger as the winter grows colder.

The turkeys wander off the hillside toward the barn. They fly onto the top rail of the fence, then hop, one by one, into the corral. Pecking with staccato bobs, they eat the grain we have scattered about and the grass seeds from the horses' leftover hay.

I sit by the woodburning stove and look at my grandmother's bone-handled carving set, which sits in the china hutch next to our wedding portrait. No family stories accompany this carving set. I never saw my grandfather use it, never sat by his side as a youngster, mouth watering in anticipation, while he carved the Sunday roast.

To have no tradition is to be without a culture. Perhaps that is why Mark's family history, five generations on the original homestead, is so important to me. He was linked to his forefathers' land—to the cottonwoods that grew in the shadow of Wildcat Mountain and to the towering peaks of the Rockies. Here, in Wyoming, he reconnects, while I, for the first time, begin to truly understand the Lakota expression, *mitakuye oyasin*, "we are all related," to one another, to each creature, to the sky above and the earth below.

The expression is foreign to me, though, and I struggle with its pronunciation—it reminds me that I have no tribe, no ethnicity. I am colorless, transparent. There is a stigma in being white near the turn of this new century. Perhaps that is why the environmental movement is funded mainly by upper-middle-class white women who seek a cause. We sip freshly ground mocha java from thin-lipped cups and stare over the rims at our hybrid skin. Perhaps we are in search of color—green for the begetting of new seed, sky blue for ancestral souls, nurturing yellow for family legacies, red for passionate births and deaths.

I am tired of being colorless, of looking to other cultures for a reflection of my past. My ancestors must have left tracks, cast shadows. I ask questions, but the answers are incomplete, skeletal.

Lacking ancestral roots, I borrow from others. I cleave to Mark's history. Like the bird who lacks the genetic intelligence to build her own nest, I claim a deserted patch for my own. There is an advantage in being colorless, though. When I hike to the top of the ridge, the reflection of the Bear Lodge Mountains passes through me like a breeze through an open window. I sift the sandstone soil between my fingers, breathe in the scent of sage. When one is transparent, colorless, it is easier to absorb.

I surround myself with historic-looking mass-produced objects. A battery-operated pendulum clock hangs above the woodstove. Lace valances hang from the tops of our log windows, and friends ask me, "Did your grandmother crochet these?" I answer no, confessing they were mail-ordered from a catalogue. I caress the soft lace before taking the curtains outside and carefully shaking the dust from the woven fabric, pretending they are irreplaceable.

My few family heirlooms guard their stories well. A small gold pocket watch, resting on black velvet and framed in gold-painted pine, hangs next to the woodstove. It belonged to my father's father. But I never saw him hold it in his rough logger's hand, never heard it tick. Perhaps that is why I framed Romie's horse blanket and hung it on the wall, for woven into the red-and-brown-striped fabric are many stories, stories I know well.

I was fourteen when I bought Romie. She was only four, a strawberry roan mare with bay markings. The hair on her body was flecked with reds and browns. Her legs, mane, and tail were black. The half-Arabian heritage was evident in her small bones, dished face, and large, intelligent, almond-shaped brown eyes.

We spent every summer day together. I took her from the confines of her dark stall at the county fairgrounds and we sought out patches of morning sun. We were young, full of daring energy. Astride her bare back, I soared through open farmland. We splashed through narrow, deep canals, green wet willows whipping the water. Our passage echoed from the packed dust of deserted country roads. Strands of barbed wire snaked across our path. A front hoof became ensnared. Romie stood, trembling but still, while I knelt to free her. We crossed the South Platte River, only a few miles downstream of where Mark's own rite of passage was taking place. Fast-sucking quicksand crept knee-high on Romie's legs; I slid off and coaxed her onto harder, dryer land. We jumped over fences ahead of fancy-bred hunters who pursued the wily fox. Only etiquette kept the hunt master in the lead. We were an unbeatable pair. I can still feel the frothy horse sweat beneath my bare legs, can still hear Romie snorting and blowing as I shoot pretend arrows from her back at imaginary buffalo racing with the wind.

But those were younger, faster days. The bareback riding gave way to a saddle and blanket and, little by little, carefree summer days were replaced by part-time jobs and college semesters.

The future was given to me, promising and exciting. Opportunities abound. But without a legacy there is no heritage, the future lacks depth. Romie's blanket is, at least, a beginning.

Outside, the turkeys begin to climb through the corral and head out past the barn and down into the draw. Leaving linear tracks in the snow, the birds disappear one by one. Mark is still clearing the driveway as I decide to go outside.

The wind is blowing. Imprints clutter the new-fallen snow in the corral. I follow the trail down into the draw, but the turkeys have vanished. Their footprints mark only the surface of the snow, while mine sink thigh-deep into the drifts. A single tail feather with banded markings lies in the path; the quill is hollow and tough. I turn and head back to the house, taking the feather with me. Smoke rises from the chimney and the wind sends it spiraling upward. I stop near the woodpile and bend to pick up the ax. The wooden handle is slick and smooth, and I decide that I like the balanced feel of the double-bitted ax head.

Back inside, I open the china hutch and carefully place the turkey feather between the bone-handled carving set and the wedding portrait. Perhaps, when Matt and Sarah wake from their naps, we will go outside and I will show them where the wild turkeys gathered on the hill. I may even put a braised roast in the oven to slow-bake, then sharpen up my grandmother's bone-handled carving set while I tell them stories of *my* younger, faster days.

13

Red Suspenders

ARCTIC AIR ENGULFS US. Vapor escapes from the tractor's exhaust pipe and hangs above the ground, forming a cloud that does not rise or move. Chunks of once-thawed snow have turned to ice, fossils of frozen footsteps that map out yesterday's chores, immortalizing the path from the barn to the house and the haystack to the pasture. They become a legacy to the hardness of winter, which lasts until the first melting reveals a lost glove or empty grain sack hibernating beneath the snow.

The temperature is an even zero degrees. The sky is a pale blue and the earth a subdued white. The bare branches and wet bark of the oaks appear in black and white, like an old, weathered photo. Only the telltale blue shadows in the snow and the cautious sky speak of color.

The horses bury their noses in piles of strewn hay, and steam rises warm and moist from their feeding ground. A saddle of white powdered snow rests upon Romie's back. Silhouetted against the white background, her slightly swayed back appears concave as her spine disappears into a distant snowy ridge.

Just when it seems this relentless cold will last forever, a warm wind blows across the eastern edge of the Rockies: a Chinook. It brings a brief January thaw—to the Bear Lodge Mountains and to our winter-worn souls.

Icicles hang from the eaves and snow falls from the limbs of Sassy's tree, landing with heavy wet thuds upon the ground. She has stolen the keys to the tractor, hiding them within the deep recesses of her oak tree. Hondo and the cats bask in the sun on the wooden deck. Snow begins to recede from the tops of the ridges, exposing bare buttes and dry winter grasses, and Sassy appears on the edge of a limb, disgruntled by the intruding noise when she hears a spare key turn over the tractor's motor. Farther west, Lois and J. W.'s cattle loosen their humped-up gaits and follow his feed truck with supple enthusiasm.

The deer appear in the draws and on the horizon. They scatter themselves across the meadow like winter-birthed wildflowers; over twenty graze in the small hay field and more than sixty feed in the large meadow. Though they will provide no calf crop for us to market in the fall, we are glad to be able to share what drought-weakened winter feed there is. The deer prefer the tender short grasses of the meadow to the taller, wolfy grasses that have not been grazed by cattle. They are reckless with hunger, eating with the abandonment of storm-sequestered creatures.

The deer are not the only ones to venture out. Dry asphalt highways invite us to town. We splurge and take the kids out to eat, arriving at Higbee's, the local coffee shop, which is already crowded with restless ranchers exchanging stories of storms and stock shows. It is impossible not to eavesdrop. Winter drifts, like summer trout, are measured and compared.

"This country just doesn't get the snow like it used to. No, siree. Why I remember when the drifts used to stand taller than a horse's back!"

"Folks nowadays don't know what a snowstorm is. Hell, this is just a skiff!"

We watch one old gentleman kick the mud from his feet as he enters the cafe. He pulls leather work gloves off gnarled hands; the skin over the knuckles is cracked and white. He removes a Scotch cap from his head, revealing a pale forehead. He has weathered many winters.

Soon he is joined by another gray-haired man. Unbuckled overboots flap loosely as they walk to a table. The waitress brings coffee while they loosen their neckerchiefs and take off their lined canvas jackets. The first gentleman wears bright red suspenders, and I smile at the surprise. They lift their coffee cups in unison, and hot steam forms a temporary fog between them. Blowing to cool the hot coffee, they talk in low voices and their gnarled hands shake slightly. The cups rattle as they come to rest on the saucers.

A third man appears in the doorway and spots his friends sitting in the corner of the cafe. Unnoticed, he walks up behind them. He grabs hold of the red suspenders with his hand and pulls them toward him quickly. Then he lets go with a sudden jerk and the suspenders snap back with a loud thwacking noise. The two old friends look up, their eyes sparkling, and a few playful cuss words are exchanged.

"Damn, where the hell you been all winter, anyway?" The three men settle into the cracked vinyl booth for an hour of reminiscing and shootin' the bull.

Hanging on the fading plaster walls around them are original Sarah Rogers watercolors depicting horses, buffaloes, and eagles. The townspeople claim "Sally" as *their* artist (though she's originally from Florida) and proudly point out to tourists that she was recently chosen as Wyoming's Wildlife Conservation Artist of the Year. The painted canvas face of an Indian stares down at our table. The painting is entitled *Teal Shirted Red Banded Yellow Shafted Flicker Winged*, but Jinx and Steve, the cafe's owners, affectionately call the Indian simply "George."

"Remind you of the B & B?" I ask Mark, not referring to the paintings but wondering instead if he is thinking of the local cafe back home and the old-timers who took him under their wings after his father's death.

"Does the B & B really have a bullet hole in the ceiling?" Matt asks, interrupting.

"Yep," Mark answers, stirring the tall glass of iced tea, which he drinks summer and winter.

"Did the sheriff really get killed?"

"Yep. He was my cousin's relative, way back when."

"Wow. A real gunfight. Like in a saloon." Matt looks at the somber face of George and then takes a bite of his hamburger.

Nearly one hundred years ago, the B & B Cafe (located in Castle Rock, Colorado, about eight miles southeast of Sedalia) had been a drugstore and soda fountain with a marble countertop, fancy mirrors, twirling stools, sarsaparillas, healing liniments, and elixirs. For the next century, the locals had gathered at the B & B. Then an ambitious reporter from a Denver newspaper did a feature story on the colorful and historical cafe. It became the "in place" to eat for business people making the half-hour commute from the city, and now the old-timers begrudgingly eat at a nearby restaurant with less atmosphere and fewer memories but more elbowroom.

A cold draft invades the cramped cafe as the door once again swings open, and in hobbles old Charlie, our water witcher. Watery eyes peering from beneath unruly eyebrows scope out the interior of the cafe, and he nods at several customers, then makes his way toward our table.

"What'd you have to do, come to town for a drink of water?" he ribs us.

"Naw," Mark teases back, "town ran out of water and asked us to bring in a few hundred gallons."

Charlie laughs, rubbing the back of his bare neck with a calloused hand. He wears only a lightweight jacket.

"Where's your winter coat, Charlie?" I ask.

"Don't need no winter coat yet. Ain't cold." He tugs on Sarah's ponytail. "Ain't cold yet, is it?"

"No," she answers in barely a whisper, a broad smile on her face.

"You buy yerself a snow machine yet?" he asks Mark.

"Those snowmobiles cost too much, Charlie. Can't afford 'em."

"Well, then, you'd better make yerself some snowshoes. You folks live in snow country up there. Ain't gonna stay nice forever."

"The wife got me a pair for Christmas, Charlie. Bear Paws they call 'em. Not as good as a horse, but they'll get me around."

Knowing it infuriates my liberated friends, I admit to liking it when Mark occasionally calls me "the wife." The term suggests a permanently bestowed title, somewhat like queen or duchess, a rare endowment in this easy-divorce era.

"Heck, a horse ain't gonna do you no good when the snow's ten feet deep. Better get you four pair of them Bear Paws. Unless you kids don't care 'bout missing school?"

Charlie tugs on Sarah's ponytail again, blinks his watery eyes, and then says "See ya, folks," before sauntering back to the corner table where the three old-timers sit huddled around their coffee cups.

"See ya, Charlie," Mark and I say, raising our hands in a half wave.

I turn back to face the children and suddenly hear the loud, familiar thwack of red suspenders, answered with "Hell, Charlie, you old trapper, you. Been holed up somewhere? Haven't seen you since the creeks froze up. What've you been doing, anyway? Hunting trap lines? Sit yer carcass down, you look ornery as hell. ..."

14

The Dance Goes On

Approach the maiden as one would approach any shy creature of the earth, gently, slowly, one step at a time, as one approaches a young antelope trembling in a cactus patch, for the shy heart is the same.
—Mari Sandoz[1]

WINTER HANGS ON but has grown weary, reminding me of a discourteous dinner guest who knows that it is time to leave but lurks at the door, one foot in, one foot out. The half-frozen melody of a meadowlark travels through the treetops, lighting note by note on the bare limbs of the big oaks. Then the forest grows still—for one noticeable moment.

The sky blackens with dark clouds that bear down upon the pine trees like monstrous locomotives, roaring past, one after the other. Wind howls, swirling snow across the yard and against the barn, then out into the pasture. Romie and the other horses huddle close to one another, bunched up in the trees, tails turned to the wind, eyes closed.

Mark and J. W. ride hard to gather in those cows who, restless with impending birth, wander away from the herd. The luckiest of the newborn calves suckle their mothers in the safety of the calving shed. For two days the winds blow. Clear skies come and go; snow falls when the clouds gather only to be whipped away, filling the cracks and crevices of the land as Winter purges himself one final time. At last he heads north, dragging overbooted feet across the meadow, leaving trails of muddy snow in his wake.

The meadowlark knows a new season is about to begin. He sends his call out across the open meadow where the sleepy roots of the prairie grasses and mountain asters listen for his song, waking and warming to the melody. The bare limbs of Sassy's oak tree vibrate gently as the notes bounce across their tips, rousing her from her nest. Sassy finds Sarah's cotton jump rope surfacing from a melting snow drift and hauls it—like a snake soggy with spring— into her hole. The next morning the jump rope is draped across the upper branches of the tree and left drying in the sun.

Sarah, too, is stirred into action by the sound of the meadow-lark. Forced to stay indoors by the storm, she dresses up and asks me to put on some music. She dances as if in a trance, barely old enough to be self-conscious. I watch discreetly from the kitchen. A violet dress with ivory lace drapes her young torso like apple blossoms on a slender sapling. As she moves noiselessly across the carpet on feet clad in pink satin ballet slippers, I am reminded of when her father and I first danced together, our bodies touching one moment, then separating—held apart by a few lonesome but hopeful notes. Spin, Sarah, spin. Someday, too soon, a young man will fall in love with you, and he will steal your heart away from me, and I am not sure that I will be able to stand it.

I wish I could freeze this moment in time, clasp it to me like a golden locket—keep this picture of her forever within my reach. Twirl, Sarah, twirl. She holds her long skirt in her hands, pointing her toes and pivoting on graceful legs. Her long ponytail flies behind her, leading the way or racing to catch up—I cannot tell which. The music ends, but she does not seem to notice. Twirl, Sarah, for me. But not too fast, nor too far, so soon. ...

There was a yellow tomcat out in the corral this afternoon. He left the barn and climbed on top of a large hill of manure that has been accumulating as Mark has been chiseling out the floor of the barn. Years of use have layered themselves on the dirt floor in the animal shed, and Mark hacks away at the frozen manure, carrying it out by the wheelbarrow to the corral. The yellow cat climbed to the top of this mound and then disappeared down the other side— a wandering tom come to visit Simon now that winter is heading out.

Simon has been responding to the coming of spring, greeting the meadowlark's call with her own heat-like cacophony, not nearly as melodious as the lark's but just as stirring. I look forward to new spring kittens.

The tom brings back thoughts of the mutilated kittens in the barn. A tomcat, apt sometimes to kill his own offspring, can be as dangerous as a raccoon. The yellow tom may have even been the culprit. Last fall, after the incident with the kittens, we baited a box trap and left it in the barn. The first night we weren't successful: the bait was gone, the trap empty. The next night Mark rigged the trap up a little differently, and in the morning a large ring-eyed raccoon hissed at us, caught inside. Matt and Sarah were excited to see a coon up close. Matt, angry at the raccoon, felt relocation too lenient a sentence.

We hauled the cage into the back of the pickup and took the coon several miles up the road to a small pond in the national forest. He watched us warily from inside the trap, hissing when we got too near. Mark set the cage on the ground with the door facing the pond, then cautiously opened the door and stepped back. The coon took off, running awkwardly through the tall grass, diving into the pond as he reached the water's edge.

That night we set the trap again, and again in the morning were greeted by a sullen masked face. We caught four raccoons in total, a family, and turned all four of them out up at the pond, hoping they would not return.

The yellow tom is not a loyal suitor. His actions are motivated by hormones, triggered by Simon's vociferous mating calls and feminine feline odors. Simon is driven by instinct and the ancient need to procreate. Romance does not enter into their relationship. Yet her insistent calls stir the female in me, tug at the mammal within, help me remember a passion as urgent as spring. I think of Sarah twirling in her violet dress while a storm ravages the countryside, and for a brief guilt-twinged moment, I envy her. Her dance card is yet unfilled, her tunes yet unsung. This twirling is but a prelude, an overture.

Simon is not troubled with ponderous thoughts. She is like a rhapsody, eager to improvise, willing to be spontaneous. She rubs against my leg and arches her back at my welcome touch. I know the feeling—I have arched my own back, more than a time or two, at Mark's welcome touch. Ours is a continuing ballad, a narrative in the process of being sung, the Chinook a promise on the horizon.

Not all men have the ability to elicit from me a maiden, virginal blush. This special quality endeared Mark to me early on. He recognized the shy heart, the trembling, wary stance, and I, thank God, recognized him—a clear, honest note.

Does the age of maidens, the age of innocence, exist only in our memories? Or can we find relevance in the words of Mari Sandoz even today? "Approach the maiden as one would approach any shy creature of the earth, as one approaches a young antelope trembling in a cactus patch, for the shy heart is the same."[2]

Sarah—slender-limbed, doe-eyed, creature of the earth. She deserves to be approached slowly, gently, one step at a time.

15

Growing Velvet

The higher power, the Great Mystery, is identified by all energies in life. The Great Mystery is in a blade of grass, an animal, a fowl, the thunder, or a rock.

—Dallas Chief Eagle[1]

AFTER A BALMY SHIRTSLEEVE DAY yesterday, a damp wind cooled today's temperature back to a seasonable forty degrees. Matt and Sarah had both been sick with the stomach flu, keeping me cooped up. When Mark came inside in the late afternoon, I eagerly pulled on my mud boots and jacket, paused at the door to debate the need for gloves and earmuffs, then headed outdoors bareheaded and bare-handed.

Hard winter was gone, taking the snow with it. The spongy earth succumbed to my weight, and the grasses, shortened by never-ending freezes, could be measured by the quarter-inch. The air, clear and new, filled my lungs, and I was grateful for the chance to finally walk the high ridge where two old smooth-barked trees stood side by side.

Everywhere, hanging like a dropped net over the grass and occasional pile of manure (horse, cow, and deer), was spread a cottony silver web. I stooped to get a better look. The gray cloud spread over the scaled-down universe at my feet, making an overcast day of a sunny one for all its miniature inhabitants. I peered closer, wanting to find at least one of the ambitious females who had helped to spin such a sky. Movement disappeared a split second before my eyes relayed the message, and I stared at a deserted city. The alarm caused by my footsteps traveled quickly. So hasty was the retreat, though, that the most prized possession was left unguarded. Rolled inside several layers of fine, sticky fluff awaited a cocoon of eggs, the future generation of this diminutive universe.

I did not resist the temptation to pluck the spider womb out of the low-hanging sky but carefully tore it open. Instead of finding tiny eggs full of tiny infant spiders trapped impatiently inside, I found dried, lifeless hulls. No future generation here. If any female had placed her aspirations in that imposter cocoon, she would soon be disappointed. The hulls crumbled in my hand, the strands of web clung stubbornly to my fingers. I wiped them on my jeans and stood up, towering above the gray ghost town below me. I knew a secret and felt godlike, my hand of fate powerful, the child in me disillusioned. Maybe there was no secret and all the spiders knew this town had no heirs. Maybe it truly was a ghost town after all— the fleeting movement only imagined.

I raised my vision from the ground and looked around. Knit here and there among the grasses of the pasture were small universes hidden beneath silver clouds with gray linings, surely not all of them ghost towns with barren wombs. I looked down at the film of web by my feet and the torn hole where the cocoon had rested, then walked on, up the hill toward the ridge.

Before going much farther, I came to another place where the spiders had woven a huge ground cover of sticky thread. Curious again, I knelt for a bird's-eye view but discerned no movement, no mad scramble for cover at the sound of my approach. Two small twigs lay just below the surface of the web, giving it a slightly peaked roof. Nestled in the cross that formed where the twigs met was another bundle of eggs. This time, no destructive urges goaded me to break apart the cocoon.

Then I saw her—a small brown spider, oval of belly and furry of back. She had not run away but steadfastly held her post, appearing to stare straight at me, an anchor line trailing behind her. This was no ghost town. Beneath the overcast sky of web, life teemed with potential heirs and future architects of the heavens— and she was there to protect them.

The spider did not fear me, nor I her. We stared at each other, one mother to another. Matt and Sarah entered my thoughts, small children with tummy aches and cranky dispositions who awaited my return. I stood stiff-legged, wordlessly said good-bye, then hurried up the ridge where the two old smooth-trunked trees also awaited my return. The winter had been long—I needed to rest in the circle of solitude that surrounded these trees that stood as sentinels high upon the ridge.

The trail was a steep one, narrow where the deer walked up and rutted where the waters ran down. On either side, oak brush, tall enough to be trees, lent privacy to the path as the pasture receded into forest. I stopped twice to look around and breathe in the smell of the woods, to catch my breath before cresting the last rise where the trail ended and a small clearing opened up. The trees stood on the steep north side of the clearing, precariously close to the edge of the ridge. I averted my eyes, not wanting to glimpse the trees until they were in full view. In order to see them from exposed gnarled roots to silhouetted barren crowns, I stood in the middle of the clearing and tipped my head back.

A familiar hallowed feeling overcame me—for I had felt the same sense of awe the first time I climbed this ridge—a feeling of reminiscence, of not being alone. The intuition had been strong, but I had yet to learn enough about this land's earlier inhabitants—the other two-legged creatures who once may have traveled beneath these same trees—to place the intuition in perspective.

Generations of winter cold and summer heat had become an intrinsic part of these trees; they had felt the rain of many springs, sensed the rising of many moons, perhaps even absorbed the keening cries of a grief-stricken bride or the melancholy prayers of a young impoverished girl.

Slowly, my eyes cut a path toward the trunk of the largest and closest of the two trees. Many small pieces of wood were scattered about the base of the tree. Instead of the dark gray color I remembered, the lower portion of the trunk was yellow, almost gold in places. Streaks of black receded into the core of the tree where lightning had struck decades ago. The tree was wounded— I had not noticed this before. I began to walk toward the tree but found my eyes again averted to the ground.

I knelt, clasping my hands together, doing what had been done thousands of times before by scores of ancient people—

doing what is still done, even within the most modern of cultures.

I was not the first to pray in this protected clearing high upon the ridge, kneeling not to worship two trees but out of humbleness. For a moment, I cast aside my elevated two-legged status and bowed my head. The spider's universe, suddenly, seemed very grand.

Plucking a supple strand of silver sage, I smelled the pungent scent, thinking again of the young Lakota girl who had nothing to give White Buffalo Calf Woman but a bouquet of dried weeds. Could the legend be true? Had the girl's simple faith really turned the weeds to silver sage? Had my own grandmother Effie, deafened at the age of eighteen, possessed enough simple faith to turn tragedy into opportunity? How many times had she knelt on the baked earth of the Mojave and clasped a stalk of sage between her hands? How many times had my grandmother Helen knelt on the bluestem prairie of Oklahoma and listened to the lonely notes of her own keening?

I am told that after Helen's mother died (around 1903), her father went to Washington to make his fortune and left her in Oklahoma as an indentured servant to a family he thought would treat her well. After months of brutal treatment, Helen was able to smuggle a letter to her father, telling him of her plight. He threatened the family with severe consequences if they did not send her to Washington immediately. She fled, traveling partway by wagon, partway by train. Years later she would say little about her servitude, except that she used to put padding in her clothing to cushion the blows.

My grandmother never told me this story—I heard it from my great-aunt. Two questions came immediately to mind: Would the beatings have been as severe had it not been for the Cherokee and Irish blood that flowed through her veins, and, more practically, with what did she pad her clothing? Old rags? Duck down? The soft, white silken fibers of cattails? Was it then that her soft cries floated across the bluestem prairie? Could I hear her keening, even now? In the wind? In the trees?

Rising, I approached the tree and reached out my hands, touching the trunk. The bark had peeled away years ago; what came loose now was the flesh of the tree, and it fell away in long strips of splintered wood. The lightning had struck deep, turning sap and sinew to hard charcoal. It had happened late in life, for the strike was low and close to the ground.

No visible life remained, no growth of new rings, no budding clusters of pine needles—not a single fertile pinecone, no smooth strand of sap. I put my cheek close to the tree, feeling its rough surface next to my skin. I inhaled deeply, taking in the smell of damp, cool wood. Overcome, I backed away and circled. The smaller branches of the tree had long since fallen off, leaving only the larger main limbs. These radiated out from the tree in great majestic sweeps. I stretched to touch the very end of the lowest, longest limb. Gently, I moved the branch— up an inch, down an inch. The wood moaned softly, brittle with age. A large branch across from where I stood responded in slow, graceful motion—an inch up, an inch down. Again, I swayed the branch. Again, from at least thirty feet away, the opposite limb answered.

In wildlife management terms, this tree is known as a "snag." Live trees are sometimes killed in order to create snags. Birds of prey roost high in the skyward branches. Deer rub the velvet from their antlers on the smooth lower branches. And I, I grow velvet on my soul, which has been worn smooth by the human friction that robs me of my intuitiveness.

I walked over to the other tree. It, too, was dead, but I saw no sign of a lightning strike. Sometimes, when two people have been married for half a century and one of them dies, it is not too long before the other follows. Could this be true of a pair of trees who have stood side by side for more than two hundred years?

The bits of wood that were strewn about the larger tree saddened me, for I could foresee a time when this old tree, witness to so much, would become dust. I bent and gently picked up a piece of wood, and then, again, another piece. I placed the shorter length of wood crosswise on top of the longer piece, much like the two twigs in which the spider had placed her cocoon.

I knew that these two souvenirs would accompany me back down the mountain. And I knew, too, that I would return soon—whenever the worldly friction that started at the end of the trail began to rub me raw, I would come here to rest. I would kneel and breathe deeply, smelling the perfume of this holy place, listening for the whisper of a young Lakota girl and the gentle breathing of my own grand-mothers, listening for the timeless wind that carries all hope.

16

Sassy

ASSY AND I BEGAN OUR spring housecleaning today. I awoke to squirrelish chatter and the industrious song of a blue jay, the pre-dawn notes bouncing in through the window.

Sitting at our wooden table in the dining room, I looked out the half-circle window to Sassy's tree. She scampered along the gnarled limbs of the tree, busy inspecting every budding twig, every wandering ant, and just plain busy being a busybody. When benign Hondo ventured too near the base of the tree, Sassy hurried out to the edge of the lowest branch and scolded him severely. When the cats sidled up next to the old oak, rubbing their winter fur against the rough spine of the tree, she bluffed them into believing that her tree was not for climbing.

This morning I sat at the birch table by Sassy's window, coffee cup warming the early morning chill from my hands. She was having quite a time. A large robin landed in the tree—much like parking in a no-parking zone. Sassy appeared suddenly, thrusting herself out of the small entrance to her nest, tail twitching, voice scolding, eyes flashing. I expected to see her shake her finger at the offending robin.

The robin flitted up to the next branch, parking himself again in her territory. Sassy disappeared into her nest, then surprised the robin by reappearing from another hole, a little higher up.

Then the blue jay surprised Sassy, landing on the branch where the robin perched—and where Sassy sat, erect and angry. The blue jay, unlike the robin, was every bit as vocal and opinionated as Sassy: "This tree is public domain and no puny, rust-colored fox squirrel is going to tell me any different!" I chuckled as the three faced one another in a standoff over public lands—politics on a real grassroots level.

The robin succumbed to the pressure and moved to a lower branch. The blue jay, contradicting his public domain speech (in true political fashion), flew after the robin, flapping his wings in aggressive pursuit as if to say, "This is blue jay territory, buddy, no robins allowed! I don't care if you were here first."

Even from my indoor view, I could tell Sassy's temper had flared. "First? Why I was here first! I'll have you know I've raised three litters of fine youngsters right in this very tree. First? Why of all the notions! Both of you, out right now! Off my tree!"

Sassy's tail pumped madly up and down in rhythm with her ceaseless chatter. The blue jay scolded in retaliation but was no match for her. The robin left, confused. The blue jay hopped a little closer to Sassy, as if to say, "I could stay if I wanted," then flexed his wings, flashed a blue parting at Sassy, and was gone.

Sassy sat and pulled her tail to her, combing it with her long fingers and claws. She smoothed her whiskers and rubbed her petite ears, and as she exhaled a deep, long-held breath, the raised fur on her back settled down. I watched, enjoying her regained composure. She peered at me through the window, her shiny brown eyes smart with recognition.

"Housecleaning," she challenged me. "You had great intentions this morning, and there you sit, coffee cup in hand—not getting a thing done. Woman, it's spring, don't you know. Time to get busy! Can't laze around all day."

Sassy was a squirrel of action, the earlier confrontation over territory only a minor intrusion in her plans. She scooted back into one of her holes, turning at the last minute to give me a "Well, let's get with it!"

The morning was in full swing. The sun, bright and alive after its winter sojourn, flexed its territorial muscles, scaring off the chilled night air. I rose from the table and got on with the day.

Sassy was not to be outdone. For every curtain I freshened, for every window I cleaned, Sassy, too, cleared the winter debris from her corridors and rooms, from her kitchen's cache. I watched her discreetly and with brief stolen glances. If she caught me as she poked her head out, her mouth full of the fuzzy linings of her winter bed, she mustered up a chattering of, "Get going, get going! Can't you see the day's a-wasting?"

I found excuses to go outside, past the growing pile of debris at the base of her old oak. At least a hundred empty acorn shells were scattered about. Among the lint and little wads of fluffed nest lining, pieces of Sarah's jump rope appeared. Dried and crumpled leaves were tossed here and there, a torn corner from a newspaper floated down to the top of the pile.

I went back inside our log home, where cobwebs clung to the rafters and wood chips dirtied the floor by the stove. It was time to invite another season to come and set awhile, time to open the windows and let the early breeze waft through my hollow corridors.

On the deck again, I shook out the kitchen rugs, enjoying the rhythm that traveled from my slightly bent knees to my fingertips, watching the pile under Sassy's tree grow. A woven tangle of discarded hair, mine perhaps, had been added to the collection. Dust from the rugs puffed up and away, blown by the brisk breeze that threatened to turn to cold wind. Overhead, light gray wisps gathered into heavy dark clouds. Fewer blue patches could be seen. I hugged my sweater to me tightly, then went inside to close the windows.

Sassy perched silently on the end of a limb, her nose pointed nervously toward the darkening sky. She leaned over, looking down at the clutter she had swept from her nest, then trotted back to one of her entrances and disappeared into her own hollow tunnel. A few minutes later she appeared again, nose held high, one paw raised and curled in anticipation. The breeze brought an unwanted message, and she disappeared back into the heart of the tree.

I returned to the dining room table, a fresh cup of hot coffee in hand. The windows were closed, the rugs rested upon newly swept floors, the wooden chips had been placed in the woodburning stove, kindling for the next fire. I wrapped my fingers around the warm cup in anticipation of the storm we both knew was coming.

Our spring cleaning was really only a late-winter washing, impatience oozing forth in little bursts of energy. A cozy comforter still stretched across my bed, but poor Sassy's winter quilt lay scattered uselessly about the base of the old tree.

Out Sassy came again, scurrying down the trunk. She arrived at the bottom of the tree and looked quickly around before grabbing a mouthful of discarded jump rope and shoving it into her cheeks. Then again, another mouthful. Soon her cheeks bulged; she turned and ran up the tree, Ol' Man Winter on her tail. She pivoted and looked at me one more time before going into her hole. Her brown eyes held a warning. I held my tongue.

Sipping my coffee, I watched her make four more trips down the backbone of the oak, returning four times to her nest. The sky had grown dark, the curtain drawn on the sun. Snow began falling, and I faced the fact that I must light another fire in the stove.

Sassy stood on the edge of the limb. My thoughts were apologetic. "No need to feel silly, Sassy. I was fooled too."

She looked at me, I filled in the dialogue. "Silly? Ha! Nothing silly about it. Why, in this country you've got to grab at every opportunity. If you have a chance to freshen up your bedding, then freshen it you'd better! Didn't you know I was expecting a suitor? Why, before you know it, I'll be running more than blue jays offa this tree. Might have me another litter of young 'uns, too. And you thought I was doing spring housecleaning. Why, any fool knows Winter never beats a hasty retreat! What are you doing just standing there gawking? Don't you have a fire to build?"

No sense in arguing; Sassy always got in the last word. I went to the woodbox and picked out three dry logs and set them down next to the stove, then opened the damper and built the fire, placing the logs on top of the crumpled paper and kindling wood. I lit a match and the paper caught fire quickly. The splintered kindling crackled and sparked in the heat. Closing the doors to the stove, I began sweeping up the fresh wood chips that were scattered about, once again, on my just-swept floor.

17

Purring

Women are revered in our society, you are constantly giving, not only to your children, but to all living things ... in the human body every organ vibrates to a certain song ... a song of power. It is the spiritual purpose ... the healer calls people to remembering their songs ... everything vibrating is consciousness.

—Dhyani Ywahoo[1]

WITH THE COMING OF SPRING and the yellow tom, Simon's belly does indeed swell again, and she walks with the heavy gait of a pregnant female, her long back slightly swayed in the middle. She has a new mark on her right shoulder, a sign of where the tomcat gripped for dominance, and balance. Her wheat-colored Siamese fur has a small patch of darkness on the shoulder blade that moves up and down in feline rhythm as she walks.

Each day I hold her to me and she nuzzles under my chin, making deep purring noises. I cup my hands around her growing belly and guess at the size of the kittens inside.

Finally, several weeks after the yellow tomcat climbed the hill of manure out in the corral, Simon appears up by the house looking thin and haggard. I kneel and pick her up. Her stomach sags low, heavy with milk-filled teats instead of kittens. She purrs and nuzzles, and I talk to her with quiet, private words—one mother to another. *Ah—good girl, good girl.* No fanfare, no flowers, no cards, no proud father standing by, no one to share the midnight feeding. So much endured in solitude, the pains of birth as life swings round again, and again. *Such a brave girl you are Simon. So little you ask in return, just a rub here and a rub there.* Her chest-deep purring vibrates the tips of my fingers and I feel her song of power become my healing.

This time I will leave the mothering to Simon, the fate of the kittens to her instinctive wisdom. Each day when I get home from work I mix a raw egg with milk and carry it to the barn. If Simon is not there, I call to her and she comes quickly, close by. I pour this treat into her dish in the barn and she laps at it ravenously before returning to her hidden kittens, sharing her milk with them.

Mothering, nurturing—one of the things we do best, animals and humans alike.

My grandmother Effie writes briefly about two tragedies that occurred during her homesteading days on the Mojave, both involving mothers:

> Mrs. Hannam, the mother of the boys, was killed instantly when her horse became frightened in a storm, reared up and struck her in the chest as she was tying him to the hitching post in front of the store. The other was a young Austrian woman who died at childbirth because she wanted to have her baby like I did mine—without benefit of a doctor. The baby died as well.

My grandmother describes her own experience in an abbreviated postscript: "P.S.," she writes,

> My husband delivered our baby with my help and was thereafter called Doc Corum. Ralph, my brother-in-law, went for the doctor in his model T Ford. Couldn't find the road off the lake till daylight. Arrived in time to cook me a breakfast of T-bone steak and hot biscuits and coffee. I was starved, and the doctor shocked, when he arrived on the noon train.

I love the image of my strong deaf grandmother devouring a thick, juicy steak with a newborn babe suckling at her breast. It portrays a lust for living and helps to ease my own anesthesia-clouded memory of Matt's Cesarean birth. It also helps me to appreciate birthing Sarah—the feel of Mark's hand supporting my back, and the sound of my own doctor's voice, with her strong East Indian accent and long black braid trailing down her back, yelling excitedly, "Bear down, Page! Bear down!" Together, we sang *my* song of power.

One kitten remains of the eleven Simon gave birth to last year. Tuffy, the gray kitten who huddled in the corner of the manger, the only survivor of the mutilated kittens, has grown into a perky teenager. She has eyes the color of new grass, as green as her mother's are blue. Her ears are small, her cheeks tufted slightly, and her tail kinked at the tip. Independent, she is no longer interested in Simon's mothering. She wants a playmate. Occasionally Simon succumbs and they tussle about on the ground until Simon jumps self-consciously to her feet. Tuffy chases after her, swatting at the retreating tail, until Simon turns to administer an admonishing swat with her paw. Black Jack, if nearby, joins in until the females overwhelm him.

Each evening when I carry the egg and milk to the barn, Tuffy races ahead, waiting impatiently for me to reach the door. I pour the mixture into their dish, holding Tuffy and Black Jack away so Simon can have the greatest share. Tuffy wiggles out of my arms and lands with all four feet in the milk.

Every evening it is the same, every evening Simon shares this milk and egg with her offspring before returning to the new kittens. She takes and gives unselfishly, only to give again. *Ah, good girl, good girl.* I pet her and she purrs. Her vibrating body rubs against me. She nuzzles my chin and I purr inside, not minding the sharp pricks of her affectionate claws in my skin.

Hondo stands patiently beneath one of the large oak trees at the front of the house. Simon trots around the corner and I call her to me. She meows when I pick her up, looking nervously into a large hollow knothole. Curious, I place her on the tree. She grabs hold and climbs up, disappearing into the knothole. I call to her and she reappears. Faint, plaintive cries come from inside the tree. *Silly girl, you've got your kittens up a tree. Think you'll keep them safe up there, huh?*

Simon turns and disappears back into the tree. I reach down and pat Hondo's head. He looks up into the tree and wags his tail, a slight whine coming from his graying throat.

The yellow tomcat was a cradle-robber as well. Not only is Simon a mother again, but Tuffy has become pregnant. Her adolescent tummy swells, appearing too large for her gangly legs. The tomcat, like a thief in the night, has stolen Tuffy's youth. She no longer wrestles with Simon and will have nothing to do with Black Jack. Instead, she walks the path from the barn to the house and climbs the steps to the deck, one labored step after another. Once there, she stretches out on her side and lets the cool wooden planks support her heavy belly.

Simon still mothers her. When she isn't in the tree with her new kittens, she sits consolingly down next to Tuffy and proceeds to groom her about the face and ears. "I know," she seems to say, "I know." Tuffy finds comfort in this brief retreat into kittenhood.

During the quiet of the night, Tuffy has her kittens. In the morning she climbs out of the manger and meows plaintively at my feet. The bones of her hips force her gray fur into angular shadows. Her torso is thin and gaunt. I pick her up. She is kitten-light.

"So you chose the manger, huh, Tuffy? Where you were born?" Three dark, motionless shapes curl together in a furred ball. I gently place the palm of my hand on top; the warm bundle rises and falls in breathy unison. I hug Tuffy.

"Ah, such a little girl you are." The words have a familiar echo. Simon, grandmother to the newborn kittens, stands at my feet and rubs against my legs while Tuffy purrs at my throat. *How silent they are in their procreation.*

I think of my own grandmothers: Helen, muted by shame, afraid to speak of her own Cherokee grandmother, and perhaps her Irish grandmother, afraid to remember the beatings and the prejudices, finally laid to rest in a smooth pine box in San Francisco; Effie, deafened by accident, a desert bride, turned to ash and scattered across the Mojave—both long gone. Yet despite the lack of detailed family diaries or letters to share, somewhere in all this cycling of generations there still exists a bond, a cohesiveness of spirit. I share their womanness, feeling hungry to know more yet satiated with emotion.

Wilma Mankiller of the Cherokee Nation speaks about the written history of native women in ancient tribal societies. In her book, *Mankiller*, she points out that almost *all* written history was recorded by men and influenced by a male perspective. The oral stories about women that do exist are often dismissed because they lack *written verification.*

> No wonder our written history speaks so often of war but rarely records descriptions of our songs, dances, and simple joys of living. The voices of our grandmothers are silenced by most of the written history of our people. How I long to hear their voices![2]

Cats are experts at appreciating simple joys. And it is difficult to be oblivious of this joy when petting a purring cat. Tuffy jumps back into the manger with her kittens, waking them with a low maternal meow. Roused, they find her warmth and root for her swollen nipples. I stretch one hand across the row of nursing kittens and place my other hand upon Tuffy's chest. The purring vibrations resonate up both arms to my own chest, filling me with energy— tempting me, for a moment, to loosen the female purring so long stifled in my own lungs. How would one record such a sound?

"We place a great emphasis on the role of the honored woman in our culture," writes Dhyani Ywahoo, Cherokee Priestcraft Holder of the Ani Gadoah Clan,

> That is the woman who holds dear the thought of family and turns aside whatever enmity there may be in the community and transforms it to love, and that is very much the power of mother's energy. ... It is most important to remember that the empowerment of the voice cannot come from anger. It comes from the certainty of the gentle power within ourselves. It comes from the certainty that nurturing, giving, receiving, also requires a fierceness to see that the children grow. What is more fierce than the mother protecting her child? To be a woman and to recognize her gentle nature is also to recognize her strength and power ... .[3]

I leave the barn and head toward the house. Simon, with Black Jack on her heels, comes in from the deep grass and crosses the driveway. She carries a brown field mouse in her jaws. She stops at my feet and lays the mouse down. The mouse is not dead but remains dropped on his back. All four feet twitch, the mouth gapes open. Arching his back, he makes frantic motions and turns over, too stunned to flee. The fur around his neck is wet but not bloody. Black Jack and Simon watch as the mouse tries to maneuver an escape, inch by inch.

Hondo, watching from nearby, can stand the curiosity no longer. He pushes his muzzle at the mouse, flipping him over. Simon, motionless, allows the intrusion. The mouse squeaks and Hondo moves quickly. The mouse tries vainly to protect himself with bared teeth. He leaps upward in spastic jumping motions. Hondo, *gentle Hondo*, lunges again at the mouse, closing his large black muzzle over the rodent in one quick motion before tossing the mouse into the air. The mouse drops to the dirt, rights himself, and squeaks. Hondo feigns a growl. Simon and Black Jack continue to watch Hondo's antics. Again and again Hondo feigns a growl and then attacks, tossing the mouse into the air.

Each time the mouse lands he becomes less paralytic in his escape attempts, running in straighter, longer paths, only to be grabbed up again. In one last valiant, frightened burst of energy, the mouse almost outruns Hondo. Simon, from a stationary position, springs ten feet through the air and recaptures the mouse. Hondo wanders away, the game over.

Tuffy, fur matted from the routing kittens, walks stiffly up from the barn. Purring, she rubs against her mother. A low sound comes from Simon's clenched jaws where the mouse dangles—a growl or purr, I cannot tell which. Simon drops the mouse at her weary daughter's feet and steps away. Tuffy gratefully picks up the meal in her teeth and deftly decapitates the mouse, biting small, delicate mouthfuls from the head of the still-twitching rodent.

The crunching of the bones is muffled by feline growling or purring—I still cannot tell which. Thinking I ought to feel slightly repulsed by the decapitated mouse, I think instead of my grand-mother Effie devouring a juicy T-bone steak, her afterbirth still warm, and find my own stomach growling, my own mouth watering.

18

The Picture Window

I SURPRISED A SLENDER DEER standing in the driveway when I drove home for lunch. At the sound of the car she retreated to the edge of the yard. She did not, as would have been normal, flee into the early, knee-high spring grass and the camouflage of the tall oak trees.

A few days later, this time with the kids loaded in the car, Matt pleaded with me from the backseat. "Mom, why can't I have a Nintendo? All the other kids have them."

As a child, I had quickly learned not to argue that logic with my father. The fact that all the other kids had something provided reason enough for my independent dad to decide I didn't need it.

"Matt, you spend enough time in front of the television as it is."

"But Mom, they're only eighty-nine ninety-five. I saw them advertised."

Only $89.95. That would pay the electric bill, or buy one new snow tire for the truck, or ... .

"Please, Mom?"

"Matt, when your Dad was growing up, his idea of a treat was going to Sedalia to buy a candy bar once a month from his Uncle George's old mercantile store, and he had to wait until all his Saturday chores were done before he could eat it. And when his Uncle George was a boy, *his* idea of a treat was spooning out the leftover sugar from the bottom of a New Orleans molasses barrel."

"M-o-m ..." Exasperated, Matt stretched the word out, hoping to end the lecture.

"Look, kids, over there in the grass. The doe is back, the same one I saw at lunch the other day." The deer watched our car as I slowed and turned into the driveway. As before, she did not run but meandered farther into the tall grass.

Sarah is not as full of "I wants" as is Matt. Still a preschooler, there is no peer pressure yet with which to deal. The television exerts a more sophisticated pressure, but it is pressure we at least have some control over. Matt, an average grade-school kid, has already succumbed to the "everyone else has one" ailment. Mark and I are sympathetic to the causes of this disease but have very little patience with the symptoms.

"Mom, when am I gonna get a new bike?" Matt asked this question, like the Nintendo plea, in the car on the way home from work, occasionally the only place where the children have my undivided attention.

Matt's first bike lasted him three years, and Sarah now rides it. The training wheels, reattached for half a day, came quickly off as Sarah mastered the art of riding. Matt was left, however, with no bike at all.

"Mom, Nate has a five-speed but he's gonna sell it and get a ten-speed for his birthday."

"A five-speed, huh?" I remembered the three-speed bike I had as a teenager. I thought I was pretty hot stuff sailing down the paved road toward home, doing at least sixty miles an hour, perfecting a smooth handlebar shift from second to third. Here in the country, though, the driveway was part gravel, part dirt. The road to the stockyard was weedy and all dirt. What Matt really needed was an all-terrain vehicle.

"Maybe we could buy Nate's old bike when he gets a new one?"

I patiently explained to Matt why a five-speed bike would be not only an extravagance but also pretty impractical on our dirt roads.

"Besides that, Matt, you've already got a five-speed horse. He walks, trots, lopes, runs, and sometimes bucks."

"Come on, Mom, I'm *serious*."

"So am I, honey."

"Mom," Sarah interrupted, "look at that hawk. He's got babies flying with him!"

A red-tailed hawk rose from the pasture, quickly gaining altitude. He cut a straight, purposeful path toward the pine-dotted hills. Two smaller birds flew above him, frantically beating the air.

Their wings pumped much faster and harder than the wings of the larger, more powerful bird of prey. We watched as first one, then the other, dive-bombed the hawk. The hawk flew on, unflinching, and then I noticed that he clutched something in his talons. Those in pursuit were not young hawks; it was too early for even the most precocious to have grown flight feathers. The small birds that dove frantically at the hawk were parents. And what the hawk clutched in his talons was their fledgling, perhaps a young killdeer snatched from their prairie nest.

I pulled the car off the road and we continued to watch this drama unfold until the birds became mere specks that disappeared into the afternoon sky. How much farther did the killdeers pursue the hawk? When did they give up, realizing the futility of their chase? Or did the hawk finally, hassled beyond hunger, drop the fledgling in midair? Would the prairie nesters follow this downward death spiral, scratching and sniffing at the remains, making sure their offspring was truly dead? Would they return to an empty nest?

The following weekend we bought Matt that new bike—a one-speed, leg-powered, wide-tire, good old kid's bike. Matt loved it. He loved the bright "hot" green color, he loved the newness of it, and he crashed and burned on it just as he would have on any high-geared racing bike.

"Wow, Dad! My new bike goes just as fast as any five-speed can go!"

We were proud of him. He set aside his temporary disappointment and fell head over heels in love with his new bike. He and Sarah spent the entire day racing up and down the dirt driveway, and *I* only had to race outside once.

"No, Matt, you can *not* play chicken!" *Chicken?* I didn't think kids learned about "chicken" until they were at least sixteen!

That night, sitting at the supper table, we saw the doe again.

"She's got a fawn with her!"

We scooted our chairs back as quietly as we could, for the deer who venture near are able to hear vibrations from within the house. Matt grabbed the always handy binoculars.

"She does, Mom. There's a little baby deer with her. Dad, the fawn's nursing!"

We spent the next twenty-five minutes standing at the picture window passing the binoculars back and forth, watching the mother deer lick and clean the fawn. She stopped occasionally to browse while the fawn sucked and nuzzled and stared, wide-eyed, at the world around him.

This was entertainment—better, even, than Nintendo. True, the price of a home in the country is more than $89.95, but then, good things don't come cheap. They don't come easy either. It takes a lot of saying no, not just to fancy bikes and mesmerizing Nintendos, but to new trucks and new cars and late nights out.

There are also a lot of ways to protect one's young. The killdeers tried bravely, but in vain, to save their fledgling. The thieves who rob our human children are not so blatant. Sometimes they come disguised as expensive toys whose real costs are not measured in dollars and cents but in the time we must take to earn the extra money—time away from our spouses, time away from our children.

I am glad we have a picture window. Big and wide. Sometimes, when the light is just right, we see our own reflections in the glass: a foursome standing shoulder almost to shoulder, facing the outside world. When the light shifts and a cloud floats beyond the sun, the brief image is gone. Once again, the oak trees fill the picture window with green wildness, and we peer, as wide-eyed as the fawn, into a world full of surprises.

19

Black Jack

We can come to the wilderness to feel what is possible and naturally beautiful—but we must stand rooted in the Earth and face the crying issues right where we live.

—Brooke Medicine Eagle[1]

BLACK JACK SAT ON THE DECK of the house, his haunches tucked under him and his head hanging down. Mucous saliva fell from his mouth in two long, wet strands. This morning he was fine, but now this drooling and listlessness. Out in the country, with the raccoons, skunks, porcupines, and Sassy and the other squirrels, the threat of rabies was frightening.

Sarah, only four, had scratch marks made by Black Jack when he vaulted himself from her arms at feeding time. And Mark had been bitten when he forced a worming pill down Black Jack's throat last week. Neither of these were aggressive acts on the kitten's part, but they left wounds even so.

I called the veterinarian's office to find out at what point a diseased animal begins to drool. The assistant answered the phone.

"The Doc is gone and won't be back until late this evening. Yes, you'd better have the cat tested for rabies." Her opinion was definite. The cat must be tested.

"The lab in Laramie will have to do a biopsy," she continued, "from brain tissue."

Oh, God. I hung up the phone. Surely it isn't rabies. An animal isn't healthy and energetic one minute, then sick and diseased the next. I looked out the window. Black Jack still sat hunched up on the deck. In only six months he and Sarah had become inseparable. She loved him. *Please God, help me get through this.*

I called the next closest vet, thirty miles away, and hoped for a more optimistic second opinion.

"Well, you could quarantine the cat for ten days," he said.

"Both my husband and daughter were scratched. Would that make a difference?"

"If the cat's rabid, they should both start on the series of shots right away. There's no other way that I know of to check for rabies besides the brain tissue test."

Mark went to the only medical clinic in town and spoke with one of the local doctors. Her opinion was harsh.

"Well, unless your wife cares more for the cat than she does her kids, tell her to kill the cat."

Though I kept telling myself that Black Jack's only symptom had been drooling, something else with ominous implications nagged at me: We still didn't know what had mutilated Simon's litter of kittens. Raccoons, even healthy ones, will kill kittens, and so will old toms. *But what if it had been a rabid animal?*

Public opinion was overwhelming. I spoke with the local game warden, and he confirmed the serious threat of rabies in this part of Wyoming.

"I've got a small cage you can borrow if you want, maybe isolate the cat until you make a decision?" he suggested. We borrowed the cage.

Later, down at the barn, Mark and I examined Black Jack. Mark put on thick leather gloves and I pulled on long rubber ones. Black Jack, no longer drooling, looked the perfect healthy specimen. Mistakenly, I had thought kittens must be six months old before having a rabies vaccination, but the veterinarian told me they can be given the shot at twelve weeks. *If only I had checked sooner.*

We hoped to find an explanation for the drooling—ulcers or lesions in the mouth, or maybe a porcupine quill. Porcupine quills—Mark pulled them from the horses, the dogs, the lessee's heifers. We wrapped a towel around Black Jack, immobilizing his feet and claws. Mark held him as I pried his mouth open with one hand and held a flashlight with the other. We found no sores, no ulcers, no sign of where a quill might have become imbedded and then later worked itself loose—no explanation for the drooling.

Mark put Black Jack down. Taking off my rubber gloves, I called him to me, picked him up, and gently pressed his thick, glossy black fur to my cheek. He began purring, then wiggled impatiently out of my arms.

We walked back to the house to get the game warden's cage from my car with Black Jack and Hondo following along. Sarah and Matt stood inside the house, watching from the bay window. They had been told not to go near the kitten.

I held the cage upright as Mark dropped Black Jack into it, tail and hind feet first. The small cage prevented him from even turning around. We carried him back to the barn and put the cage down. I placed a small dish of water and some cat food inside. He looked up at me, trustingly, from inside the wire cage. A few minutes before, Sarah had stared at me accusingly from behind the glaring window.

There are times when the human mind protects the heart by compartmentalizing difficult decisions so that we only have to deal with one problem at a time. Now was one of those times. The thought of Sarah having rabies was inconceivable. The series of shots were painful—the disease sometimes fatal. I worried about Mark as well, but he was my husband, not my child. I focused on Black Jack, the key. The domino effect would begin soon enough.

Most people did not understand. They thought that barn cats were a dime a dozen. They didn't know that the issue was about playing God, about responsibility, about trust and love. Maybe they had never seen a child hold a small black kitten in her arms, a kitten who magically responded to her every touch. This was Sarah's world, a world where four-legged creatures can become best friends. A world where parents can be trusted.

Mark and I opened *The Merck Veterinary Manual* and read everything we could on the rhabdovirus that causes rabies:

Probable means of spread to man—bites of diseased animals, possible inhalation. Is usually localized in the brainstem and spinal cord. Virus may be present in saliva and transmitted several days prior to onset of clinical signs. Incubation period within 15 to 50 days but may be longer, even several months. May be present in the paralytic form with early paralysis of the throat and profuse salivation or may take on the Furious Form, better known as the "mad dog syndrome." ... Disease sometimes causes irritation or stimulation to the urogenital tract as evidenced by frequent urination, erection in the male, and sexual desire. When man is exposed to an animal suspected of having rabies the animal should be killed in such a manner that will not damage the head. Rapid laboratory evaluation is essential ... .[2]

Hondo barked a warning as the local wildlife biologist turned off the county road onto our driveway and came up to the door.

"Just wanting to get a count on whitetail deer," he said, taking off his cap. "Mind if I spotlight your hay fields?"

"No problem," Mark answered. "How 'bout counting the coyotes while you're at it?" The biologist, a friend, laughed.

"Having trouble with coyotes?"

"No, but the deer might be. Want to come in for a glass of iced tea first?"

"Thanks, but I'm on government time—better be getting after it before they bed down for the night."

"Say," I interrupted, "you know much about rabies?"

"A little. What's the problem?"

"Well, we've got a cat that's been drooling. The vet says we should get him tested for rabies—have a brain biopsy done."

"Barn cat?"

"Well, yeah, and Sarah's pet."

"Tough deal," he shook his head, then put his cap back on. "But the vet's right. We've seen a lot of rabid skunks this year. It's too big a risk to take."

"Know any other way of testing for it?" Mark asked.

"Sure don't."

"Well, thanks anyway."

"You bet," he said, turning to go. "Sorry I couldn't help. I'll let you know how the deer count turns out."

Later that evening, as Mark and I lay in bed, I wished only to be able to sleep and wake to the realization that it had been a bad dream. But we knew what we had to do; the wildlife biologist only confirmed it.

Mark, in a moment of levity, teased about already having one of the "male" symptoms. The humor momentarily eased the tension, and we finally drifted off to sleep, trying not to think of Black Jack huddled in the wire cage.

His only crime had been the misfortune of letting me see him drool. For this he would die, even though the chance of rabies was slight. For Sarah's sake, and Mark's, we had to know. Early the next morning we talked to Matt and Sarah and told them the time had come for the lab to test Black Jack.

Mark went down to the barn. A few minutes later he walked back to the house with Black Jack running carefree at his side. During the night an animal had bent open the cage and eaten the cat food. Black Jack escaped unscathed. What kind of animal had the dexterity and cleverness for this? A raccoon?

I followed Mark into the bedroom. He pulled the gun out of the drawer and the hidden bullets down from the top shelf. We did not talk. Mark's jaws were clenched, his teeth clamped together—not letting words escape when nothing really could be said. He angrily put the bullets in his gun belt.

Matt saw him leave. "Where's he going with the gun, Mom? Is he going to kill Black Jack?" He hurled the questions at me point-blank. Sarah just stared.

"Hush, Matt, hush. Come here, Sarah. Come over here, too, Matt." I held them to me, not because they needed to be held so much as I needed to hold them. Outside, Mark walked toward the barn. Black Jack scampered ahead of him, oblivious. As they turned toward the trees, I turned the children away. A sharp crack split the air.

Mark returned five minutes later carrying an old gunny sack the color of wet sand. The sack swung rhythmically, close to the ground. Mark's head hung low, as Black Jack's had that day on the deck. *Had it really only been yesterday?* He put the gunny sack into the back of the pickup and came to the house. Once inside he went straight to the bedroom. I followed him.

"Are you all right?"

"I had to shoot him three times." It was all he said.

"That's quite a sack you've got there," the vet's assistant said to us as we walked into the clinic. "We won't ship him out 'til Tuesday. Monday's a holiday and the mail doesn't go out on Saturdays." I stood there in the sterile office, silent, not trusting my own voice.

"I thought the test had to be done as quickly as possible."

"Oh, it should be. But we'll refrigerate it. It'll be fine."

Refrigerate it? All of Black Jack, or just his head?

We left. I wanted to get outside, to breathe in new air, to feel the kindness of the sun on my face. I needed to fill up this dark hole inside that ached and threatened to become more than just a sad place where a kitten had died.

Later, Mark and I sat across from each other at the cafe, alone except for the portrait of George the Indian staring down at us.

"Some guys could do that and it wouldn't even bother them." He paused before continuing. "I hope I don't have to live with that scene in my mind for very long."

I watched Mark, sitting across from me in his cowboy boots and old 3X silverbelly beaver-felt hat. Dark sideburns framed his brown eyes. His mustache hid his upper lip and moved slightly up and down when he spoke. His shoulders leaned toward me over the table, and he watched the glass in his hands as he talked, not looking at me or touching me. The space between us filled with quiet intimacy, bent inward with mutual pain.

Softly, he finally spoke again.

"The thing that really got me is that he trusted me—thought we were going for a walk. I shot him right where I needed to the first time—then he jumped up and started running for the barn. I couldn't let him get under that barn or we'd never have gotten him out."

The ice shifted in his glass as he lifted it to his mouth to drink. He sucked the tea from his mustache with his bottom lip and lowered the glass again to the table. Then he reached for the check.

"You should have seen his eyes."

The state lab called Wednesday. The tests were negative. Black Jack had not had rabies. Sarah and Mark would not have to be treated; there was no disease. We had been lucky. The next day the news reported that a stray rabid kitten in Rapid City, only ninety miles away, had scratched and bitten several people, including an employee from the animal control center. Everyone exposed was being treated, especially the children.

20

The Red Shirt

We Sioux ... see in the world around us many symbols that teach us the meaning of life.

—John (Fire) Lame Deer[1]

SUMMERS IN WYOMING are never long and lazy. The path the swather cuts may be long, and our lessee's cows move lazily from one water hole to the next, but the summers are gone almost before the neighbor's branding irons have cooled.

Mark's own branding irons, with an unusable Colorado brand, hang dust-covered in the barn. Looking down the road toward the day when we finally save enough money to buy our first cows, Mark applied for a Wyoming brand. After several rejections, the state brand office finally accepted a Lazy VJL: a V lying on its side next to an upright JL. The J is for Joseph, a name shared by at least five generations of Lamberts; the V had to be added because no two-letter brands were available.

Unlike summer, October smells of cold pine-scented breezes that blow down from the Bear Lodge Mountains, disguising the faint odor of cows and the sound of their restless, age-old urge to move to lower pastures. For cattlemen like our neighbor J. W., one cycle leads to the next in a pattern that is woven by birth and weight-gain, weaning and shipping.

Veteran cows will go back up into the forest next year with new calves at their sides, but first the cattlemen who hold forest grazing permits will spend frantic days repairing fences, checking riparian areas, and developing springs and dams. For the rancher, the cost of a federal grazing permit is only a small portion of the *true* expense involved when leasing forest land.

Younger, less experienced replacement heifers will have to bide their time in the lower pastures close to home until they, like their mothers, can return to the high country. And so the ritual is preserved, the traditions continue.

Crisp fall temperatures lead me back indoors where neglected chores await. Stacks of unattended papers beg to be sorted and filed. Seed packets of picture-perfect flowers sit unopened on the counter, signs of an optimistic but unrealistic gardener. I add them to my growing collection of seeds from last year, and the year before.

The iron and mending beckon also, unpatched Wranglers and worn-out coveralls. My grandmother Effie, in her brief biography, mentions her laundry chores during the early years in the growing Mojave settlement: "Soon we were having church services in our home," she writes proudly, "and everyone who came brought a picnic lunch. All stayed for the baseball game afterwards. The uniforms were gray with red stripes ... it was my job to keep the team suits clean and repaired."

I wish she had been able to pass on her seamstress skills to me. A bright red shirt sits on top of my own pile of laundry. Matt wore it only once. It was his favorite shirt—a brand new long-sleeved western shirt with pearl snaps. The material is still stiff with starch, the factory creases still run down the length of the arms.

The tag inside the shirt tells me it is a size 6. The need to mend the shirt has passed: Matt has grown much too big for it now. *Have two years really passed since we had that argument?*

When you're young, traditions come easily. Do something more than once and a tradition is born. That's how rides up into the forest with J. W. began. He and Lois, instead of enjoying their retirement years, run their ranch alone. My father, Matt's only living grandfather, lives in San Francisco, fifteen hundred miles from Wyoming and worlds apart in lifestyle. Matt feels a distant kinship with his grandfather and seeks a closer bond whenever the distance can be traversed—but a boy without a gray-haired friend close by is a sad thing. Matt grafted himself to J. W. as surely as an orphaned calf to an old milk cow.

One evening the phone rang. With an easygoing drawl, J. W. asked to speak to Matt. "How's my pardner?" Matt's face lit up at

J. W.'s mention of alliance. "Thought I'd check and see if you wanted to ride up in the woods with me tomorrow?"

Matt, ecstatic, insisted on wearing his good red shirt. "But, Mom," he argued stubbornly, standing with feet spread and fists anchored to his slender hips, "it's my *favorite* shirt—I've just *got* to wear it!"

"You're only riding up into the forest with J. W. to check cows. You'll be horseback and getting dirty—there's no need to wear your best shirt. Besides, it's supposed to be saved for special occasions."

I tired of arguing before Matt did. He left the house decked out in his good red shirt. That night he came home tuckered and close to tears. It had taken the two of them hours to trail a lame cow down out of the forest. The minute he stepped into the kitchen I knew something had gone wrong.

"Mom, I couldn't help it," he pleaded. "We were in all this brush and there was this low-hanging branch and it almost knocked me off my horse."

"Couldn't help what?" I asked.

The confession spilled forth. "I tore my shirt Mom!"

He turned slowly around on dusty, dejected heels. The shirt, torn almost in half, hung from his young, lanky shoulders. A telltale thin bloody scratch ran down the length of his spine. Hoping he had learned his lesson, I couldn't resist the temptation to point out that Mom had been right.

"Maybe next time I tell you to save your good clothes for special occasions, you'll listen." I bit my tongue the minute the sharp words pierced the tense air.

Large, solitary tears rolled down Matt's smudged and sunburned cheeks, the frustration finally overwhelming him. He shuffled down to his room, shoulders drooping, head hung like a scolded pup.

Not until bedtime, when Matt's tears had dried and my high and mighty attitude had succumbed to remorse, did he tell me of their day.

"Yeah, it was pretty fun. We talked some, but mostly we just rode. Then we ate our lunch under some pine trees and took a nap. Only J. W. says cowboys never admit to taking naps. J. W. says it sure is a good thing we brought that cow home—couldn't a done it without my help, he said."

I pictured the two of them beneath the tall ponderosa pine trees that shade the deep draws and high-country creeks. Their horses are tethered, cinches loosened. Matt and J. W. recline in the pine needles, cowboy hats tipped to shade their eyes—one a tiny version of the other. Twin blades of dying fall grass, plucked from the ground, rest between their lips, the roots still succulent and vital. The forest squirrels skitter about, filling their winter caches with wild grapes and pinecone seeds.

Now, instead of lying among the pine needles, our exhausted but exuberant son snuggled beneath his bed quilt. I picked the dirty, torn red shirt up off the floor and hugged Matt good-night.

"I hope I get to go with him next year," he said, anticipation bright in his eyes.

A new radiant sound enhanced Matt's voice that evening—the faint melody of a boy on his way to becoming a man. I refold the torn red shirt and place it back on my neglected stack of sewing, having finally learned what it is young boys and old men share— an impatience to experience it all pairs up well with the patience needed for such desires.

It is easy to think, because of my adult perspective, that I am somehow wiser. But I am too busy with the pressures of unplanted seed packets and unmended clothes. Sometimes it takes the passing of two years and the holding of a shirt that is now too small for me to see the wisdom of my children's ways.

If J. W. calls and invites Matt to gather cows and bring them down out of the forest, I think I will let him wear his best shirt. I may even get out the mink oil and polish up his good gray Ropers—the boots I used to make him save for *special* occasions.

21

Nothing Between Us

HEAVY AIR HUNG LOW between the hills, muggy and still. I started to head out past Mark who lay half under the pickup with his tools, an oil pan and filter nearby. Hondo rested in the sliver of shade cast by the old Ford, and Simon's kittens peered down at us from their hollow knothole in the old oak.

"Mark," bitterness edged my voice as I slowed my steps, "silence is not golden. Don't expect me to know what you're thinking if you don't tell me."

I didn't wait for him to reply to my caustic comment, the tail end of a petty marital quarrel. The air between us, too, remained heavy and still. I needed to get away—away from the work week's fast pace, away from the irritable image of myself. Hondo lifted his head, wagged his tail, looked from me to Mark, then settled back down, his difficult choice made.

I turned on my heel and continued on my way. A single female bluebird perched on the fence between the stackyard and the pasture, and the relentless sun beat down, fading the blue from bird and sky alike.

The fence line led to a cattle path that is used by the turkeys and deer as well. I hiked along past the heat-faded bluebird, across the pasture, and finally into the oak brush. The sun filtered through the leaves, casting veils of black lacework upon the path. Cool shadows soothed my mood, lightened my steps. I eased up, leaving the bickering behind while reprogramming myself to Saturday's slower pace, shaking the ten-second sound-bite mentality from my consciousness. Here in the woods no clock ticked away the minutes, no quarrel echoed from the trees.

Ironic, a deception of life, that the years a married couple spend together and that give depth to a relationship are the very years that separate them. When Mark and I first dated, the spinning was so intense that we fused, became inseparable, like the front and back of a newly budded leaf. There was nothing between us. Everything remained external and outside our realm. Pressures drove us together, not apart.

What changed? Do all relationships have a dark underside? Do the tedious tasks of raising children and paying bills become like unseen fungus growing in the dark? Does the natural law that leads to the setting of each risen sun apply even to us?

We had raised Hondo from a pup, giving him chew bones for his milk teeth and love for his loyalty. Now we soften his food with warm broth and stroke his head with callused fingers. We have seen friends begin their families, watched some divorce their dreams. We have buried mutual loved ones. We shook the Colorado dust from our boots and stepped side by side onto the Wyoming soil. *Where, in all these experiences, is the knife that cleaves?*

After twenty minutes of hiking I left the trail and veered uphill, deep into a draw and a grove of silver aspen. Gooseberries, plucked cautiously from nettled stalks, quenched my thirst. A fallen log lay across the narrow ravine, bridging the overgrown sides of the draw. I sat down.

This wooded world, so different from the sage-covered prairie above me, was thick with flora and fauna. Chickadees and phoebes darted away, landing on the upper limbs of the aspen. The insects quieted. I sat motionless. Soon a daring dark-eyed junco darted between trees. A cautious dialogue resumed: *fee-bee-ee*, answered with *pweer, pweer*, until the chatter and buzzing reached normal pitch.

The rustle of leaves and swishing of grass made me turn—just my head—ever so slowly. A red fox with nose to the ground and white-tipped tail held aloft meandered down the draw toward me. A lingering scent kept him focused on the trail; his black nose twitched and his white-furred throat rippled. I dared not move. When he passed, head bent beneath the log on which I sat and within ten feet, I could hear his breath. The birds continued to chirp and dart, the insects buzzed—their behavior did not give me away. Finally the fox wound his way through the gooseberries and brush until he disappeared into the shadowed aspen.

His presence hung golden before me, a gilded gift suspended in time. I stared into the trees, wanting to re-create him, to retrieve the moment of first encounter.

I hiked back down the ravine through purple blossoms of horsemint and ripe blades of canary grass. The ravine widened; silver aspen gave way to gray-trunked bur oak. I retraced my steps down the shaded cattle path where filtered sunlight still cast black lacework upon the trail. A bright turquoise male bluebird had joined the female, and they both perched, waiting, on the taut wire.

I arrived at the house hot and sweaty. My shirt clung to my skin; the morning's quarrel clung to my conscience. Mark stood in the driveway next to the truck. He wore an old western shirt with ragged tails and torn-off sleeves. His arms were bare, his tanned hands streaked with grease. He wiped them on a flannel rag, then leaned on the pickup.

We glanced self-consciously at each other, testing the wind. Then we looked away, averting our eyes to the old oak where Simon's kittens nested. Simon sat at the base of the tree, meowing.

"Has she been there long?" I asked.

"All morning. Won't go up. Wants the kittens to come down, I guess."

"Looks like the striped one's about to try."

The most robust of the litter, with front paws extended and head pointed down the trunk of the tree, meowed plaintively. He inched his way downward toward his mother, digging his quill-like claws into the rough, furrowed bark. The effort shook his entire frightened body.

"He's gonna make it," Mark said as the kitten passed the halfway mark. Then he stopped and hung suspended from the tree.

Meooowwww, he wailed, as if still expecting Simon to climb up.

Meow, she answered, not budging.

Meooowwww, he pleaded one last time. Then he released his grip and sprang from the oak, landing with all four feet spread and tail flared like a feather duster. Having never walked on flat ground before, he took a tentative step, using his flared tail for balance in the manner of a tree squirrel.

"Looks like Sassy," I said, and we both laughed for the first time that day. We looked at each other across the short distance and, this time, did not avert our gazes but faced each other full on.

"Hi," we said in soft-spoken apologetic voices.

The acrid smell of gasoline and oil tainted the air, accented by Mark's sweat and the sun's heat. The odor, alien to aspen-thick ravines, assaulted my senses and shocked me into the present. I forgot about Simon and the kitten, forgot about the fox. Mark stood before me. A mere five feet of space lay between us.

Suddenly, overwhelmed with a desire to strip from us all petty quarrels, all burdens of parenting, all responsibilities, I wanted only to lie with him in the late summer grass. I wanted to bed down—naked, bare-skinned—upon the black lacework path beneath the forest trees, stripped to our very souls. I wanted to cleave to him, spun into fusion, with nothing between us—*not even ourselves between us.*

Instead, I walked to the barn.

Romie nickered as I approached, following me into the corral. I haltered her and fed her a handful of grain. I curried her roan hair with a brush, using long, smooth strokes to massage her tired flesh. I brushed the dust from her back and the flies from her eyes. I ran my fingers through her black mane, untangling the coarse hairs. Mark appeared in the corral, reading my thoughts.

"Want me to saddle her for you?"

"You think it would be all right? If I took it easy?"

This would be our last ride together. I knew it. Mark knew it. Romie's brittle bones and emaciated muscles sensed it.

The lightweight Heiser saddle settled on her back. The cinch, too loose, had to be tightened to fit her gaunt ribs. I eased the metal curb bit into her mouth and mounted her, wishing I were a lithe girl of fifteen again—wishing she were barebacked and I bare-legged.

Her unshod hooves kicked up puffs of red dirt. Mark, standing alone in the corral, waved good-bye as Romie and I headed east, away from the afternoon sun. I spoke to her of younger, faster days, of racing with the wind, of chasing imaginary buffalo. She nickered into the breeze, her ears pricked forward, and together we trotted up the hill, heading for the sky-high butte that crowns the ridge.

The next time I climbed to the top of that butte, I did so on foot. A new season had arrived and I wore a down coat, insulated leather gloves, and a red wool scotch cap. I thought about that hot summer day and the black lacework upon the path; I thought about my petty quarrel with Mark but could not remember the cause of the argument. Below me, in the pasture across the road, Romie grazed alongside Cindy and the geldings, and I realized that I *did* remember the silent empathy in Mark's eyes that day as he saddled Romie, a silence gilded by mutual understanding.

Sagebrush and an occasional gray-green yucca plant clung to the butte's rocky soil. I knelt, removed a glove, and ran my hand over the loose chips of shale and sandstone. Rubbing the red dirt from a stone, I felt the weathered rock for signs of chiseled edges.

Could a hunter, armed with bow and arrow, have stood in this same spot centuries ago?

No, this was not a hunting place but a seeking place, where perhaps the faint tracing of a vision quester's protective circle lingered. Long ago, had another woman come here to soothe her overburdened spirit? To seek answers? To seek the past? What had *she* learned about the dark underside of relationships that she could teach me?

Did my own grandmothers face these same questions? Had my grandmother Effie, married off by her aunt to the first suitor who would have a deaf wife, ever known unburdened passion? Had my grandmother Helen, my father's mother, been able to escape the memories long enough to lie, bruised but hopeful, upon the black lace shadows beneath the trees? Were there, perhaps, even *good* memories upon which to build the framework of the future?

I put the weathered rock back on the ground. It had no chiseled edges; all had been rounded smooth by time, the rough edges long ago having disappeared.

Perhaps in time, my rough edges, too, will disappear. Perhaps if I stay in this searching place a while longer—allow the storms to work their magic—I will be able to go to Mark, once again, bare-souled.

22

Wooly Livestock

WE HAVE HAD SHEEP since Thursday: ten frightened ewes due to lamb any day. The first livestock of our own. It is a beginning.

Last night the sheep crowded into a corner of the barn, a tightly wedged woolen mass. They did not venture out of the corner except to move cautiously a few feet to the hay.

The next morning, under a silver pre-dawn moon that hung high above the ridge, I heard the coyotes howling. An obsessed, uncontrolled energy stimulated their calls—as if the moon tugged on a string tied invisibly to their vocal cords. Are the coyotes as driven to howl, I wondered, as the ewes are impelled to bunch?

Our small band of ten ewes came from the Good Ranch up in Montana, where they roamed the eastern plains with five hundred other sheep.

"A good little bunch of sheep," the sale barn's auctioneer had crooned, "due to lamb April fifteenth." I wondered how many rams were in that bunch of five hundred and how long it had taken them to cover all the ewes —there could be a lot of leeway in that April 15 date.

Edie, Mark's mother, had arrived from Colorado for a visit just in time to see our new sheep.

"Why, if your granddad knew you had sheep, he'd roll over in his grave!" she teased Mark.

"Could be worse, Edie, " I said. "My Grandmother Effie used to raise goats and White Holland turkeys out in the Mojave. Can you see Mark herding a flock of turkeys?"

"Or branding a bunch of goats?" she laughed. "How *do* you brand sheep, anyway?"

"With green paint, " Mark answered, "and it's gonna be Page's job!"

The price of cattle, even old broken-mouthed cows, remained high, making it difficult for us to get started. Except for the sheep, our new ranch remained unstocked. The cattle we pastured during the summer months helped make the land payments and gave us reason to ride and check fence, but up until a few days ago we had no livestock to call our own.

"Hey, Matt tells me you got a new horse," Edie elbowed Mark in the ribs.

"Yep," Mark answered, verbose as usual.

"A bucking horse!" Matt added with a gleam in his eyes.

"A bucking horse?"

"No, Mom," Mark shook his head, "he's not a bucking horse. He's gonna be Page's horse."

"Not a bucking horse *exactly*," I corrected.

"What's she mean, Mark, *not exactly?*"

"Well, we bought him from Calvin, a friend of mine who rides rough-stock."

"In rodeos?" Edie asked, raising her eyebrows.

"Yes, Mom. In rodeos. Calvin bought the black horse at the sale barn. They sold him as bucking stock. Calvin was hoping to practice on him, but he hasn't been able to get him to buck."

"So you thought maybe Page would be able to?"

"Right," I said, "I'm gonna ride him bareback, with only an Indian bridle looped around his jaw."

"Now, don't go rollin' your eyes. He's not gonna do any bucking. I rode him. He's foolproof." Mark was an understated optimist.

"First sheep, then rodeo rough-stock. I don't know about you, Mark."

Edie, just trying to get a rise out of her son, knew that Mark wouldn't buy a rogue horse. At least I *hoped* he wouldn't. She also knew that his granddad wouldn't really turn over in his grave, even though he had been a proud Colorado cattleman. He had also been a businessman; believing in diversification, he had added an orchard of over twenty-eight thousand apple trees to the ranch's cattle operation. A father also, he had raised four children on the ranch back in Colorado. I am sure he had watched his children, wide-eyed at the birth of a new calf, and felt a sense of rightness knowing that they witnessed life unfolding. No doubt it made it easier on his children, too, when as adults they watched their father grow older, until finally they witnessed life folding back in on itself.

Just as he watched his children, Mark and I watched ours. Matt and Sarah needed to experience that wide-eyed amazement as new life presented itself. Calf or lamb, the feeling was the same, so we had bought the ten head of Rambouillet-Columbia-cross ewes. We had a lot to learn about sheep in a short amount of time.

Matt and Sarah went to school with a boy and girl whose parents also had sheep. We knew Floyd and Veronica only slightly, but when they found out about our ewes, they offered to loan us their lambing jugs. The day Mark went over to pick up the small wooden panels, they sent him home with ten water buckets, and some sought-after encouragement and advice as well. These folks raised both sheep and cattle in an attempt to cope with the costs of ranching. They were eager to help us, and we couldn't help but be warmed by their neighborliness.

Edie and Mark reminisced about the old ranch, about his first 4-H calf, about his lanky granddad. Then we all went out to the barn to check the sheep. Matt and Sarah wrapped their own long legs around the corral posts, watching the ewes chew their hay.

A few days later Veronica and Floyd stopped by where I worked. He stayed out in the car while she ran in, carrying a plastic bag full of frozen cream-colored cubes.

"I brought you some cow colostrum in case you get any bums. We milked some extra out of one of our older cows for you."

Colostrum—Mother Nature's birthing tonic—contained in a newborn's first taste of milk, rich in protein, and a boost to the immune system.

Her casual manner gave no more importance to this gesture than that of waving to a friend on the street, but the subtle significance was not lost on me and it warmed my soul. These people, whom we knew only slightly, were sharing their equipment and experience with us, taking time from their busy and hardworking lives—all for ten ewes. And here, too, unknowingly, was some old cow sharing her lifeblood with lambs yet to be born.

I thought of Matt and Sarah and the wide eyes they would surely have when they held that first newborn lamb, then I carefully took the sack of frozen cubes from Veronica and thanked her as she hurried out the door.

"Hey, Page," she said with a grin, interrupting the sentimental moment as gritty, hard-living westerners are prone to do, "I hear you got a new horse."

"Yeah, we did," I said. "Word travels fast around here."

"Well," she headed out the door, laughing, "don't let him buck you off!"

23

Renewals

This oneness with all that live is the Indian heritage, though other sensitive people with compassionate vibrations, who breathe forth the fragrance of a holy life like Saint Francis, have it also. ... It is in the rhythm of their approach, the way they walk toward those who share the world with them ... fellow guests in the house of the Great Spirit ... .
—Evelyn Eaton[1]

PALM SUNDAY. CROSSES WOVEN of palm leaves will be given at church today, but we will not be there to receive ours. Matt and Sarah will miss this time-honored tradition.

There is an ache deep inside my chest. Not the viral ache that has plagued me all winter but the ache that comes from being confined too long indoors. It is cured only by green grass, strong sun, and ripe earth.

A hike up to a rocky outcropping, homesteaded by striped ground squirrels, invigorates my languid heart muscle. A mule deer doe watches me from the next hill. I search for her tracks, find them, and trudge off after her. She leaves shiny, slick droppings to mark her passing. Perfectly smooth, an even-colored dark coffee brown, they glisten in the morning sun. Early training makes me hesitate before picking one up, deep conditioning urges me to wipe my hand on a patch of slushy snow after putting it down. Somehow, this tactile connection eases the ache.

Later, with the sun still beating its way through the chill of a March breeze, the four of us sit half-in and half-out of the barn door, soaking up the rays that warm the sheltered east side of the barnyard. A few pieces of cat food are scattered about, left by a thieving skunk last night. Sarah sits on my left, Matt on my right. Mark has carried an aluminum lawn chair out of the barn and sits in front of us in full sun. The chair is old and dilapidated and leans unevenly to one side, threatening to dump Mark into the manure-rich corral dirt.

The sheep shearer was supposed to come this afternoon, but he canceled on us—down sick with a bad cold. Rotten timing. Mark's mother, Edie, is visiting, and we were all going to get together: Keith (Mark's brother) and his wife, Cindy, and the three cousins, too. They wanted to share our first sheep-shearing, and now we have missed Palm Sunday as well.

A time of firsts—humble as they may be. To make a celebration of the shearing of a meager ten head of sheep seems an embarrassing declaration of our modest starting over. But I am stubborn and will not let embarrassment stand in the way of recognition. This is a milestone. We bought ten old ewes for less than what one good cow would cost. Yet their lamb crop this spring will help pay for our first cows, we hope this fall. A blasé attitude would be irreverent, disrespectful.

The barn is an appropriate substitute for church with the manger in waiting and the animals gathered around. We sit in the sun and have our own private time of worship. We attempt to braid loose hay into neat crosses but don't master the technique. I think of the meticulously woven baskets of the Four Corner Anasazi and feel inept and clumsy. Perhaps this summer I will attempt weaving with yucca fibers as did those proficient Basket Makers of the past.

Tuffy is curled up on Matt's lap, her gray downy belly exposed. As Matt rubs her tummy all four feet flop loosely in the air and I am reminded of Black Jack. Sarah pets Simon, who sunbathes in the warm dirt. Hondo naps beneath Mark's dilapidated chair.

I begin reading aloud an essay by Lansing Christman. "Look at the natural world around you," the essay begins, "and witness the evidence of God's presence. ..."[2]

Another voice echoes within me, so familiar I almost confuse it with my own. *O Great Spirit, Whose voice I hear in the winds, And whose breath gives life to all the world ... .*[3]

Do the others hear this shadowy female voice? I look at them: their eyes are half-closed, their faces loose and relaxed. *Let me walk in beauty, and make my eyes ever behold the red and purple sunset.*

... Let me learn the lessons you have hidden in every leaf and rock.
I cannot help but think of the young Lakota girl standing before
White Buffalo Calf Woman, holding her bouquet of dried weeds.
Mark stretches, and glints of sunlight flash from the aluminum
chair. Suddenly, silver sage is everywhere.

Sarah giggles at Tuffy, whose foot wiggles in response to Matt's
petting. I stop reading and touch the delicate gray fur on the inside
of Tuffy's thigh, only inches from her vulnerable belly. The fur is
warm and so fine it is almost imperceptible to the touch. Like an
elusive shadowy voice.

The sheep are gathered around the feed bunk in the corral next
to where we sit. They take bites of hay, swallowing quickly, while
they stand at the feeder. A few have moved away and are lying in
the sun at the edge of the corral, their jaws moving sideways in a
relaxed cud-chewing motion. The black horse, whom we now
simply call The Black, and Mark's gelding, Tee, are tethered to the
corral fence. They stand with mellowed heads hanging low, wast-
ing no energy during this brief reprieve from Wyoming's harsh
winter.

Our two mares, not tethered, stand on the other side of the
fence. We gave Romie worming medicine yesterday, hoping to ease
her gauntness. She finally looks as old as her twenty-eight years. No
longer an easy keeper, she lost weight this winter, and her bony hips
emphasize the slightly swayed back. Yesterday, when I was cleaning dried mud from her, the currycomb raked across her thin ribs,
and as I combed the mud from her forehead, it skipped over the
deep sockets above her eyes.

I do not want to admit that she is old. Will we be able to bury
her when she dies, I wonder? I am not sure what one does with a
dead horse. Leave her bones to the hawks and coyotes? Use a winch
to hoist the carcass onto a trailer? It would be a lot to ask of Mark,
to dig a horse-sized grave. Even for an old, thin horse, it would have
to be a very large hole. Perhaps one of the deep ravines, an eroded red
washout, a place sheltered from the wind and warmed by the sun?

The auburn tips of Romie's roan hair blow gently in the breeze.
The mangy gray hairs of her winter coat lack vitality, their roots
already shriveled.

The breeze ruffles the longer hairs around Hondo's neck as well. His muzzle has turned completely gray. It will remain gray, even after he has shed his winter coat. Guilt floods my conscience as I think that perhaps we should get a young pup to fill the void when Hondo dies. The thought is disloyal—the void unfillable.

I finish reading Christman's essay. It concludes, "As Spring begins, Easter places at your fingertips a whole new universe of eternal life."[4] I shut the book and lean into the shade, closing my eyes, thinking of life's cycles of birth and death. The shadowy voice returns. *So when life fades, as the fading sunset, my spirit may come to you, O Great Spirit, without shame.*

Matt and Sarah begin fidgeting. They have grown impatient, for they are anxious to saddle the horses—Mark has promised them a ride. I contemplate saddling Romie again and going with them, but somehow our friendship gets in the way and I cannot see myself climbing selfishly on, asking her to carry me up yet another hill. Besides, I need to be alone. There are things I must learn while the teacher is willing to teach.

We stand and shyly join hands with Mark for an ending prayer. Mark, his reticence overcome in honor of Palm Sunday, thanks God for the animals, the day, and our many blessings. We say the Lord's Prayer together. Matt's voice is loud and confident, he knows the prayer well. Sarah speaks in a whisper, unsure of some of the words. But we finish with voices of equal strength, our "amen" settling on the backs of the sheep like a light dusting of late snow. *Amen.*

24

Lambing

We have a biological father and mother, but our real Father is Tunkashila, Creator, and our real Mother is the Earth. They give birth and life to all the living, so we know we're all interrelated. ... That is why you hear us saying mitakuye oyasin ... *it means "all my relations."*

—Wallace Black Elk[1]

WE KEPT A CLOSE WATCH on the ewes as lambing time approached, turning them in every night. Beginning on the night of the fifteenth we began our midnight vigil, checking them every four hours. Many ranchers check more often, some don't check at all. Had these ewes still been out on the range, they would have fended for themselves; with only ten head, we decided to pamper them.

I had my eye on one girl, identified by her squared-off left ear. Mark was used to checking on heavy cows whose signs of impending birth were a bit more evident. These ewes weren't as predictable, but I liked to think that my feminine instinct made up for lack of experience. This ewe (we called her Square Ear) had a ready look about her. She was bagged up and loose in the rear. But more than that, she moved awkwardly. I remembered the feeling well: struggling to get out of bed or rise from a chair. Once the baby settled head-down in the birth canal, everything became awkward. I was betting on Square Ear to be the first to lamb.

On the night of the fifteenth Mark went out to check the ewes. He came back up to the house quickly.

"Well, we've got one." His voice was tinged with more enthusiasm than he probably would have cared to admit. He reached into the refrigerator for the tetanus vaccine and syringe. I pulled on my coveralls and headed out the door with him, sure that my girl, Square Ear, had lambed.

Within twenty feet of the barn a high-pitched bleat, plaintive and persistent, penetrated the night air. The sound thrilled me—I hadn't expected the lamb's call to be so viable, so insistent.

Inside the barn the newborn lamb bleated, stumbling in circles as she searched for the ewe. If the ewe had been "mothering up" before we got there, she wasn't any longer. All ten ewes bunched in fright at our appearance. We scooped the lamb up and put her in a small lambing pen (also called a jug), then, stirring among the sheep, we picked out the mother.

It wasn't Square Ear after all, but a ewe we had named Stomper. Stomper always stood guard at the front of the flock, stomping her feet in warning to the others when we came too close. She had probably been at the head of the flock, too, when the bucks had done their breeding.

Blood and mucus dripped from the severed umbilical cord that hung from beneath her tail. The task now was to separate her from the other ewes and get her in the jug with the lamb.

Mark brought an eight-foot panel into the lambing area, using it as a divider. I worked my way into the center of the bunch, sorting off ewes until only Stomper remained. Then, in a panicked rush to join the others, she fled past me, half leaping and half crashing into the panel. *Dang it all!* She left a trail of blood behind her.

We tried again, clumsy in our attempts, managing to separate only six of the ewes. Stomper and three others were jammed wedge-like into a corner.

"What would happen if I just tried to grab her?" I asked. Tackling her might work—if I could hang on.

"Couldn't hurt. Grab a hind leg."

I made a flying dive, zeroing in on her left hind leg. She kicked frantically, the other three ewes fleeing to the safety of the herd and leaving Stomper to protect herself. I held on with both hands, determined not to let go. Mark grabbed on, but the frightened ewe flipped herself over, landing with a thud on her side. I winced sympathetically. Meanwhile, the lamb continued to bleat.

I opened the gate to the jug and Mark dragged Stomper inside. She got to her feet quickly, eyeing us suspiciously. We backed away.

"Real smooth, huh," I said sarcastically, not impressed with our finesse.

"Well, let's doctor the lamb and leave 'em alone."

We weren't done yet. Mark picked up the lamb, turning her over onto her back. I poured iodine solution into her torn and dangling umbilical cord, squeezing more of the reddish brown liquid around the outside. Then I held her while Mark, more experienced at shots, injected one-half cubic centimeter of anti-toxin into the wriggling lamb. I started to put her back in the pen when Stomper saw me reach toward her and came at me head-on, not about to be wrestled to the ground again. The lamb got caught in the middle, crushed by the ewe against the wooden planks of the pen. I jerked the lamb up out of the jug. Stomper pounded her hoofs into the dirt and glared.

"Easy, girl, easy." I lowered the lamb again, slowly. Stomper came at me, catching the lamb full-force this time. I jerked her out.

"She got her good that time. Think she'll be okay?"

"I imagine." Mark reached in and held Stomper at bay while I placed the lamb gently in the straw. We backed off and watched. Stomper sniffed the lamb suspiciously but made no aggressive moves. The lamb knelt motionless, all the spunkiness knocked out of her. After a few minutes, she bleated, and Stomper answered with a low throaty rumble. The lamb bleated again, struggling to her knees. Stomper rumbled and sniffed. The lamb's weak legs wobbled as she made her way to her mother, then pushed her nose instinctively between the ewe's hind legs and butted forcefully at the swollen teats. Stomper became more vocal, talking in a low gurgle as she licked the birthing fluids and nibbled the pieces of torn sack from the wet yellowish wool.

The next night, the sixteenth, it was my turn for the midnight watch. Mark would check the sheep at 4:00 A.M. As I approached the barn, I heard plaintive bleating. Standing on tiptoe, I peered through an opening into the lambing barn. The flashlight's beam cast eerie circles of yellow into the darkness. In the far corner, by herself, stood a ewe, busy inspecting the shivering lamb that had just dropped unceremoniously from her posterior. Deep maternal rumbles answered the plaintive bleating.

Deciding to give the pair time to adjust to each other, I headed back to the house and woke Mark—not exactly what the midnight watchman was supposed to do.

"We've got another one."

"What?" He sat up in bed.

"We have another lamb. Do you want me to handle it by myself?"

"Sure." He buried his head beneath the pillow and turned over.

Back at the barn, I walked quietly inside the enclosed lambing area. "Easy, girls, easy." I inched open the door, my vision adjusting to the dim illumination of the flashlight. The ewe and lamb stood near the door. Then the ewe circled around the lamb, allowing me room to maneuver my way to the light switch, placed high on the wall. I used the end of a broom handle to flick it on.

"Why, it's you, Square Ear. I wasn't far off, was I?" She watched me curiously but without panic.

"Easy, girl. I'm just going to open the gate on this pen for you." I reached slowly toward the lamb, keeping a wary eye on Square Ear. The lamb bleated loudly at my touch, and the ewe answered quickly, possessively. Placing the lamb inside the jug, I angled the gate open.

"Here, girl. Go on, go inside with her. That's a girl, go on in." I moved aside, and Square Ear followed the sound of her lamb, trotting neatly into the pen. I eased the door shut and was twisting a wire to secure it, when I heard Mark.

"Looks like you've got everything under control."

"Almost everything. Stomper's lamb doesn't look so good." I turned my head in their direction. The lamb had not roused herself. The image of her being butted forcefully against the wooden panels nagged at my conscience. I should have known better.

Working in town only four miles from the ranch allowed me time during my lunch hour to hurry home and check the sheep. Arriving the next day at noon, I pulled on my inexpensive pair of black rubber irrigation boots and headed to the barn. Stomper's lamb lay huddled in the corner, ears droopy and eyes half-closed. Gaunt hipbones protruded. I reached in and stood her up, keeping a wary eye on Stomper. The lamb quickly lay back down.

Mark was working for J. W. that month, helping during calving season while he had time off from his work with the forest service. I went up to the house and phoned, catching him inside for the noon meal.

"Stomper's lamb doesn't look good." I went on to describe her listless behavior.

"Well, I'll check her when I get home tonight."

"I don't know if she'll last that long."

"I'll see if I can come down after a while and check things out."

Later that afternoon Mark called me at work. "The lamb's got the scours. I milked the ewe out and bottle-fed the lamb, but you'll need to stop by the vet's and get some scour medication."

At the vet's I spent twenty-seven dollars on scour medication, a quick-acting combiotic (a combination of penicillin and strepto-mycin), electrolyte water, a stomach tube, and a syringe—more money than the lamb would have brought at market. But by the next morning, after another round of bottle feeding and medica-tion, the lamb was up and active. By that night she was nursing well.

The third ewe handled things on her own, dropping twin lambs on the ground outside, much to Sarah's delight.

"Two!" she exclaimed as we stood just inside the door.

We sat down, dangling our legs out of the open barn door and watched the threesome. The ewe sniffed first one, then the other. She licked each, turning in circles as the lambs rotated around her hungrily, responding to that most ancient of instincts.

Not long ago I heard about a government study costing hundreds of thousands of dollars, the sole purpose of which was to discover if newborn humans could distinguish the smell of their own mother's breast milk, as can all other mammals. The results proved conclusively that babies can, indeed, discern their mother's scent. Matt, as a newborn, had nursed possessively from the very beginning. Sarah had been gentle, more lady-like. Both had turned their heads instinctively in a rooting reflex at the slightest touch of a finger on their tender cheek. The idea never occurred to me that our humanness might negate our commonality with other mammals. It is frightening to live during a time when the blood bond is doubted, when we feel such a compulsion to separate ourselves from our instincts.

Fog hovers over the valley, cloaking the town, hills, and ridges in a gossamer mist. Three inches of new snow cover the deck. I head down to the barn to check the ewes before going to bed.

The male twin from ewe number three is bloated. I go back to the house and get Mark. We maneuver a stomach tube down his throat and into the distended belly, trying to release the gas. I massage his swollen sides while Mark gently blows into the tube, hoping to clear any obstruction. The blowing creates a temporary suction, and the lamb belches, his stomach rumbles, and air bubbles move beneath my fingers. His sides stay distended—the relief only temporary. For more than three hours we take turns breathing the putrid fumes from the stomach tube. It does no good. We try soybean oil to counteract the acidity, and in a last, desperate effort, I get two old antiflatulant pills from my days of pregnancy and force them into the lamb's mouth. Finally, we go up to the house for a few hours of sleep before work. We don't expect the lamb to make it.

He barely does. Only long enough for me to hold him in the early morning chill. Yesterday he ran and gamboled with his sister, chasing sun dust. But now, at 5:30 A.M., his cries from last night still fill the dark barn.

I put him back in the pen. He can no longer hold his head up. The ewe sniffs him. His body convulses, then jerks twice. I pick him back up. The ewe takes a bite of hay, sniffs the other lamb, then goes back to eating. She has given up on him. I hold his limp body in my arms. The wool on his long legs is clean and white and I think of crew socks. His head flops against my neck. He presses his wet nose against my cheek, and I think of my father rubbing my stomach when, as a child, my spastic colon would awaken me during the night. Why didn't the ewe care? She did not lick him or comfort him, despite her otherwise strong instincts.

The lamb and I, nose to cheek, look at each other. His eyes go blank. He is gone. I am mad at the ewe. The grief should be hers, not mine. The lamb startles me by exhaling. Our faces are so close that his last breath becomes my next breath. Is this what life is, the beginning and ending so close that they form a circle that flows on and on—an invisible exchange of breath? The lamb's life was short. He lasted only long enough for eternity to reach out and grab him. Maybe it was, after all, long enough.

I place the dead twin on the haystack, planning to bury him after work. By the time I get home, the cats have gnawed away his mouth and nose. Nothing else has been touched, only the milk-drenched woolen muzzle.

The barnyard has become a nursery, an entertaining place to be. The fifth ewe lambs easily and has a healthy buck lamb. Stomper and Square Ear enjoy roomier accommodations, while ewe number five suckles her youngster in the lambing jug. Ewe number three and the remaining twin are turned out in the corral.

Branding sheep is quite different from branding calves. Before the lambing began, Mark, with Matt and Sarah's help, bent pieces of wire into the numbers zero through nine. Before turning each ewe and lamb out of the small jugs, we paint them with matching numbers. We vaccinate the lambs again, this time with an "overeating disease" vaccine. We place elastic bands on all tails and on the testicles of the buck lambs.

It is necessary, in this day of animal rights activists, to analyze common and habitual practices. One should do this even *without* animal rights activists hammering at the door. Is it really necessary to dock the tails of lambs? Can this be done more humanely? With only ten sheep, we have options. A herd of a thousand is a different matter. When Stomper's lamb scoured, we had to scrape crusty yellow foul-smelling manure from her tail and hind end. I understood then what the sheep manual meant when it stated that sheep with docked tails had less trouble with flies and maggots.

I watched Stomper's lamb carefully as we stretched the green elastic band over the base of her tail. She stumbled and lay down when the band constricted, confused by the sensation of pain. Then numbness set in and she got to her feet, punching angrily at her mother's bag before settling down.

When Matt was a newborn I read that the immature blood vessels in a baby's fingers and toes should be kept covered in cold weather. Is it the same with a lamb's tail and testicles? Do they lack complete sensation? When Matt was circumcised the nurses took him to another room, and I tried not to think about the surgical procedure. The decision had been left to Mark, who knew what went on behind closed doors in boys' locker rooms. The film we had been shown graphically portrayed a doctor cutting away the foreskin of a newborn who, outraged, howled briefly. Later, when the nurse returned Matt to my side, I held him closely and offered him my breast. He, like the lamb to the ewe, latched on fiercely. Only after he had fallen asleep did I dare to gently undo the diaper and look at where his first scar would grow.

Branding our sheep does not test my conscience. The kids help, dipping the appropriate wire number into a can of green water-proof paint, then placing the wire carefully on the lamb's ribs before repeating the procedure with the ewe. A bright green L, for Lambert, marks their hips. Had I been the Queen of Hearts and Alice in Wonderland my guest, I am sure we could have invented a clever corral game to play with the painted, cud-chewing creatures.

A month later, by the time most of the lamb tails have dropped to the ground, the tenth ewe lambs. I can think of no witty metaphor to describe a lamb's dismembered tail, and I can think of no way to describe the feeling I get when holding a dozen such tails in my hand, except perhaps as a quickening awareness in the pit of my stomach of the mortality of the flesh.

The night the tenth ewe lambs we do not set the alarm. I fall asleep quickly and dream of Pocatello, Idaho, and childhood family vacations. I carry with me a stuffed animal—a musical lamb with curly wool on long, stiff legs and a pink satin ribbon around her slender neck. I cling to her during the long drive to our friends' home in Pocatello. When we arrive, the daughter, a paraplegic, pushes her wheelchair into the living room and meets my questioning gaze with a challenging stare. She eyes my lamb, spins her chair around, and exits the room, only to return a moment later with a stuffed poodle. The next day, when it is time to leave, I cannot find my lamb. I know the girl has hidden it, but I say nothing as I walk to the car. She waves at me from her wheelchair and, for a moment, I hate her.

I awake in the pitch-dark. The clock's iridescent letters glow red—2:00 A.M. I get up and tiptoe out of the room, pull on my coveralls, and grab the flashlight.

Everything is quiet at the barn; the lambs nestle next to their dozing mothers. Square Ear baas at me, and Stomper glares suspiciously as I sit down on the feed bunk. Square Ear's lamb raises her tailless hind end in the air and struggles to her feet. She wobbles over to me. I hold out a finger, and she takes it in her mouth and begins sucking. I turn off the flashlight, wanting to blend into the dark world of the sheep. The lamb's muzzle is the first thing to fade away in that brief instant between light and dark. I feel the lamb's strong wet tongue curl around my finger and am glad for the reminder that this lamb is whole and vital and alive.

25

Layers of Time

I am tracing my roots to my grandmother's heart, to her sacred fire … .
—Dhyani Ywahoo[1]

A WYOMING SUMMER DAY can be as hot as a Wyoming winter night is cold. Overhead a white disk glared in a wilted sky from which even the blue had faded. The sound waves of a supersonic jet pierced the noon air. I stood up from where I knelt in the garden and tipped my head back. The jet trail, a thick frothy line, crossed from the eastern horizon to the western coast. Dizzy from standing too quickly, I closed my eyes. The radiant heat and the sound of the plane brought back memories of a California day fifteen years ago.

The Mojave's borax-rich earth was warm beneath my feet. High overhead, a military plane tipped its wings in a final salute to the First Lady of Edwards, Effie Corum Pelton. They called her the Mother of Edwards Air Force Base; I called her grandmother.

A low-flying helicopter circled above me. The contents of an urn were being spilled ceremonially from the aircraft. The resulting sky-trail—bits and pieces of calcium—dispersed as the particles filtered through the hot California air to the desert floor. These ashes, my grandmother's remains, fell among the sage beyond my reach, beyond my meager memories.

First distance, then death, robbed me of my grandmother. We lived two thousand miles apart and were separated by sixty-five years of living. Our bond was thick as blood yet as elusive as the long-distance voice that reached me on Christmas and birthdays. I needed to hear her stories. I was finally ready. But it was too late—death had taken her to a higher place and left me stranded, earthbound.

The air base museum was full of newspaper clippings about her. Old photos filled the walls. I longed to step through time, through the camera's lens and into her life.

Her pioneer home stood among the California sage where her ashes now rest. I see her, deaf, in the quiet stillness of the Mojave, searching her arid garden for a half-hidden rattler. A snake shakes a warning, but only the desert scorpion hears.

What part of me stood in the dusty yard with my child-mother as she watched the deaf woman in the garden? Did my essence lie dormant, even then, within my mother's youthful seed, fertilized by the memories of generations gone by and the hopes of generations yet to come?

Deafness was a part of my grandmother's life long before she homesteaded in the Mojave. But I have no pictures to tell the story. Skeletal facts form a structure, but the fleshing out I must do on my own. Closed eyes and deep breaths allow transcendence to soak through the cracks and soft spots of my soul. I imagine her on that fateful day, a young girl of eighteen … .

She looks with trust at the doctor who treats her recurring ear infections. She sits in a heavy leather chair. He reaches into a glass-fronted oak cabinet while at the same time glancing down at the bottom of the chair and a lever he pumps with his foot. As the chair rises he takes a small amber-colored bottle from the cabinet.

"Lean your head to the side, Effie." She tilts her head so the medicine will not run out, and he gently puts a cotton ball in her ear.

"Good girl," he says. "Now the other side." He pours clear liquid into this ear also. Her eyes grow wide. She bites on her bottom lip but says nothing.

"There we go. That should have you feeling better in no time."

Her eyes fill with tears as she gets slowly out of the chair, which the doctor has lowered. The walk home takes forever, the dusty California streets blurring through her tear-filled eyes. The pain in her ears penetrates her skull. The trees that line the streets are filled with birds, but they make no noise. A dog barks silently at her from behind a picket fence. Finally she arrives at her aunt's home. She climbs the steps onto the porch slowly, exhausted by the effort required to lift each weighty foot. The door swings heavily open but she does not hear the creak of the brass hinges.

Her aunt comes to the door. "Ah, Effie, you've returned. What did the doctor say? We simply must get rid of these constant earaches. You really shouldn't be expected to endure them any longer."

Tears brim over the lower lids of young Effie's eyes, the pain finally too much. Inside the foyer she slides to the floor, landing at her aunt's feet.

Bolivar, Missouri, was hot in the summer. Located in the middle of Polk County, with reservoirs to the north and south, the humidity was unbearable, even to eleven-year-old Effie. She kicked at the hot dirt on the path that led to the outhouse behind their home. Things hadn't been the same since her daddy died. Momma never smiled anymore and forgot to tend the garden. The roses, which the gardener was not allowed to touch, grew in wild disarray. Effie plodded on, thinking about her half-finished lemonade waiting on the porch.

Earlier, Momma brought out the good silver tray and set it on the glass-topped wicker table. Water beaded up on the outside of the lemonade pitcher. Three bowls of fresh strawberries and cream sat on the tray next to the lemonade.

"Pearl," Momma said to Effie's older sister, "you're a big girl now. Why, you'll be thirteen this fall." She gave Pearl a hug and then kissed her on the forehead.

"Effie," she said, walking over to the porch swing where Effie sat, "what a pretty one you are, but always so serious. What's behind those eyes of yours, child? Here, sit on my lap for a moment. I know it's hot, but sit, just for a moment." Momma held Effie tight. Their skin was clammy where they touched. She smoothed the hair away from Effie's forehead and kissed her gently on both cheeks.

"George, you come over here, too." Effie's little brother climbed slowly up on the swing. Momma stared at George for the longest time before whispering to herself, "So much like your father, so much like him." Effie was hot and wanted to climb down and drink her lemonade, but the faraway look in her mother's eyes made her sit still. Then her mother stood, gently pushing the children aside. She walked into the house, the screen door closing abruptly behind her.

A little while later, Effie headed toward the outhouse. It was painted white to match the fence, and her daddy had cut the design of a daisy out of the clapboard walls for better ventilation. Effie pulled the latch on the door toward her, and a beam of sunlight cut its way into the darkness. Her mother sat inside, her head slumped backward.

"Pardon me, Momma. I'll wait outside."

Her mother didn't answer. Effie saw an ink-like stain on the front of her mother's apron. A trickle of dark liquid ran down her skirt and collected into a pool at her feet.

"Momma? Momma, you alright?"

Effie pushed the door open wider, letting in more sunlight. She didn't scream when she saw the blood that stained her mother's breasts crimson. Her mother clutched her father's rusty razor in her hand. It, too, was colored red with the blood that seeped from her throat. A deep, thin cut stretched from ear to ear.

"Effie, Effie, the doctor's here." Her aunt is shaking her awake, pulling her away from the awful memory of her mother's suicide seven years ago. Effie lies in her bed in the upstairs room of her aunt's home, where she has lived since the death of her mother. Her sister and brother were farmed out to separate homes.

The pain in her ears is terrible. She sees the doctor's mouth move but hears no sound. Her aunt stands rigidly by the bed, eyes wide, fists clenched. The doctor lowers his gaze to the floor. Effie does not hear him explain to her aunt how he mistook the bottle of acid for the bottle of ear medication. They were both in amber glass of the same size. It was a tragic mistake. Tragic indeed. Effie does not know which is worse, the pain in her ears or the memory of her mother in the outhouse.

The California desert retreated and I found myself again standing in my Wyoming garden. The jet trail was gone, disappearing into white wisps. I, too, retreated—away from the heat and into the house. Inside, I opened the china hutch and gingerly took out a cup and saucer from my grandmother's antique cocoa set, wishing we had, at least once, sipped cocoa together. I ran my finger down the length of the turkey feather, smoothing its edges, then carefully stroked the dull edge of the carving knife.

It is the next night, and Sarah and I are saying prayers. She lies beneath the covers, freshly shampooed hair still damp, smelling of raspberries. I kneel to be close, at her level, only a whisper apart. This moment between us becomes the day's fruition, making it all worthwhile. I breathe in her sweet raspberry smell, remembering how cool and chilled her bare arms felt that evening when I lifted her off the corral fence. The sound of another jet racing past had shaken the ground and I thought again of my grandmother Effie.

Now, in the quiet solitude of Sarah's bedroom, we bask in this moment of aloneness. She puts her small arm around my neck and kisses me softly on the cheek. Still kneeling by her bed and wanting to hug her to me, I close my eyes and put my head gently on her chest. I feel her small hand pat my back much like I have patted hers at least a thousand times before. For a moment I am the child. I imagine that it is my own mother, hundreds of miles away, comforting me, patting me on the back. Then I become not the child but the mother again. Only now I am an old and fragile mother, my tiny daughter suddenly grown, and it is she who holds me in her capable arms. Time fuses and floats away.

Grandma, speak to me. Loosen the strands of time—pluck the knot and unravel this seam that stretches between us—these layers of life and death that form the haze that keeps us apart.

As I was lifting Sarah off the corral gate, a jet plane flew overhead. I remembered the way your ashes fell from the hot California sky fifteen years ago. Tonight the Wyoming air is still, the sun gone. In its place is dusky coolness, dusky quiet. Diurnal creatures retreat to their hidden borrows and nests while night hunters flex their muscles, stomachs tight with hunger.

How many times did you lift my mother off the mesquite wood fence whose posts stood buried deep in the Mojave? When the desert moon rose icy-white, did you hold your child to you, warming her chilled flesh?

For you, the dusky silence was forever. There was no pause in the noisiness of your day. You knew anyway, though, didn't you? You could smell the evening breath of the Mojave. You held on to the side of the barn and felt the sand shift beneath your feet as Night stretched and began to rise from his slumber on the desert floor.

Today is cooler and I am working in the garden again, planting seeds that a friend stored in white envelopes last fall. She wrote the names of each of the flowers on the outside of the envelopes.

Coreopsis. Marigold. Foxglove. Black-eyed Susan. Shasta daisy. The seeds were family heirlooms, the original flowers had been her grandmother's. Each fall she gathers the seeds and stores them away in her winter pantry. Each spring she plants them anew.

Today, I will plant her grandmother's seeds. I will pretend that they are yours. Do Shasta daisies grow in the desert? I will pretend that they do.

It is connections I am wanting, more than blossoms. I rise from the bare garden, brushing the caked dirt from my legs. I walk away from the thick oak trees and the draw where the grass has already grown knee-high, where the fawns lie hidden, past our barn and across the pasture where the buffalo grass grows low and the wild iris wave their lavender crowns. I cut through a gathering of oak brush, staying to the deer and cattle path so as not to crush the leaves of the Oregon grape. *I smell skunk and remember you telling me, during one of our rare times together, that it was one of your favorite scents—this musky odor of skunk.*

I come to the edge of the thicket and walk out into the open pasture, closer now to the sage-thick ridge where I am heading. The blue harebells are in bloom already, gracing the hillside. As the incline becomes steeper, the soil thins, exposing small rocks and gravelly places where an occasional rose grows. Wild strawberry plants cling to the slope, their dainty white blossoms turning toward the sun.

Finally, on top of the ridge, I sink to my knees. The dark wet dirt that still sticks to my jeans blends with the eroded red soil of the washout.

This is it, this is the link. These rust-colored minicanyons absorb the heat of the sun just like the borax-rich earth of the Great Basin's Mojave. If I were a snake I would come here to rub my lengthy body along the abrasive shale-like ground. I would push and slither, grinding my nose into the gypsum dirt until the old, unwanted skin tore loose. A few more feet of exertion, a rock to rub against, and finally the paper-thin skin would be gone.

You would not hear the rustle of discarded rattlesnake skin as the wind blew it across the open desert, though, any more than you heard the rattles shake a warning. But were you able to smell the new skin, see the fresh and vivid pattern?

Here, I could melt into this rusty sandstone soil—where the earth's skin, too, has been stripped away, exposing the raw generations beneath. Cinders—their pale red color hinting at the molten mass that burned eons ago. Born again.

Was this why you loved the desert so? Where there were no treetops to catch the wind? There, a deaf woman would not need to look skyward, haunted by the sound of the wind blowing through the tall cottonwoods back in Bolivar, Missouri—back when you were a child, back when the wind was so loud that even the daisy-carved walls of an outhouse could not quell the noise. In the desert it would be easier to forget your sudden growing-up. Easier to forget that fateful day when the doctor poured acid in your ears. Easier to just be. Shed your memories, begin anew. Be reptilian for a while, let the new skin thicken.

When you pioneered in the Mojave, you cleared the land by chaining railroad ties together. Your horses dragged them, weighted down, over the sagebrush, pulling up great clumps of the stubborn plant. You grubbed out the greasewood by hand.

Here, the sage grows too. It grows close to the red washouts. It grows among the buffalo grass and the wild roses. It is a versatile plant that sinks its roots into a variety of soils.

I avert my eyes from the green fields and pine-topped hills that are only a hawk-glide away. They are a distraction. I enter the washout and pretend to be surrounded by desert.

In the eroded gully a narrow path leads me to the private depths of this high-walled canyon. I sit and look at the rock walls, which are cocoa brown, not red. I try to count the tiny fissile slabs but give up after counting fifty in only twelve inches. Three feet farther up a single gray band stretches down the length of the gully.

An occasional leafy weed clings to the steep-sided walls. They become more numerous, but still scarce, toward the top, where the prairie edge folds over the rim of the washout. I touch the soft, feathery leaves of a young sagebrush whose stalk has not yet grown woody but is pliable, like the single plants of silver sage that grace the pasture. A pungent odor remains on my fingers.

I pull the tenacious bush from the rock wall. Slender roots, three feet long, first refuse to let go, then snap. Reddish brown dirt remains adhered to the heart of the plant. Glancing up, I see a wild rose, pink, in bloom. I leave it alone but take the sage with me.

The path upward narrows. It is necessary to place each foot directly in front of the other. I look at nothing but thinly layered walls, variegated clay-stone that forms this cuesta-like ridge. Finally, I reach the end of the path. Each hand, when I extend my arms, touches an opposite side of the washout. Using the walls for leverage, I climb out. Flakes of rock fall onto the path below.

On top, the breeze brings a faint odor of skunk. *I think of you, clearing the sage to make room for the board-and-batten shack that was your first desert home. A rattlesnake hisses, a scorpion arches his back. Both seek the next nearest circle of shade.*

The trek down the hill, through the thickets and across the draw, goes quickly. Back in my garden I clear a large space for the long roots of the young sage. The reddish cocoa-colored soil mixes with the fertile black dirt, mulched for decades with oak leaves and acorns. The red dirt is warm and grainy, the dark soil moist and cool. I carefully place the sage deep into the prepared hole, covering it with the marbled earth. Patting the soil down gently, I stand and compact it with my feet, needing to push the tubers deep into my garden.

I dig small pits next to the sage plant and drop in the quill-like seeds of the marigold, the heart-racing foxglove, and the black-eyed Susan. I save the Shasta daisies for last.

Where are you, grandma? Where were you when I was just a child? Why did we never walk the hills together, hunting for wild roses? What took us so far apart, what modern fission of families is to blame? Pretend as I may, I know that these seeds did not come from your garden in the Mojave.

I look up at the corral fence, and a brief image of Sarah, perched there in the cool evening, passes through my mind. She is your great-granddaughter. She is your flesh and blood, your seed sprung to life. Someday I will explain to her why I have become accustomed to the musky odor of skunk, and I will tell her why there is sagebrush growing among the daisies.

But for now, I breathe in the pungent minty scent of this prairie sage, taking its essence, its very history, deep into my soul. I close my eyes and listen for the silence of your world.

26

Porcupine Dusk

KIDS CAN BE KIDS; Matt and Sarah are no different. And dogs are dogs, including Hondo and our new puppy, Freckles, a red-and-white border collie whose presence a few weeks ago Hondo accepted gracefully. Still, I am surprised to hear the four of them down in the draw poking a stick at the dead porcupine.

Last summer we watched a mother and almost-weaned baby move their ponderous bodies slowly across the lawn. In brazen proximity to us, they nibbled and nosed their way along. The youngster gravitated toward his mother, pushing his face into her soft underbelly. She reared up on her hind feet, trying to push him away. He persisted, unwilling to give up her sweet milk. They stayed upright for several minutes, and she parried with him gently, allowing this dance of weaning to continue. Finally the youngster gave up and returned to the grass. From that day on, they appeared each evening at dusk, their noses to the ground, chewing on new undergrowth. A pile of broken tree limbs, saved for kindling, served as their den.

Now the mother lies dead in the draw, a bullet in her head, and the kids and dogs gather around. Matt's and Sarah's irreverent voices filter in my open window and Freckles barks incessantly, last week's mouthful of quills still a vivid memory. They are having too much fun. I head outside.

"Hi, Mom. See where Dad shot the eye out? He shot it in the mouth too—and once in the stomach. It was right here under this tree. Sarah and I dragged it out."

The porcupine is over two and a half feet long from head to tail, and as big around as a basketball. She looks like the female who nested in the kindling wood last summer.

"Matt says it's a boy, Mom."

The porcupine is lying belly-up.

"No, Sarah, she's a girl, a fat one, too—getting ready for winter. Pet her here if you want to. See, she's a girl."

"Is that where the babies nurse, Mommy? There's no quills on her tummy."

"That's right Sarah," I say, remembering how much Matt and Sarah had loved watching the porcupines in the yard.

"Get back," I scold Freckles. "We'd better move her out of the draw and get her away from the house. Think you can help me carry her, Matt? Here, grab the feet like this while I get hold of her on the other side."

We lug her up the steep side of the draw, past the stackyard holding this year's hay crop, and over to the barbed wire fence that separates the big pasture from the small pastures close to the house. I stop several times to readjust my grip and pull an occasional quill out of my jeans.

Quills. One of the many problems. As the porcupines became accustomed to us, they no longer even waited for dusk. Some of them nested up high on the broad limbs of the oak trees. Each evening they lowered themselves down slowly, inch by inch, using their tails as a third hind leg. They browsed in the new growth at the foot of the tree before wandering out into the yard.

Mark and I had hoped they would migrate away from the house up into the hundreds of acres that surround us. But they did not. Instead, they became more numerous, less cautious. Five or six usually waddled from the oak trees to the garden, to the salt lick at the barn, or to the short grass beneath the swing set.

The horses got quills in their legs. The heifers got quills in their noses. Sarah and Matt got quills in their jeans. Freckles tangled with the porcupines several times, and after six mouthfuls of quills and an abdominal operation that removed five inches of quill-infected muscle, she still did not learn. Hondo, older and wiser, stayed clear.

Sarah is dawdling behind and finally stops altogether as Matt and I slide the porcupine under the fence.

"What's the matter, honey?" I ask. "What's wrong?"

"She's making me sad."

"Who?"

"Her." Sarah points to the porcupine.

I am glad she no longer wants to poke the dead animal with a stick. Matt too grows quiet.

"It's okay to be sad, Sarah. It's a sad thing Daddy had to do."

We continue our trek across the pasture, heading toward a grove of tall scrub oak. I tire often from bending over and carrying the weight sideways. Hondo and Freckles trot behind, leaving to trail fresh scents, then returning.

Hundreds of acres and thousands of trees surround the house and barn. Gnawed scars half encircle an occasional pine, marking porcupine territory. Surely the woods could handle a few more. But a conversation with the game warden several weeks ago was disheartening.

"Anywhere to take porcupines if you use a live trap?" we asked.

"No, there sure isn't. It's open season on porcupines. They're considered predaceous animals—you can shoot them anytime. But I don't know about releasing them. They're overpopulated as it is— aren't enough natural predators around anymore to keep them under control. They sure create havoc with the trees, though."

We knew they did. During the springtime they gorged them- selves on tender grass shoots. During the summer, they sampled our garden fare and nibbled on my flowers. Fall brought a covering of acorns, which they crunched between strong jaws. None of this caused problems, but winter's food was scarce. The porcupines rarely moved from the oak trees that held them cradled above the ground. We watched as the bark from the old oaks was slowly stripped away. Last winter the upper branches on three of the trees that separate us from the county road were slowly devoured. These trees provide homes for squirrels like Sassy, and blue jays, robins, and chickadees. They shelter the does and fawns.

"Have you noticed those trees?" Mark had asked me a few days ago.

"Yeah," I said, hating to admit it. "Think they'll die?"

"Hard to tell. Guess we'll have to wait and see. But I think we're going to have to do something."

Matt, Sarah, and I, with porcupine in tow, reach the grove. "Let's put her down by that dead tree over there. That one, Matt, where the two logs are."

"Will the coyotes come and eat her?"

"I hope so. At least here they will be able to smell her. Help me pull that other log closer to her, Matt. I don't want the heifers messing with her."

"Should we turn her over, Mom?"

"No, Sarah, she's fine."

"Mom?"

"What, Matt?"

"Could we maybe say a prayer or something for her?"

So Matt's perspective has changed a little too since helping to carry her up the hill and across the pasture.

The porcupine lies on her back between the two logs, paws reaching toward the sky. Her dark brown claws are long and curved, the pads of her feet tough and smooth.

"If she had babies inside her now, would they be dead yet?"

"Yes, they'd be dead now too."

"Oh."

The three of us sit next to the dead porcupine. The dogs settle into the comforting shade. It is quiet, the time of evening when the shadows stretch across the field as the sun recedes behind the hills. I am glad we decided to move her, glad for this chance to absorb her death.

"Let's hold hands, Mommy, when we say a prayer."

"Okay, Sarah. You want to say the Lord's Prayer?" Together, sitting beneath the scrub oak, we begin.

"Our Father, Who art in heaven … ."

I am surprised when the tears come. While I was busy watching Matt and Sarah, my own feelings sneak up on me. I regain my composure as we finish the prayer.

Sarah, too, is crying. Small tears turn into great sobs and a heaving chest. I hug her.

Then Matt says, "I'm sad too, Mom, only I'm not crying."

"I'm glad you're sad, Matt. We *should* be sad."

Less than an hour ago it was laughter I had heard, and Freckles's frenzied barking. They had been curious and excited about this dead porcupine, staring at the shot-out eye and poking at the long, sharp spines. What a shift has taken place, how different they are now, sitting on this log holding hands. I pull them closer, drying Sarah's tears with the end of my T shirt. I think of Mark and the roles we each play in life's unrelenting duties.

The breath of the meadow reaches us, rustling the soft fur on the belly of the porcupine. Her paws, still stretching toward the sky, cast long shadows in the grass.

There is a three-legged porcupine who makes his home in the forest above our small hay field. I have seen him several times waddling slowly across the field as he heads toward the spring to drink. He has learned to function well with only a single back leg.

Driving home one evening at dusk, I found him waiting in the middle of the road that separates the forest from the hay field. I braked, got out of the car, and knelt. He stared at me intently before swiveling on his back leg and continuing across the road. During the next few weeks we encountered each other three more times. He sat in the middle of the road. I braked and got out. We stared at each other for several long moments. Then he turned on that strong single leg and sauntered away, leaving brush marks in the dirt with his spiny tail.

I could not help but feel that this porcupine was connected in some way to the dead porcupine. I tried to make my eyes convey remorse, but his penetrating gaze was unforgiving. *We are different*, I wanted to say. *We are not like some, who would bludgeon your slow-moving body because they have nothing better to do on a lazy summer day.* He read my thoughts and replied, *It does not matter. We have become accustomed to death.*

Hoping for spiritual insight, I checked my American Indian reference books but found few mentions of porcupines. I asked my friend Jeanne to ask her Lakota professor for an interpretation. The professor, probably wondering why I didn't consult *myself* for inner revelation, simply said, "If it was happening to me, I would think of taking up quillwork."

27

Home Fires

DEER ARE FLEET AND NIMBLE. They appear out of nowhere. They disappear like an illusion, the flash of their tails a brief memory that hangs momentarily in thin air before fading into the pine trees. Their elusive quality teases, inviting one to follow, to chase.

According to Oglala beliefs (as described in the book *Prayers of Smoke*), Mark and I are in the sixth cycle of life, when temptation comes in a form as seductive as the tawny deer. Usually by now a woman has already been tempted by the deer. At first she is impressed by his prowess and the carriage of his impressive antlers. If she does indeed succumb to his charms, the moment he succeeds in leading her away from her family, he disappears.

For men, the temptress usually appears later in the sixth cycle. The Makaha believe that a man needs a woman's gentle guidance during this time, a gentle nudge back toward the direction of wisdom. She does this through ceremony and prayer. The appearance of the deer does not come as a surprise. A wife expects her. She comes swiftly but is elusive, as difficult to stop as the passing of time, as impossible to hold on to as youth.

This is a time of restlessness, when true friends are needed, when sweet grass is burned and sage is scattered in the winds.

Our anniversary is tomorrow—fourteen years of marriage, and Mark spent the last twenty-eight hours fighting fire. No sleep, nothing to eat but forest service fire food: prepackaged energy snacks full of high-caloric no-taste foods. I wonder what it would be like to be out there on the fire line with him. I envy the girls, the women, who stand next to him, shovels in hand, the comradery they no doubt share.

Hoping Mark would be home last night, I put four pork chops in the oven to bake—one of his favorite foods. When I headed out to do chores, a red-tailed hawk circled high above the barn, then flew off to the hay field in search of gophers. And while I was outside putting the sheep and mares in the corrals before turning the geldings out, the pork chops overcooked. Mark didn't make it home for dinner, so Matt, Sarah, and I ate the too-dry chops without him. Around 9:00 P.M. his boss called.

"Just thought I'd better let ya' know Mark'll be out all night with the fire crew. We aren't expecting a replacement crew until morning."

The storm yesterday afternoon, which dropped little moisture but brought numerous lightning strikes, left its calling card throughout the forest. Scattered "smokes" were spotted all over.

The women's movement is a two-sided coin. What was once a man's occupation, firefighting, is now a woman's domain as well. For those on the fire line, those who have passed their "step-test" and stayed in shape all winter by running or working out on the exercise equipment in the shop (or burning logging slash piles and hefting hay bales, as does Mark), a fire is an exciting thing. It is the climax to a drawn-out preparation. Green fire pants are donned, heavy boots laced, yellow lightweight jackets worn like secret handshakes at a fraternity gathering. And then there are the "hot shots" of this special club, the fire crews who spend their summers flying from one "smoke" to another, sporting shirts that say simply, "I was at Yellowstone."

Even the local crews compete with one another, each fire attended becoming like a notch on a gun belt—signs of experience and a big paycheck. I suppose the rivalry is necessary, for crews are expected to work nonstop, to be ambitious and tireless. And nowhere is the rivalry more evident than in the various Indian crews.

For the spouses who remain at home, the experiences are different. This morning the sun, even at 8:00 A.M., is hot. I am thankful the night was cool, giving Mark some relief from the heat of the day. What must it be like, standing at the edge of a fire line, feeling the rubber soles on your boots begin to melt while the white-hot sun beats down from above? What a reprieve it must be when the sun finally slips behind the tips of the orange-flamed pine trees.

Again I wonder. Does he lean against a tall ponderosa, yards away from the burning trees, drinking water from the melted ice in his water jug? Does some seasonal fire fighter, female, younger, and fitter than I, with fewer battle scars to mark her flesh, watch with him as the sun disappears, while the children and I eat our overdone pork chops, adding calories to conjecture?

Trusting Mark has little to do with it. I trust him—trust his love for me and the kids, trust his faith in the returning Chinook and in this ranchland we now call home. But even after fourteen years of marriage I still notice the way his Wranglers cover his muscular rear and thighs. I still appreciate how trim his waist is, how strong his arms are, still admire his dark wavy hair and the sexy mustache that is so much like his grandfather's. Surely other women must, too. If I sat next to him, quenching my thirst with the roar of the blaze cresting above us—in the heat of the fire, so to speak—I would notice him. I would be tempted to make more of this bond of firefighting than would be wise.

In bed alone, without Mark, it takes forever to get to sleep. Morning comes, and he has not returned. I make coffee, filling the pot half-full. Doing morning chores on Sunday is a luxury. I bask in the relaxed pace, having no need to hurry. Able to do these things without him, I feel self-sufficient. I feel inefficient because the water level in the tank has gotten too low for the sheep to reach, and I did not notice last night.

"Damn," I say out loud. Why the heck didn't I pay attention when he told me how to turn on the timer to the well pump that runs water into the tank? I go and get one of the black rubber tubs from inside the barn that we use to feed corn to the sheep. I get a bucket and carry them both out to the tank. Then, putting the tub on the ground next to the tank, I use the bucket to scoop water into it.

Mainly, though, I luxuriate in doing the morning chores. I walk the path Mark walks each morning and am greeted by the low throaty baas that the sheep greet him with each day. I open the gate to the pen on the east side of the corrals and call to the geldings: "Here, boys. Heeeere, booooys!" I try to keep my inflection like Mark's, the tone an octave lower than normal. The geldings surprise me by turning at the sound of my voice and slowly sauntering into the pen. They go directly to the small feed tub, and

I remember that Mark grains them each morning. Latching the gate closed, I return to the barn to hang up the unneeded halters and get a bucket of grain.

Mark's presence is everywhere, his touch apparent. The floor of the barn is swept; the bridles and halters hang neatly on the wall. There is no more sweetmix for the horses, only oats. I wonder when he switched to oats, and why. Too much protein in the other, too high-powered a feed for hot, lazy summer days?

I think of the women he works with, especially the pretty blonde that he hired for his range crew. She's a ranching girl, knows about feed and water tanks, no doubt. She doesn't know how Mark calls the geldings in, though. They wouldn't know her voice either, the way they know mine.

The lunch hour comes and goes. I feed the kids and me tuna, same as yesterday. I mix up a batch of chocolate chip cookie dough called "sweet dreams." Too hot to bake, I decide to wait until tonight, when the temperature will cool. Baking is a wifely thing to do, and today it gives me pleasure.

More than twenty-eight hours have passed now since Mark left. I picture him in my mind. He bends down to retrieve a tool, sweat dripping from his brow. He wipes his face, leaving a telltale streak of ash on his forehead. He is dead tired but works at the same steady pace as always. Others, less disciplined, lean too long on their shovels.

Hondo is sitting sentry in the front yard with Freckles next to him. He stands. Freckles studies him, then gets up also. I look up the driveway and see the old green Ford pickup pull in.

"Daddy's home!" Matt yells, and Sarah runs out the door.

I walk outside and take his thermos from him. All the water jugs are empty. His face is whiskered and sooty. A gray smudge of ash streaks his forehead. I think of other women but ask only, "Have you eaten?"

He smells of pungent, acrid smoke, and the mudroom fills with the strong odor as he takes off his fire clothes. I hug him, wishing I had been with him up in the forest.

"Yeah," he says, "I ate in town. I just want to shower and get some sleep. They could call me back anytime."

I rinse out his water jugs and set them on the counter to drain. Then, changing my mind, I fill the sink with hot soapy water and cleanse the jugs thoroughly, scrubbing the black marks from the plastic.

"The water in the stock tank is too low for the sheep to reach," I say to him after his shower, "and I couldn't remember how to turn the pump on." I fill the jugs with fresh water and put them in the freezer.

"There's a black switch on the pole that turns the power on. Then you have to rotate the dial in the control box ... ." He continues to explain, and I listen carefully this time. Then I go into the bedroom and turn down the covers. The sheets are clean, tight and crisp. Closing the blinds, I unplug the telephone and sit down on the bed. The room is cool and dark and I wish that, for at least a moment, I could be just a wife and not a mother. I want to share his bed with him, enjoy the coolness of his skin next to mine while he drifts off to sleep.

He comes in the room and climbs into bed. "It's sure good to be home," he says, stretching beneath the covers.

I know he isn't just referring to the comfortable bed. He means that it is *good* to be home, where his family is, where his wife waits. I wonder if he can sense my presence in the house as I sense his presence in the barn. Do the thoughts that kept me awake last night still linger beneath the sheets?

We kiss.

"I missed you."

"That's good," he answers.

And it is good. It's good to miss each other. For fourteen years it has been good. And for fourteen years he has been glad to come home, and I have been glad to have him home. We are lucky to have been able to resist the tawny deer, to be able to gently nudge ourselves back toward the direction of wisdom.

I close the door softly behind me. Outside, the sun glares in my unshaded eyes. I can hear the *kee-r-r, kee-r-r* of the hawk but do not see him. Down at the water tank, I climb the corral fence, flip the power switch, then reach for the pump's control box. I adjust the timer and water gushes into the tank.

Next time, I will remember. I put my hand into the shooting stream of water. It is cold and wet and forceful.

28

Gifts

*That night the old one told stories by the fire again and the children
sat very still as they listened, their eyes big in the gleam of the flames.
And it seemed that there was in the air a new thing, a new feeling, as
if the spirit of the Indians, withdrawn far into the mountains, hidden
in the mountains, came down into the valley again.*

—William Willoya and Vinson Brown[1]

IN MY HANDS I HOLD a hardback copy of *Jules Verne's Classic
Science Fiction*. Torn airmail packaging is scattered at my feet.
I open the book and read the inscription: "To Matt, with love
from Grandpa Loren, San Francisco." *Why is my seventy-five-year-
old father sending my nine-year-old son a 511-page book?* The
inappropriateness of the gift irritates me. I chalk it up to careless-
ness, a gift hurriedly bought with too little care given. But perhaps
it is unfair of me to expect my father to know what a boy of nine
would like. Then I remember last spring, when we were able to visit
San Francisco. Dad sprinted after a cable car, grabbing Matt's hand
and leaping safely aboard. Later he plucked a nickel off the street.

"Matt, look here! See what happens when you put a coin on the
track—the cable car almost cuts it in half!" I can still picture them
standing there, heads bent in mutual admiration.

Less irritated, I stare out the window. Hondo lies sleeping on
the deck. He has been with us since he was eight weeks old. Gray
hairs cover the muzzle of his glossy black head, and the lids beneath
his deep brown eyes droop slightly. His huge Lab feet splay when
he walks, more telltale gray hairs grow from between his pads. I
think of my father's beard and how I have watched the streaks of
gray widen until gray is all there is.

Freckles rests next to Hondo on the deck, her red-and-white border collie fur ruffling in the breeze. Much of her puppy freckling has faded. I thought back to last summer.

Fourteen years represent a full life for a dog. Hondo's moon had begun to wane, growing weaker with the setting of each sun. The time for a second dog had come, but it was not without guilt that we brought Freckles home to the ranch. When she scrambled out of the truck, puppy legs trembling, Hondo was a perfect gentleman. He sniffed and she cowered. Then she whined and he licked. Tails wagged, and a friendship was born.

He was a gracious teacher. Down at the barn, Freckles watched Hondo sit patiently while we saddled the horses. She sat down as well. The cats rubbed up against Hondo's legs and Freckles learned that, here, one does not chase cats. We rode out to check heifers, and Hondo trotted faithfully behind. Freckles learned that it was all right to follow a fresh scent, but it was not all right to harass a cow or deer. Freckles grew lanky, and a new sprightliness came to Hondo's step. Years fell away. We began throwing sticks for him again, and he fetched and fetched until his panting jaws could no longer hold the stick. Freckles never learned to love the game, but she cheered him on anyway. He was given a brief reprieve, a second wind.

The reprieve did not last. A hot summer day and too many miles traveled on dusty cow trails took their toll. Hondo collapsed in the corral. Twenty minutes of soft coaxing and gentle stroking brought him around. Matt and Freckles looked on, watching him stagger to his feet and shake the dirt from his coat, as if shaking off a bad dream. Hondo drank deeply from the bucket by the house before climbing to the deck and taking up his post near the door. He recovered, but we continued to worry. The next time we saddled the horses and rode out into the pasture, we locked him in the horse trailer. He peered through the wooden slats, his feelings hurt beyond comprehension.

"It's all right, old boy," I said to him, "we'll be back." But he had become deaf and did not hear me. After that we continued to take him with us on our rides. His moon will wane, no matter how protective we are.

I set the heavy volume of Jules Verne on the table and begin to pick up the discarded packaging. Outside, a car drives by on the gravel road. Freckles hears the car and she stands, ears pricked forward. Hondo still sleeps. Then Freckles barks, a quick and high-pitched sound—unlike the deep, chesty warning that has guarded our home for fourteen years. It is not the noise of the car that finally awakens Hondo; the high-pitched bark penetrates his increasing deafness and he lifts his head to look about. He sees Freckles on duty, poised and ready. With a deep sigh of resignation, he lowers his head back onto his paws and closes his eyes.

I want to go outside and take Hondo's gentle black head in my hands. I want to look into his brown eyes and speak softly, letting him feel with his heart those things he can no longer hear me say. I want him to cling to my world a little longer.

Instead, I pick up the Jules Verne book and reread the inscription. "To Matt, with love from Grandpa Loren." Suddenly the gift makes sense. Fourteen years separate Hondo and Freckles. Sixty-five years and more than a thousand miles separate my father from his grandson. Only a few more years of gift-giving stretch before him. He, too, counts the setting of each sun, watches the waning of his moon. Time does not allow him the luxury of sending only those gifts that are appropriate. If in ten years Matt opens this book, ready to dive twenty thousand leagues beneath the sea, it will be his grandfather's words wishing him bon voyage.

Putting the heavy volume down softly on the table, I open the door and walk out onto the deck. Hondo's fur shines in the sunlight. He feels the vibrations of my steps and his tail begins to move slowly, back and forth.

29

Gathering Bones

... there is a great strength in the earth and in nature that the old Indians knew about, but which is almost all lost to present generations. This power of the spirit gained from the wilderness most people who live in cities know nothing about.

—William Willoya and Vinson Brown[1]

THE DEER CONTINUE TO FLOCK to the meadows in the lateevening and early morning, grazing on the short stubs of mowed hay. Hunting season arrives in two weeks. The deer will scatter, fleeing to the brush and deep ravines.

I leave for work Monday morning and see the body of a fawn heaped in the borrow ditch, probably a victim of the paralyzing sound and speed of the gravel trucks that careen down our unpaved county road. I wonder if it is the fawn we watched all summer, the one who stood at her mother's side, half-hidden in the tall grass beyond the house. The doe grazed, unaware of our scrutiny, while the fawn nursed in distracted and impatient bursts.

As I arrive home for lunch, the carcass of the fawn greets me. Hondo and Freckles have pulled her onto the lawn. She is intact except for the intestine and stomach area. That, the juiciest and choicest part, has already been devoured. Glassed-over brown eyes stare unblinking through delicate lashes. Only the faintest hint of newborn spots remain a part of the tan fur. Tiny split hooves lead up to slender long limbs. Freckles kneels possessively over the fawn, chewing on one ear.

By that evening the deer carcass is torn in two. The head and upper half are separated from the hips and lower legs. Both ears are gone. The eyes, still intact, look dully off into the distance.

Both dogs have the entire night to gnaw on the carcass. By Tuesday morning the hide is stripped from the fawn and lies in a curled mass off to the side of the steps. The head is still attached to the shoulders by a thin strip of hide. The neck and pectoral muscles are exposed, the hide gone from the small rib cage. One hind leg is on the deck, the other in the grass. The meat from the rump area has been eaten.

Coming home again for lunch twenty-four hours from the time the fawn first appeared on the lawn, I step up on the deck and onto the disjointed bone of a front leg, the ulna and radius held together by stringy cartilage. The deck of the house has become an archaeological site; bones are scattered everywhere. On the woven mat by the back door is the fawn's head, eyes still an open foggy brown. I pick up what remains of the deer, starting with the head. I toss the pieces as hard as I can over the edge of the deck and into the trees and tall grass. The tiny-muzzled oblong-shaped head spins through the air and lands with a thud. I wince. It takes fifteen more throws to clear the deck. Finally done, I go inside and wash my hands.

The dogs are not to blame. Within a few days, the flesh that was the deer's will become the flesh of the dogs—a natural cycle. I recall a Bible verse, John 6:63: "It is the spirit that gives life, the flesh is of no avail." But still, the earless head in the deep grass is a haunting image.

Tuesday night I arrive home after work, my arms full of groceries. I walk cautiously across the yard. There, neatly gathered beneath the big oak tree, is the dismembered skeleton. The muscles and tendons and cartilage are gone now. A large tibia bone is cracked in two lengthwise, exposing the bright red marrow. Hondo and Freckles snooze contentedly near their pile of retrieved treasures. I inspect the bones quickly. I find no skull, no brown eyes. But peeking out from beneath a detached piece of hide I see the jaw with tiny lower teeth still intact.

I am reminded of the bison bones that lie buried within the sinkhole walls of the buffalo jump east of Sundance. When archaeologists unearthed the first several layers, they discovered that most of the larger marrow-rich bones had been removed from the killing site—probably pulled in travois by dogs up the steep spiral path and then cooked, providing a rich, hearty broth. The archaeologists also discovered, amid the chaos of crushed bones, a circle of prayerfully positioned buffalo skulls —an offering of thanksgiving to the Great Spirit.

The groceries grow heavy. Once inside the house, I set them down and begin putting the food away. Twelve small, perfectly oval eggs tucked neatly inside a Styrofoam carton go in the refrigerator. Canned tuna, deboned and dolphin-safe, goes in the cupboard. A twenty-four-ounce loaf of honey-and-bran bread, sliced into twenty-two identical pieces, goes in the bread drawer. A plastic-wrapped package of ground beef, weighing 1.12 pounds, 80 percent lean, goes in the refrigerator next to the eggs.

Last fall we bought a heifer to butcher from J. W. and Lois. The fresh beef lasted all winter and most of the summer. We kept the heifer in the corral, where we grained her and fed her homegrown hay until she was sufficiently meaty. She eyed me warily each evening as I carried the feed bucket to her. But once engaged in chewing her corn and barley, she let me rub her nose and scratch the hard flat place between her eyes. In the end, she rested in our freezer wrapped in white butcher paper marked with Mark's handwriting.

I liked unwrapping those frozen, white packages of beef. When the writing got wet and smeared, I would have to guess the cut of meat inside. The heifer once surprised me with a standing rib roast when I had expected soup bones. I always knew she was 80 percent neighbor's grass, though, and 20 percent our hay.

Finally I put the last of the groceries away. A sack of wax-coated red delicious apples goes in the fruit bin. I carefully fold the biodegradable plastic sack and store it in the kitchen cupboard.

Outside, the dogs still sleep contentedly in the fading afternoon sun. Their consciences are clear; no haunting questions bother them. Their paws jerk and their noses twitch almost imperceptibly as they dream of running in circles, chasing fleet-footed deer. I envy them their intimate acquaintance with life's circles.

The next morning, early sun cuts through scattered clouds and sends shafts of light to earth. Driving to town, I think I see a black-baldy calf lying in the north pasture. But we have no cows yet, and we have been resting the north pasture—allowing only a few horses to graze there. The grass, though not overused, is stressed from drought.

The calf is out of place and attracts my attention. I stop the car and peer across the distant field. The calf rises, his white head stretches upward, and his black body struts forward. This creature is no calf at all—wings sprout from his sides and cast broad shadows in the grass. He is a bald eagle. And he is insulted that I did not recognize him.

With open wings, he steps, king-like, into a shaft of brilliant sunlight and is lifted from the field. Flying eastward, he disappears.

Death, I am beginning to realize, will always be a dominant part of living on the land, especially here on the Great Plains, where the signs of death can remain for years, where deer bones, porcupine fur, stiff cowhides, and the skulls of coyotes become integral but unmistakable parts of the landscape. Death likes to be noticed.

The same cycle of renewal—birth, life, death, and decay—exists here, just as anywhere. But on the grasslands, where rainfall is scarce, the decaying process slows down, sometimes by decades.

It is the hoofed animals—the deer, the buffalo, the domestic cattle and sheep—who speed up this critical part of the cycle. They stomp the earth with their sharp feet, break up the hardened soil, tread on decaying organic matter, defecate and urinate in places where no moisture may have fallen for months. Seeds germinate, plants begin to grow, new life rises from the parched land.

My perception of death is changing. The smell of death, which can linger for days on end, makes it difficult to forget that a living creature has died. The pungent odor drifts across the meadow, clings to the leaves of the oak trees, penetrates the pores of one's skin. "Notice me!" it demands; "I was once flesh and blood!" it reminds.

Life, like the bald eagle who stepped regally into the brilliant shaft of sunlight, also likes to be noticed—to be recognized, to be celebrated. It is understandable to sometimes confuse the black-baldy calf with the bald eagle, to confuse life with death, for they blend together as day blends into night. The rejoicing comes in the glory of each sunrise, in the magnificence of each sunset.

30

Redy's Foal

IT SEEMS TO BE ABOUT mothers and daughters. Some women would have it differently. But there is an intrinsic fact that cannot be altered. The womb belongs to the woman. I came from my mother's womb, my daughter came from my womb. No test tube, no alternative lifestyle, no tampering of humankind will make the womb obsolete. With each menses, with each waning and waxing moon, with each ocean tide that comes in and goes out, the cycle is perpetuated.

We knew Redy was young when we bought her. Mark had said, "No more mares. They're too much trouble." I parleyed, "The mares are no trouble when the geldings aren't around." The half-earnest sparring continued. Then Redy was ridden into the sale ring, a pastel gray-and-white paint horse possibly bred to a black-and-white stallion.

"Look how she handles, folks," the auctioneer crooned. "Not bad for a greenbroke horse. With a little work she'll be smooth as silk. See how gentle—works from either side. Why, you can climb all over her and she doesn't mind a bit. Now that's a gentle mare. And pasture-exposed, it says. Why, folks, there's probably a little paint foal in there just waiting for spring. Who'll start the bidding? Do I hear six hundred dollars?"

She reminded me of Romie. Small head, kind brown eyes, petite build. I nudged Mark. "Bid on her, bid on her," I whispered. The program in Mark's hand moved slightly and the ring man caught the motion. Mark nodded his head.

Miss Redy Cash, a blue-roan tobiano paint mare, sired by Par for Cash and out of Miss Redy Cube, a coming-three-year-old. She needs a lot of work, but she's gentle and kind and small—she'll make a good horse for Matt or Sarah. And a foal besides. A foal. Wobbling to its feet. Curious, prancing, mischievous, ornery. A dream come true.

But nature doesn't agree. Too young to be a mother, Redy doesn't carry full-term. The unexpected labor pains, three months premature, come during the night, while she's alone in the corral. In the morning, the dirt shows signs of her struggle, the frightened thrashing. Her first breeding, her first foal, a late-term miscarriage. She's only two herself, still a filly. "Pasture-exposed" the sale papers said. Three more months and the foal would have been resting on new spring grass. It's for the best, we console. Gives Redy a chance to grow a little more. Pretty hard on a young horse like that to be bred so young. We'll keep her in with Romie for the rest of the winter, close to the barn, where we can hay them and grain them each day, let her put a little weight on. Keep Romie and Cindy company. We can always breed her again. Work with her this spring, ride her a lot. Then maybe next year we can think about breeding her again. After that, who knows?

The image of Redy's aborted foal will not leave me. I see the fetus over and over again lying on the cold ground, a black-and-white stud colt. His hooves are soft, like fingernails after a long bath. His translucent skin is pink and gray, already mapping out where the hair will grow black or white. His face is well marked, the pigment around his nose and eyes dark. Whiskers already sprouting from his muzzle are soft and delicate. I want them to twitch, to move. But he lies still. The membrane is gone from around his body. How long did Redy lick and clean him before she accepted his inertia?

When I get home from work at noon, the dogs have carried the dead foal up on the lawn. Burying him would have done no good. Unlike the tempered bones of an animal who has spent a lifetime walking and running on the hardened earth, the foal's immature bones are soft and porous. By evening, there is nothing left but the head.

That same day a local high-school girl, blonde and blue-eyed, pretty and athletic, gave birth to a baby boy three weeks prematurely.

The girl's parents were not happy; she was unmarried, too young to be forced to settle down. The father was several years older. And darker—a tall, long-limbed Indian from a northern tribe. At 5:00 A.M., during the early morning hours, while others slept—while Redy struggled in the corral—a baby boy was born.

I see the baby often. He has a wonderful head of thick black hair and perfectly formed fingers tipped with tiny nails still soft. I watch the young mother nestle this child in the crook of her neck. He buries his dark head against her long blonde hair and nuzzles. The mother is proud, a survivor. The father is proud too, eager to provide. They are becoming a threesome.

On my walks, I stop by the barn before heading into the hills. I stroke Romie's nose and rub her ears. She hangs her head down and rests it against my thigh. We have hugged like this for nearly thirty years. I touch the deep hollows above her eyes and try not to notice the gauntness of her hips. Then I walk over to Redy.

She stops chewing her hay and greets me. I think of the black-and-white paint stallion and imagine him sniffing her, his nostrils flaring and snorting at the scent of her first heat. The odor would have caused him to arch his muscled neck and let loose his great phallus. Or maybe Redy, in her restlessness, jumped the fence and approached him, tail held high and quivering.

I stroke her belly. For several days it remains swollen, and I harbor a secret wish that a foal, perhaps a twin to the aborted colt, still grows safely within her.

Childhood dreams metamorphose. Only a hint of the young girl remains. My womanness spirals around me, sometimes like a cocoon, sequestering, sometimes like a spinning top that breaks the bonds of gravity, flying off into space on a solitary journey, only to return, earthbound, womb-bound, the spinning having slowed to a pregnant pace.

31

Our Own Cows

I have spent the night on sheepskins piled on a hogan floor, and felt
at my back many generations of animals milling in the darkness. ...
—Trebbe Johnson[1]

THE TIME HAS COME for us to acquire our first cows—Lois and
J. W. are thinning their herd, and we decide to buy six old
short-term cows from them, cows whose feet are not sound
enough to make the trip up into the forest next summer with the rest
of the herd. But they're good enough cows to keep close in, where
they can winter fairly easily and walk a gentle path during the
summer months. All six are due to calve April 1 or within a few
weeks of that date.

We buy the cows despite pressure from misinformed but well-
intentioned radicals who wish to remove all cows from public lands
and eventually even private lands. This mania seems to be a passing
fad and will eventually phase itself out as truth prevails, as the
voting public begins to understand how the cycle of birth, life,
death, and decay works in the West. And truth is beginning to
prevail, for the land herself is casting a gracious light upon those
ranchers who have nurtured her for generations, who have understood her needs, and a dim light upon those (in all walks of life) who
have *not* been good stewards.

Mark has waited a long time for this. And though six old cows
are a modest (and humbling) beginning, they will at least be all *our*
cows—the banker will hold no note, no upper hand. I think of
Mark's great-great-grandfather, the stonecutter, and wonder how
he must have felt when he purchased, or traded for, his first cattle.
In 1862, when he settled on the land beneath Wildcat Mountain,

herds of buffalo still roamed the valleys of the Platte River country. It wasn't until the railroad went through in the early 1870s that buffalo disappeared from the grasslands. Perhaps the seed stock for Mark's grandparents' ranch came from some of Oliver Loving's cattle, which were herded through the eastern plains of Colorado as early as 1859. I wonder also if Mark's great-great-grandmother Cynthia spoke of her cows as affectionately as Lois does about hers.

"See that old red one," she says on the day we go up to get them. "Now she's a purebred. And that other big one, we call her Big Red."

We help them sort off the older cows, about twenty, destined for the sale barn. Mark has helped calve out these cows for the last three years. Some have bad feet, some have bad bags, most are just plain old. We pick out our six, listening carefully to J. W. and Lois's subtle suggestions.

"Look over there," Lois says, pointing, "see that old girl with her ears perked forward? She always does that. Just watch her. Now, that other smaller cow, the one over there, well, she may not look like much, but she always has good calves. She gets scrawny and the calves get fat. But she'll do all right by you."

By that evening six of their cows stand in our corral. Mark moves easy and sure among them, securing the gates and checking the water. He scatters the hay and stands back, giving them room to breathe. The breeze blows down from J. W. and Lois's place, carrying with it the scent of ponderosa pine, and we keep the cows in the corral for several days, fearing that if they are let loose they will surely try to crawl the fences and follow the familiar smells back home.

Within a week the cows have adjusted to their new location, and to the strange baaing wooly creatures. Mark turns the cows out into the pasture. He is able to approach them, his presence is nonthreatening, but they retreat into the trees whenever I come too close, staying remote and aloof. Then the snow comes and they greet Mark with low bellows in the early morning, calling for their hay, the purebred Reisland cow always the first to come, the first to bellow. Big Red is second in line.

Lois inquires often, "How're my girls doing?" J. W. teases Mark when he sees them in the same pasture with the sheep.

"Now, you know, I wouldn't have sold you them cows if I'd known you'd be keeping them in mixed company." But he smiles when he says it and squeezes Mark's shoulder with his strong, bent hand.

Naomi joined us today—a yearling Rambouillet ewe who does not know she is a sheep. Bottle-fed by some ranching friends who raise cattle, not sheep, she was supposed to have been butchered this fall. But despite their penchant for cows, Naomi became a pet, and they found it difficult to butcher an animal more at home in the kitchen than in the barn. Thus Naomi joined our growing flock and the two old bucks temporarily running with the ewes.

The bucks, teetering on the brink of senility, were unattractive, unlovable, and very smelly. None of which, we hoped, would affect their fertility. Our spring lamb crop depended on it. But the bucks were not impressed with Naomi's eweness.

She followed on our heels constantly, baaing nervously. She never buried her nose in the feed bunk like the other ewes but demanded instead to be hand-fed.

A few days after we got her, Mark had to walk out to the small hay field to do minor repairs on the stock tank. Hondo went with him, of course, along with Freckles and two of the cats. Matt and Sarah skipped ahead, and bringing up the rear was Naomi, befuddled and bewildered. Mark didn't really mind the entourage, but I know that when the neighbors drove by he silently cussed the stock tank for being in plain view of the county road. He would much rather have had one of our newly acquired cows traipsing behind him.

I have become the shepherdess. Mark, although he likes all livestock, has never wished to be a sheepherder. It simply isn't in his genes. Nor do these six cows make him a rancher. But the ancient scent of their dung and their bass bellowing voices stir Mark ancestor-deep, and he at last feels at home as he watches the cows walk among the stark oak trees, snow blanketing their haired-up winter backs. They stand patiently beneath the towering fenced-in haystack, seeking shelter from the north wind, waiting for him to come.

I rub Naomi's long nose and sink my fingers into her lanolin-rich wool, massaging her hard-to-find back muscles, and think that I am beginning to understand Trebbe Johnson's words when she writes about the Navajo sheepherding families: "... they look upon their sheep as an asset that is not just physical, but metaphysical ... the most prized gift a person can offer at a ceremony. They are an outward and visible sign of the family's inner, spiritual health."[2]

I herd Naomi and the rest of the flock out into the pasture, calling "Let's go girls!" though they need little prodding. Stomper, the head ewe, leads the way down the now-familiar path while Hondo and Freckles trot behind.

The early sun casts warming rays across the meadow, and the ewes' hooves make soft pounding noises, leaving small cloven hoofprints nestled within the larger tracks of the old cows. I find that I envy Trebbe Johnson the night spent on sheepskins piled on a hogan floor, when she felt at her back "many generations of the animals milling in the darkness, their warm life lingering still, their essence permeating the small, earthen, cavelike room."[3] But at least I, too, am beginning to feel at home at last. And I am beginning to feel what all shepherds must feel, as if I have been herding these sheep for a thousand years.

32

The Longhorn Calf

Mitakuye oyasin the Sioux say in ceremony: We are related to all things. The new mystic warriors will be strong in their love and powerful in their compassion. They will be imbued with the willpower to save the voiceless ones, the plants and animals, because they understand our earthly relationship.

—Ed McGaa, Eagle Man[1]

IN THE CORRAL NEXT TO WHERE Romie and Redy graze, a heifer peers at me through wire fencing. She has a mixed-breed look—almost Hereford, but not quite. Standing on knock-kneed legs next to a pile of hay, she glances up at the sound of my voice. I hold out a handful of hay. Curious, she steps forward, then, leery, steps back.

She does not know, of course, that she has an appointment in a week at the meat-locker plant, is destined for the supper table because of flawed bone structure and poor breeding. The hay she chews and the corn and oats she savors are all part of the plan.

Lois and J. W. raised her as a replacement heifer (a young cow kept as a replacement for an older cow). By the time she was a yearling, they realized she should have been culled as a calf. In the fall, after she had been turned out all summer with the Longhorn bull, they decided to sell her.

Our freezer stood empty, the deer meat gone, the pork eaten—only a huge chunk of unrendered lard and a slab of frozen sidepork remained. We needed beef. We told J. W. we would buy the heifer. Several weeks passed before Mark finally hitched up the stock trailer and brought her home.

I peer through the wire fence. Steam rises from the hay, in which her nose is deeply buried. Her impending death does not drive me away. I look at her critically. Her front legs are too short, her chest too narrow. Not good breeding stock. The Longhorn bull wouldn't have cared, though; in the heat of summer and the cycling of cows, the bull wouldn't have minded. Tough and rangy, he bred them all.

She watches me watching her. Her jaws move in circles, grinding the hay into saliva-drenched pulp. The obvious finally occurs to me. Inside her rounded Hereford belly, a calf grows. She is no longer a one-year-old but rather a first-calf heifer; the emphasis has changed, shifting her from progeny to producer. Mark calls the veterinarian and makes an appointment to have her preg-checked (tested for pregnancy).

Connections surprise me, catch me off guard. Unbidden, they demand attention. Suddenly, no action is without repercussion; all action is the business of others. I watch the heifer eat her hay and wonder if the Longhorn bull did indeed plant his seed deep within her. Does the fetus of a spotted calf float in amniotic fluid beneath her leathery hide? The image of Redy's aborted foal, black-and-white and tiny-hoofed, lingers in my mind.

The heifer is scheduled to be butchered, the appointment at the locker plant already set. Three months ago the decision had a rhythm to it, a natural flow. I do the arithmetic, count the weeks. If there is a calf, it is more than two-thirds developed. The decision has become complicated. We spent $750 for her. She was to be meat in the freezer.

More memories come unbidden. When Matt was six he asked about freedom in America, and what it meant. A television cartoon (unusual in its educational merit) inspired him to ask about the lack of freedom in China and its meaning.

"Well, for one thing," I answered slowly, "in China a woman is limited in the number of children she is allowed to have. She is not expected to have more than one."

"You mean, if we lived in China, you wouldn't have had Sarah?"

"Probably not."

He was quiet, then asked, "What if it just happens? What do they do if it just happens?" He knew where babies came from, knew how it was with the bulls and cows. He repeated his question, "What do they do if it just kinda happens?"

My answer, regretfully, came automatically. "Well, honey, they do an operation on the mother. They go up inside her where the baby is growing and they kill the baby." The bluntness of my words, which stripped the issue of its political cloaking, shocked even me. I did not tell him that Chinese law also requires that babies delivered alive, if the second-born to a family, also be killed.

Matt does not know about politics yet. But he knows about babies. And he even knows about fetuses. He too saw the foal's delicate whiskers and soft hooves. He had watched my belly grow for nine months, had placed his small hand on his baby sister's hidden heel and felt her kick. He brought me a granola bar in the hospital and placed a tiny fur horse next to Sarah in the bassinet, carefully adjusting the calico cloth bridle.

The heifer is scheduled to be preg-checked at 9:00 A.M. She is scheduled to be butchered at 4:00 P.M. I return home from work at 4:30 and find her grazing in the pasture, reprieved.

The heifer's walk becomes a sway. She settles her growing bulk often onto the thawing soil. Resting becomes more important than eating. Every day for two weeks I come home on my lunch hour to check her. Kicking off high heels and donning ranch boots and an old jacket, I hurry outside. Sometimes the heifer grazes with the ewes in the small hay field, sometimes she rests in the shade by the old cabin. We do not turn her out with the older, more experienced cows.

Finally, swollen udders show signs of making milk. Her pelvis shifts and the hollows by her hipbones deepen.

"Any time now," Mark says.

One evening, the heifer begins walking restless circles in the corral, twitching her tail. She lies down, she gets up, she lies down. A flashlight illuminates two white hooves protruding from beneath her tail.

"Easy, girl." She lifts her head. The ewes baa loudly, hoping for a late snack. The heifer struggles to her feet.

I remember the feeling—the muscles pulling and pushing, the rock-hard abdomen—birth as imminent as the incoming tide, resistance as futile as clinging to a retreating wave. *Rock hard— sacred red rock.* Tunkashila, *ancient Lakota word meaning both God and Stone. Original life.* Inyan.

"Easy, girl, easy."

The temperature drops to twelve degrees. We ease the heifer into the barn, sorting off the curious ewes. We stand outside in the cold night air and peek through knotholes in the wood. Hondo and Freckles nudge their way between us, poking their own noses through a crack in the wood. The heifer circles the feed bunk, then settles down onto the leftover hay scattered by the finicky sheep.

"Look, Matt. See the feet?" I whisper.

The heifer groans. Quietly. Slow breaths come between contractions. The front hooves slide back inside, then reappear. Two wet, membrane-free nostrils quiver, and steam rises.

"You're doing fine, girl," Mark whispers to himself.

A smooth lull slows the waves. The heifer relaxes. Her belly lifts and lowers with each breath. We shiver in the cold, arms circling one another. The heifer stretches her neck and curves her head around, sniffing the calf's feet and nose, smelling the tiny puffs of steam. She throws back her head and pushes. A brown-and-white-spotted head appears, lanky wet legs leading the way. The shoulders come next. Then the entire calf slips gently onto the dry hay. More vapors of steam rise as cold night air meets hot wet calf. The calf shakes her head and her ears stand up.

An unexpected gift, perfectly timed; a waxing moon hung high in the night sky; newborn heat warming ill-born memories. The tide comes in and the tide goes out.

Shadows fall in the deep birth-caused hollows of the heifer's hips. They darken the hollows above Romie's eyes and shade her gaunt, fleshless flanks. Hondo's blackness disappears into the shadow's depths. The silver hairs of his muzzle catch starlight.

The black-and-white foal is gone. Redy stands alone beneath the night sky. In a nursery, the dark hair of a baby boy glistens in cascading beams of moonlight while, miles from town, a wet calf struggles to her feet.

33

Rites

PERHAPS THERE ARE MORE ceremonies in my life than I realize. I am learning, slowly, to discern these rituals, to recognize them for what they are.

Mark has been elk hunting three times since we left Colorado. The first two times he came home frustrated and discouraged.

"Too many people," he complained. "You can't get away from them. Roads are everywhere—and pickups racing down every road." This comment surprised me, since the entire state of Wyoming has fewer people than live in just one Denver suburb.

"Didn't you pack up into the high country with the horses?"

"Hell, no. We set up camp in the middle of it all. Might as well have been camping in town."

"Didn't you even ride the horses?"

"Oh, yeah, we rode. Up and down the roads."

"How did Chris's tipi work out?" I asked, shifting to a more pleasant topic.

"That part was great. Except Chris didn't have a tipi liner," Mark finally smiled, "and things got a little smoky, and a little damp."

"Didn't Craig remind him about getting a liner?"

"I don't think Craig has slept in many more tipis than Chris, even if he is Gros Ventre." Traditionally, in the winter camps of the Plains Indians, an interior dew cloth would have been tied to the bottom of the tipi poles for enhanced insulation and water resistance.

Earlier that year a member of Craig's family had been killed in a highway accident, and his family had invited Chris (our wildlife biologist friend) up to the reservation to attend the give-away ceremony—the traditional "giving away" of possessions by the family of the deceased. Chris, honored by the invitation, accepted. It was with humbleness and embarrassment that he also accepted the generous gift of a tipi, which in turn honored the departed Gros Ventre. Mark, Chris, and Craig had all looked forward to using the tipi during the elk hunt.

The fact that two elk were killed and the meat shared didn't seem to lift Mark's spirits. It wasn't until the following year that I realized what *really* was bothering him.

When Mark had gone elk hunting back in Colorado, he had gone with a group of friends who had hunted together for years, always stalking the same ridge of the Continental Divide, bordered by Cochetopa and Saguache Creeks. They returned each year to the same campsite where the same cookstove sat in waiting, undisturbed from year to year. Old Ed Curtis was the elder of the hunt and in over fifty years had missed only a few elk seasons. His presence set the tone and preserved the rituals. He had known Mark's grandfather, and in fact, Ed's own grandfather, Henry H. Curtis, serving as justice of the peace had married Mark's great-grandparents back in 1874.

Several weeks before hunting season, the men would begin discussing the upcoming hunt. *Are we leaving the same day as always? Will Ed still be able to make it? Is he still doing the cooking? Are we taking the same wall tent? The same packhorses? The same packsaddles? In short, Are we adhering to our traditional way of doing things?*

So important were these rituals, that even after Ed could no longer hunt independently, he still went along, still cooked, and still presided. It took two men to lift him onto his horse, where he would remain for the entire day despite bitter winds and howling snows. Unless aided, he did not dismount to eat or to urinate. Upon returning to camp, he would be helped, stiff-legged and half-frozen, from his horse. He would proceed to cook the evening grub, warming his gnarled, arthritic bones around the campfire just as he had for more than fifty years.

Mark was seeking ritual. I realized it when he went hunting again last fall, this time with a different close friend who invited him to join his well-established camp. Plans for the annual hunt began in September, two months prior to opening day. They spoke on the phone constantly.

"Are you taking your new range tipi?" Ron asked.

"You bet. How many horses do I need to bring?"

"Just your gelding. I'll ride Spud, and we'll pack on Shorty. Don's bringing two llamas and Doc'll have the mules."

"What do the llamas think of the horses?"

"Oh, it's more like what do the horses think of the llamas. You probably ought to bring Tee over here once before we leave—let 'em get used to each other."

"Ah, Tee won't mind the llamas. It's the backpackers that'll spook him." They both laughed, then Mark asked, "What about food?"

"Usually Don buys all the grub. We just chip in some money. He's cooking up a brisket, so we'll have that to make sandwiches with. You got any panniers?"

And so the conversations went. Night after night. When we took Tee over to Ron's one afternoon to get acquainted with the llamas, the men even pitched Mark's range tipi in the backyard, then stood inside the tipi (ambiance being important during such times) and rolled out their sleeping bags, discussing the pros and cons of foam pads.

"Mark's sure looking forward to getting away," I said to Terry, Ron's wife. "I get a kick out of listening to 'em."

"It's like this every year," she said, rolling her eyes, "just about drives me nuts."

Tradition, for better or worse.

The snow has melted off the big hay field, and we have opened the gate so the cows can come and go at will. It is a perfect calving area—open grazing, tall scrub oak for shelter, not far to water. Number Nine wasn't with the other cows when Mark got home, so he and I and Hondo went in search of her.

Mark found her hidden among the oak in a low-lying draw with still-wet twin calves on the ground. She didn't like being disturbed and held her head high, wary. Mark eased in, quiet and slow, making sure not to get between the cow and the newborns as he ear-tagged the calves and poured iodine on their umbilical cords. Just as he capped the iodine bottle, Hondo and I appeared through the thickets. Hondo saw Mark and, oblivious to the protective mother cow, sauntered over to him. The cow lowered her head and charged.

"Hondo," I yelled. "No! Get back!" But it did no good, my panicked voice did not penetrate his deafness. Like an old tractor with the bucket lowered, the angry cow plowed into Hondo, rolling him over and mashing him into the ground.

Mark hollered at the cow and threw his cowboy hat at her, distracting her long enough for Hondo to regain his footing and scurry, befuddled, to a nearby tree. Dazed and confused, Hondo hung his head.

"You okay, buddy?" Mark asked, kneeling next to him. He took off his gloves and cupped Hondo's head in his hands, then ran them over Hondo's quivering body. "You gotta watch out, old boy, you got to watch out for those old cows."

The cow stood protectively over the two calves, eyeing us suspiciously, while Mark punched the shape back into his hat and I gathered up the iodine bottle and tagging pliers. Hondo kept his eyes on the old cow this time, but he dogged us like a shadow.

"Twins," Mark said, looking over his shoulder as we turned to go. "Never thought we'd get twins."

The next morning, a Saturday, Number Nine appeared with only the heifer calf at her side. Mark saddled Tee and went in search of the bull calf, hoping to find him hidden in the grass nearby, perhaps being babysat by one of the other cows. Older cows will do that, take turns babysitting one another's calves. Often at feeding time, one old cow will stay out in the pasture with the sleeping calves while the others come in to eat.

Mark finally found the calf in the same low draw where he had been born, dry and clean but otherwise unmothered. Too weak to walk, he probably hadn't nursed. The cow, if concerned about the calf, would have been breathing down Mark's neck by now. We conjectured: Maybe he hadn't been strong enough to follow and she had finally gone on without him? Maybe she knew something we didn't? Whatever the reason, she had given up on him. Mark lay the calf over the top of his saddle and together they rode back to the barn.

Long Hereford eyelashes batted from beneath a red-and-white forehead, which was supported by a weak, floppy neck. The calf looked at us expectantly, pushing against our warmth. Sarah named him Bright Eyes, and we became the instant parents of a bottle calf—four feedings a day, seven days a week. I hurried home on my lunch hour (this was becoming routine), pulled on coveralls and boots, and raced down to the barn while sloshing powdered milk replacer into a two-quart bottle of warm water. By the time I arrived at the barn, the milk was ready to drink.

The first few days went well. Then Bright Eyes's stomach became distended, bloating from constipation. I added mineral oil to the milk and began to massage his sides and back, kneading the long muscles that ran the length of his spine. My touch caused his flesh to jerk and twitch as the circulation improved, and I realized how much he must miss the rough licking a mother cow would give. But soon his system adjusted to the artificial milk and the substitute mothering. He began answering to the sound of our human voices as he would have to the low bawling call of a cow—coming if he heard his name called, following on our heels whenever possible.

Hondo, still leery of bovines, kept his distance. But Freckles mothered Bright Eyes from the beginning, licking his mouth and neck and chest, keeping all his orifices clean and free of dirt or debris. He accepted her attention eagerly, as he did Matt's and Sarah's.

Matt, nine years old now, was ready to begin 4-H. Bright Eyes would be his first project—an orphaned calf trying to compete against well-bred, high-priced stock. I naively hoped that good intentions, coupled with gentle caring, could successfully compete with solid husbandry.

Matt spent hours with Bright Eyes, often sleeping curled up in the feed bunk in the sunlit corral while the calf napped beside him, with an empty bucket settled in the dirt next to Freckles (the two-quart bottle no longer held enough milk). Together they bucked and cavorted, kicking up their heels and pawing at the ground. Matt learned to snort and Bright Eyes learned to butt. Naomi, our orphaned sheep, began hanging around the threesome, preferring the calf's company to the other sheep.

Bright Eyes's bawling took on a baaing quality, and as he watched the horses in the adjacent corral, he began running with his tail held high. When he greeted Freckles, he lowered his tail and wagged. Bigger now than Freckles, he continued to stand still while she groomed him—then he groomed us, licking the salt from our skin with his rough, spiked tongue. When he was old enough to eat hay, he lowered his bony head and helped Matt push the bale across the corral to the feed bunk.

We were not oblivious to the fact that Bright Eyes was destined for the supper table, nor did we allow that fact to distance us from him. "Name your 4-H animals something like 'Ribeye' or 'Lambchop,' " advised more than one experienced ranch wife. "Helps you remember not to get so attached." I remained determined not to become *detached*, knowing all the while that our role in his death was inevitable.

Hanging inside the house on the log wall by the wooden banister is a miniature branding iron—just large enough to brand a sirloin or a T-bone steak. The iron was given to us by Matt's godparents before we left Colorado. The brand is an Upside Down Open Box 7, the old Colorado brand that had belonged to Mark's father, Joe. His granddad's brand, used by the ranch corporation (an Open Box L), was acquired by an aunt when the ranch dissolved. We have used this small replica only once, heating it on the barbecue and searing the heirloom brand into our medium-rare hamburgers.

Even though Mark would not be able to use the Upside Down Open Box 7 brand here in Wyoming, we continued to send the annual fee to Colorado, keeping the brand registered in the Lambert name. Then, the year before we got our cows, Mark submitted several different brand requests to the Wyoming Livestock Board and that's when they finally approved the left-rib, Lazy VJL.

"Feels pretty silly," Mark said, holding the newly arrived registration papers in his hand, "having a brand and nothing to put it on."

"Well," I put my hand on his arm, "it's not so silly. Your great-great-grandfather didn't have a brand when he left Maine, or any cows either. Just a couple yoke of oxen. We've gotta start somewhere." Mark didn't reply, just folded the official paper and put it back in the envelope.

That summer, I drew the Lazy VJL brand on a piece of paper and asked the local welder to make a set of irons as a Christmas present. The kids and I tied a ribbon around them and hid them beneath the sofa until the twenty-fifth arrived. We made Mark shut his eyes and hold his hands out, palms up, thumbs extended. When he felt the heavy weight of the three separate branding irons in his grasp, he opened his eyes.

"Do you like them?" I asked, staring at their smooth, clean blackness, wondering how long it would be before they were christened in the red-hot heat of a branding fire. "Are the letters the right size?"

"Yeah," he said, "they're great. Just the right size—three inches." He traced the Lazy VJL with his finger, then whispered in a low voice, "Joseph Lambert." He ran his hand up and down their shafts, then walked over to where the Lambert Orchard Apple Cider crock rested safely in the corner. He leaned the branding irons against the log wall next to the hundred-year-old crock, then looked at me as if to say *thank you for having faith in this legacy of mine—thank you for not letting me give up on my heritage.*

His legacy had become mine. With the birth of our children, the joining of our lives, we acknowledged this transference of history. To deny Mark's heritage, to lose faith in it and no longer nurture it would be to deny my children their heritage. But I don't think Mark realized how much my *lack* of tangible heritage played a role in my determination that he not, out of despair and frustration, abandon his. *Oh,* I thought, *to be able to draw a bit of my own past on a slip of paper and weld it into the future. ...*

Our close friends Kimmie and Andy (who ranch across the border in South Dakota) always check the moon before scheduling their branding. "The calves bleed less when the moon's just right," Andy says in a slow, deep drawl that floats down from his six-foot-four frame.

Rural people have been consulting the *Farmer's Almanac* for generations—deciding when to plant, when to brand, when to breed. Those who rely on the *Almanac*'s calendar of waning and waxing moons are not afraid to admit that nature knows more than they about such things. They do not schedule their lives around the comings and goings of man so much as their comings and goings are scheduled around the rhythms of the earth and sky. And they develop, because of this, a far more intimate relationship with the natural world than do people oblivious to the moon or the sun or the stars. At one point in the history of mankind (and among some indigenous cultures even now), humans were not perceived as being separate from nature—they did not need to develop an intimate relationship with nature because they *were* nature. It is too easy, now, to forget that at varying times in history, we were all indigenous peoples, all children of the same moon.

Our branding, which involved only eight calves, had to be sandwiched between those of J. W. and Lois and the other neighbors. Even though we had little choice about the timing, Mark called Kimmie for a consultation anyway.

"What's the moon gonna be like on the twenty-fifth?"

"Well, Mark, don't know what to tell ya. Calves might bleed a little."

"We don't have much choice. Gotta borrow J. W.'s branding stove and I broke my damn ankle helping a neighbor brand the other day. I'm not getting around too good."

Mark had been in a cast and on crutches now for almost three weeks. The lack of mobility and necessity for dependence upon others was driving him nuts, though he tried not to dwell on the disappointing fact that he would have to ask someone else to apply the new branding irons to our first calves.

When the twenty-fifth arrived and we herded the cows and calves into the corrals with Bright Eyes, I scrutinized and rationalized.

Was it really necessary to brand Bright Eyes? And dehorn him? And castrate him? Would he ever forgive us?

We asked J. W. to handle the irons. He applied them with an experienced eye and steady hand, making sure the irons were heated enough to sear the hide but not burn the flesh. Mark's brother Keith helped while Cindy and their three young ones looked on. Sarah followed Tom (who was doing the castrating) around, holding a small plastic bucket into which Tom tossed the calves' severed testicles. Mark, two crutches tucked beneath his armpits, stood by watching helplessly, a frustrated expression upon his face. And at a safe distance from the bawling calves and bellowing cows sat Hondo and Freckles.

I have been to brandings where the severed testicles, freed from the furry sack that encloses them, are simply tossed aside—thrown to the ground and trampled into the dirt—that is, if the ranch dogs who hover nearby, eyes glued to the knife and the flick of the cutter's wrist, don't get them first.

I have also been to brandings where the testicles, or oysters, are gathered, soaked in salted water, then skinned, breaded, and fried right at the branding—or saved for a later celebration. One of the first brandings I went to with Mark was at the Phipp's Highland Ranch south of Denver, where a friend of ours was foreman. Linda, his wife, had the men save the testicles (two hundred at least) so that she could clean and freeze them for a later date.

"Hey, Page," Linda said, calling on the phone a few weeks after the branding, "Warren wants to have a get-together with everyone that helped brand. What are you guys doing this weekend?"

"Nothing that I know of. What've you got going?"

"Warren wants to have a pasture roping—we figured it'd be fun to make it a campout, you know, everybody bring tents and stuff. Thought I'd fry up those oysters, cook up a brisket and maybe a ham."

The get-together, cowboy-style, took place in an open pasture beneath a grouping of cottonwoods. Betty (Matt's godmother) and I, along with several of the other wives, helped Linda dredge the thawed oysters in cornmeal while a brisket and ham roasted over low coals. The men horsed around and drank a few beers while setting up tents and chairs. We fried the oysters (Rocky Mountain–style) in hot grease, then served them, still sizzling, along with potato salad, coleslaw, pinto beans, and homemade rolls.

The following morning the men, horseback, gathered the steers, ran them in the chute, and painted numbers on their backs. Then they turned the cattle loose, picked heading and heeling partners, and drew numbers for the steers. Mark and Bob (Matt's godfather) teamed up as usual; Bob would head, and Mark would heel.

"All right, all you hands," yelled Warren to the milling group of men and horses, "here's the deal. First team to find their steer, tie the ribbon on, and get the steer back here, wins."

"Wins what?" someone piped up.

"What ribbon?" someone else hollered.

"Linda, where's the ribbons?" Warren panicked.

"Right here," she answered, holding up a handful of colored, numbered ribbons. "Don't have a fit, Warren. Who drew number one, anyway?"

"That's us, Lambert," Bob said. "You're the heeler, better go get the ribbon."

"Oh, no," Mark teased back. "Way I heard it, the header always ties on the ribbon."

"Ah, hell, quit your arguing," someone else laughed. "You guys ain't even gonna find your steer, let alone rope him!"

And he was right. Mark and Bob were the last ones in, and they never did find their steer—they came in empty-handed with gritty smiles plastered on their slightly hungover faces.

The Rocky Mountain oysters had been both tough and tender, and I remember feeling a tremendous festive sense of community that weekend. The cows had weathered the hard winter, given birth to healthy calves. The calves—up and running, their branded hides already healing—were paired up and sucking. The earth had given up a bountiful harvest, and we were partaking in a time-honored ritual.

We all celebrated that weekend—despite the fact that we danced on a dying carcass—the ranch had been sold to developers who planned to build homes for ninety thousand people. Bulldozers, already plowing up the native grasses, sat like monster sentinels of the future parked just over the next hill. They would roar to life again on Monday.

We celebrated despite the fact that Warren, as ranch foreman, would soon be without a job, and he and Linda would have to take their children and move on. We celebrated because life, new life, must always be celebrated. To forgo celebration is to give up hope.

Matt was not appeased by ritualistic behavior. He did not want Bright Eyes to be branded. He eagerly helped with the other calves, even tucked two circles of hide cut from a bull calf's scrotum into his pocket, but he would not watch when the time came for Bright Eyes to feel the heat of the irons.

There was no need to head and heel Bright Eyes. Keith simply walked up to him, grabbed a fistful of flank and shoulder, and flipped him on the ground, left ribs up. I dried my moist eyes and vaccinated him while J. W. burnt the lazy V into his hide. Bright Eyes bellowed, rolling his eyes at me. I pulled the needle out and rubbed the puncture site while Mark handed J. W. the hot J iron, and then the L. Acrid smoke filled the air.

We had promised Matt we would not cut his calf but instead would use a constricting band to turn him from a bull calf to a steer calf. Tom put his knife away, grabbed Bright Eyes's sack in his hand, worked both testicles down into it, then slipped the green elastic band over the sack. The testicles would shrivel up and atrophy from lack of circulation within a short time.

Keith felt around the top of Bright Eyes's skull for horn nubs and found two small protrusions, the beginning of horns. Matt already knew, only too well, that they were there.

"Do we have to dehorn him?" he had asked pleadingly.

"Yes," Mark had answered unequivocally.

J. W. held the dehorning iron to Bright Eyes's skull, searing the hide from the first nub. The heat popped the horn cap off, and by applying a second hot iron, he seared the nub to prevent regrowth of the horn. Keith held the calf's head still while J. W. repeated the procedure a second time. Then, finally, it was over.

Most calves scramble to their feet the minute they are given their freedom, eager to return to the comfort of their mothers' sides. Bright Eyes just lay there, his head stretched back, deep nervous breaths rattling his sore ribs. He really had nowhere to go. Those to whom he had looked for comfort had betrayed him, and his biological mother stood in the next corral suckling his twin sister, oblivious to his existence.

"Matt, it's over," I said. "Come get your calf."

Matt turned away from the corner of the corral and faced the center. He walked over to Bright Eyes and knelt down, putting a tentative finger on the burnt hide. Bright Eyes shivered at Matt's touch, then raised his head from the ground.

"Come on, Bright Eyes," Matt said, wiping a tear from his cheek. "I'll fix you a bucket of milk." I noticed that he held two small circles of scrotal hide, hair side out, in his hand. Gently, as if in a daze, he smoothed the calf hair into spiraling swirls with the tip of his finger as he turned to go.

Bright Eyes pulled his front legs under him and raised himself up, then walked stiff-legged after Matt, following the only one who had not *yet* betrayed him.

We did not dehorn the Longhorn calf. Mark, against his better judgment, succumbed to my desire to let her flaunt her mixed ancestry. We decided, also, to keep her. She would grow to be our first heifer, the first cow to be both born and bred on this land we now called home.

Kimmie and Andy, who believe in consulting the moon, would also have understood the healing power of the two circles of scrotal hide. And they would have understood why we decided not to dehorn the Longhorn calf. Andy had an affinity for Longhorns—the black-and-white-speckled hide of Old Blue, a Longhorn steer who lived out his life on their ranch, covered the bedroom floor of the hundred-year-old ranch house in which they lived. And two stately sets of well-curved horns hung above the piano and the china hutch in their living room.

In fact, their home was filled with animal momentos and western artifacts. A sense of history and traditional culture settles softly upon one, like the glow of a kerosene lamp, upon entering their home.

This sense of tradition, an integral part of Mark's elk hunts back in Colorado, is deeply imbedded in western culture—as it was, and is, in indigenous hunting cultures. The bison, which the Plains Indians first stalked on foot, then later hunted horseback, represented far more than roasts and soup bones, far more than pemmican and jerky. The buffalo represented the feminine earth-power, the womb from which all life sprang. Hunting, as Joseph Epes Brown states in *Animals of the Soul*, was life's quest for ultimate truth. And when the hunter finally came eye to eye with his prey, he came eye to eye with life's final goal—to know Truth.[1]

The honorable hunter recognizes the tie that exists between himself (or herself) and the animal that has given his life. Rituals and ceremonies—proper thanksgivings—are necessary for the cycle to perpetuate. The cycle is one of give-and-take, life continuing in another form, an awareness of the interdependence of the living and the dead.

The Lakota wrapped their dead in buffalo robes, just as the men wrapped themselves in buffalo robes during the Sun Dance. Buffalo robes were left high upon barren buttes as sacred offerings. Ceremonial pipes were sealed with fat from the buffalo's heart.

Everything used by the Lakota reminded them of their connection to the buffalo: their ladles, their parfleches, their saddles, their drumheads, their snowshoes, their moccasins, their rattles (made from the buffalo's scrotum), even the dolls with which their children played. To forget the connection, the circle, the origin, would have been impossible.

Western objects add rural earthiness to our own lodgepole pine home. A braided leather riata hangs coiled next to the miniature branding iron that Bob and Betty gave us, and next to that hangs a bridle, inset with woven rawhide. On the adjacent wall are two Wells Fargo prints. Hanging beyond the prints is a large beaver hide framed by a willow sapling bent into a circle. Carved into the hair of the hide is an elegant six-point elk. It, along with our wedding portrait, is a keepsake of our honeymoon in the Tetons.

Hanging on the wall opposite the beaver skin is a painting of three Hereford cows crossing a shallow sunlit creek. Two riders herd them placidly from behind. And at the far end of that wall is Romie's blanket, beneath which sits a lamp made of barbed wire and horseshoes. Duane, one of the few *real* old-time Colorado cowboys still around, made it for us as a wedding gift. (Mark, comparing himself to old-timers like Duane, feels ill at ease when I refer to him as a cowboy.)

A bronze-like statue of a cowboy wearing a beaver-felt hat stands on the mantelpiece. He wears cowhide boots and hugs a leather saddle to his hip. The saddle has been worn smooth from use, the rawhide strips that wrap the stirrups appear weathered. What the man wears defines who he is, and what he is.

But my favorite keepsake of all, even more than the silver-concho leather chaps Bob made for me (which lie draped across the banister), is the box Keith made.

The box is carved from apple wood Keith gathered from the old ranch, then sanded and honed to a silken smoothness. He made three boxes: one for Mark, one for their sister Kendra, and one for himself. Etched into the underside of the lid are the words: Lambert Ranch, Apple Wood, Sedalia, Colorado. Beneath a miniature apple is the year, 1986. Keith's initials are carved discreetly into the upper corner.

These are not sophisticated items, nor did they cost hundreds of dollars. Given time, they will become family antiques, heirlooms with stories to share. But I cannot help but wonder if, when considered as a whole, they don't already tell a powerful story.

Are we so different from the Bushman Laurens van der Post speaks of in his essay, "The Song of the Hunter"?

> His killing, like the lion's, was innocent because he killed only to live. He never killed for fun or the sake of killing, and even when doing it, was curiously apprehensive and regretful of the deed. The proof of all this was there in his paintings on his beloved rock for those who can see with their hearts as well as their eyes.[2]

Too often, though, the rancher forgets to acknowledge the sacred within the traditional. He forgets, blinded by government regulations and dwindling profits, to go to his beloved rock and paint anew. Yet he is not so far removed from the sacred as to make remembering impossible.

Lucky are those who still feel the sense of sacred that fills the cold midnight air of the calving barn. Lucky are those, like the Navajo sheepherder, who decide which sheep will succumb to the knife when autumn comes and take special, intimate care of the animal.

Lucky are those still able to find the sacred within two small circles of scrotal hide, salted and set to dry on the bedroom windowsill by a young boy, where they will soak up the bent rays of sun—skin turning to leather, leather turning to new story born of old.

34

Hondo

THE YEARS HAVE AGED HONDO, the winter has taken its toll. Spring snows thaw and summer flowers bloom, but for Hondo only one season remains.

He has been unable to climb the deck for three days. He sleeps in the shady grass on the northeast side of the house, beneath Sassy's tree. I watch him from the half-circle windows in the living room. We have carried his rug onto the grass, and he rests there. The cast-iron skillet that has been his food dish for more years than I can remember is next to him. But this morning he no longer tries to lift his head. He will not drink, he cannot eat.

Freckles sits nearby, and every once in a while, she goes up to him and nudges him with her muzzle. *Rise Hondo. Get up. I will play with you—we will pretend to chase Simon and Tuffy. We will sniff the deer trails for fresh scent. Rise, Hondo. Rise.*

I bring a currycomb up from the barn and sit on the grass next to Hondo. He has not completely shed his winter coat. Clumps of dusty gray fur come loose. It is the coat of an old and dying dog—lifeless, lusterless—clinging to a dry, bloodless skin. We talk. I pretend he hears me, holding his head in my hands and kissing his forehead. I lift a paw and touch the cracked, hard pads of his feet and am reminded of the dead porcupine whose paws reached toward a dimming sky.

Mark walks over to the granary and gets two shovels. Matt follows behind. Mark puts his hand on Matt's shoulder and says, "Let's go."

"Where are you going?" I ask. But I know. We decided a few days ago, when Hondo's legs gave out on him, that we would bury him across the draw by the old root cellar, where the oak trees would shelter him, up high where he could look down upon the barn and the house, near the stackyard where we come to feed the cows twice a day, near the green, open fields where the deer graze at dusk and dawn.

"Matt's going to help me dig the grave."

Being prepared for the inevitable is important. But digging the grave is more than preparation. It is a physical, empowering act during a time of helplessness. I put the currycomb down and watch them walk, arm in arm, past the barn, up the other side of the draw. Matt is proud to be old enough to help, comforted by the age-old ritual.

Digging Hondo's grave before his death does not seem morbid, nor have we prematurely given up hope. Instead, the act gives significance to Hondo's parting. Our lives revolve around his dying for four days. We are given the weekend, days when we are home together, days when town does not claim us. I pull a clump of Hondo's hair from the comb and toss it into the breeze. The wind snatches the hair, carrying the clump away, past the driveway and into the tall grass.

Vivid cameo scenes of Hondo over the years come to mind—Hondo dozing beneath Mark's dilapidated lawn chair down at the barn while Mark trims up the horses' feet; Hondo sitting sentry in the front yard for two days, waiting for Mark to return from fighting forest fires; Hondo and Sarah lying curled up together, like two leaves from a single tree; Hondo and Matt splashing together in the shallow stock pond, lunging at slick tadpoles. And the two of us? The puppy I once cradled in my arms like a stuffed animal, afraid to let outside? He had taught me to follow the deer trails, to listen to the call of the red-tailed hawk, to catch the smell of sage in the moaning wind. I learned to appreciate the smell of freshly turned earth, of damp fibrous roots, of sodden wood alive with insects. And now, the comforting smell of pungent earth overwhelms my memories and anesthetizes my grief.

The rain comes, large single drops that splash against the windows and the leaves of the trees. They fall on Hondo but he does not move, only blinks his eyes. I go down to the barn again and find an old horse blanket. Shaking the dust from the striped Navajo design of browns and golds, I walk back to the house and lay the blanket on top of Hondo. He wags his tail and blinks again. His tongue lolls out the side of his mouth, which is hot and dry. I gently close his jaws. Mark and Matt return from digging the grave, and Mark helps me carry the picnic table to the lawn. We carefully set it over Hondo, making a shelter for him.

"Should we carry him inside?" I ask Mark.

Speech is not easy. Emotions run deep. Slowly, Mark answers, "I think he is where he wants to be."

Before going back inside, I leave the comb by Hondo's side.

Hondo has always stood guard outside our home. He has always relished the freedom of coming and going, of perking his ears at an unusual noise and being able to investigate immediately, of making nightly circles around the borders of his territory. His glossy black coat has thickened each fall, the guard hairs insulating him each winter. He has slept with the soft, warm feline bodies of Tuffy and Simon curled next to him in a self-made cave beneath the granary or in a hollowed-out nest in the hay inside the weathered barn. But mainly, he has sat sentinel on the deck, listening to the comings and goings within the house while keeping his eyes and ears and nose tuned to the outside world.

He is where he wants to be. Close to us, lying on the cool earth, which has been his friend for so many years. The earth, where he buried his scavenged bones. The earth, full of rodent smells and bittersweet roots. On our walks out into the pasture, he digs where gophers have turned the earth inside out, sending cascades of dirt flying behind him as his large paws and strong worn nails dig down. The earth, where he buries his nose clear to the eyes, his nostrils snorting and sniffing as he breathes in secret dog-scents. "Hey boy, what did you find?" I ask, rubbing Hondo's head, brushing the red dirt from his mouth, from the gray hairs and the loose smile. The earth—which will soon hold him, deep beneath her topsoil.

I bring a new sponge outside and soak up a mixture of water and raw beaten egg, holding Hondo's head upright while I squeeze the sponge. The light yellow mixture drips into the side of his mouth and he laps at it and swallows thirstily. I resoak the sponge and squeeze another drink into his mouth. He swallows another four or five times, then closes his eyes, too tired to take more. I lower his head onto the rug and stroke his forehead.

"Did that taste good, buddy?" Tuffy comes over and rubs against his reclining shoulder. Freckles watches, then lowers her head onto her brown-and-white paws. She sighs. I go back in the house and clean the sponge and bowl, hoping to need them again. Later, looking through the window, I see Mark sitting on the grass next to Hondo. The glass silences his words. The horse blanket moves slightly as Hondo lifts his tail. Mark rests his hand on Hondo's head. He rubs behind the ears. They sit, man and dog, best of friends, constant companions.

During the course of the day Matt and Sarah stop to sit beside Hondo, each in turn, in their own time. Matt lies down next to him. Sarah lifts the blanket and strokes him. The rain has quit. Sarah wanders off and returns with a smooth, straight stick. She places it next to his mouth. Hondo lifts his head for a moment, sniffs the stick, then lowers his head.

I continue to squeeze beaten egg and water into his mouth, remembering the raw egg and milk Simon and Tuffy eagerly lapped up with each litter of kittens. Mark and I find a private time to talk, and we discuss our options.

"Do you think we should call the vet?" The inevitable question drapes unspoken between us like a shroud. *Should we put Hondo out of his misery?* We do not discuss shooting him. Mark asks me to call the vet; perhaps he can give us a euthanasia drug.

"See if we can just pick up the medicine," Mark says. "I'll give him the injection myself. I'm not bringing another dog home in a dog-food sack, that's for damn sure." While still living on the ranch in Colorado, he had had to have his dog Bullet put to sleep. Mark had carried him into the veterinarian's office, and after the dog's heart had stopped beating, the vet brought Bullet back out to him stuffed in a fifty-pound dog-food sack.

We tell Matt and Sarah about our decision. They do not want Hondo to suffer any longer and seem to understand. But every time we go to him, he musters up one last spark of life. He holds on, in vain. He is dying. There will be no mortal resurrection.

The veterinarian is out of town for two days. Law prohibits the assistant from dispensing the drug. The lethal injection must be given by a licensed doctor. Desperate, I call the county nurse, but she does not have access to the drug. The local physician is our last option. Almost.

Mark visits on the phone with his brother Keith, who later tells me if we need his help to end Hondo's suffering, he will help. His offer to shoot Hondo is generous, born of love and compassion, for the act would not be easy for him, either.

Mark picks up the brush and curries Hondo. His strokes are less gentle than mine, more vigorous, as if trying to force life back into Hondo, challenging death's inevitable grip.

After dinner we tell Matt and Sarah to go outside, one by one, and tell Hondo good-bye. They hug him. They kiss him and pat his head. He opens his eyes. By now they both understand that, this time, Hondo will not recover.

"Will the blankets keep him warm?" Sarah asks. She and Hondo share a special bond. While Matt and Freckles wrestled and ran up and down the cattle trails in the draw, Sarah and Hondo, more closely paced, were content to bask in the sun-filled quiet.

Dark descends and Mark goes outside. The light from the living room casts a faint beam across the yard, covering Hondo in a pale ribbon of yellow. The earth carries the vibrations of Mark's footsteps to Hondo, a reverberation he knows as well as his own heartbeat. He lifts his head and thumps his tail. He makes a valiant effort to rise but is only able to lift his shoulders. Mark sits down and slowly strokes Hondo's fur. Freckles pushes her head beneath Mark's other hand. He ruffles her fur and scratches behind her ear. She settles down next to him.

By bedtime Hondo is sleeping quietly beneath Sassy's tree, sheltered by the picnic table and the horse blanket, which covers all but his head. Freckles sleeps inches away. Our private good-byes have been spoken, our private tears shed.

"Do you think we should check on him during the night?" The question is an unfair one to ask Mark. We each must follow our own conscience. I answer the question myself.

"Maybe God will just take him tonight, and we won't have to try and figure out what to do tomorrow ... ."

We both pray for a natural end, a peaceful passing on. Twinges of guilt tug at me, thinking others might have brought Hondo inside to sleep by their bed. But somehow we cannot confine him to four walls. We cannot bring ourselves to hide the stars from his eyes. We want the moonbeams to guide him to the heavens and the night crickets to lull him to sleep.

I awake at 5:00 A.M. Mark is still asleep. I go immediately to the living room window. The blanket has slipped halfway off, and Hondo's chest is uncovered. He is taking huge, deep breaths, and his entire body shudders. *The throes of death. His body makes one last, brave effort to cling to this world.* My inclination is to rush outside and be with him. But I don't go. I do not want to make this transition any harder for him. *It's all right, Hondo. You may leave. You do not need to guard our home any longer. You have done your best. You have been a good and faithful friend. It is all right to let go.*

Dawn comes. Light pink colors the eastern sky. Dewdrops perch upon the grass blades. I should go to him, be by his side, for he is dying. *No. Don't go. He will think he must stay. He will not want to abandon his post.*

So I don't go. I wait for the last shudder to escape him, for life to ease out and death to creep in. It takes less than five long minutes. I go out and sit on the wet grass in my nightgown. I close Hondo's eyes and stroke his throat. I lay my head upon his massive chest, where his devoted heart lies still, and I breathe his familiar dog-scent one last time.

When the sun has risen, and the early-morning songs of the chickadees and the robins and the bluebirds have quieted, I pull the old horse blanket completely over Hondo and go in the house, to Mark.

Matt and Sarah help bathe Hondo. I clean his muzzle and wash his eyes. We curry his coat and use the soft horse brush on his legs. We move away to allow Hondo and Mark time alone. He girds himself for the task ahead. The time comes to carry Hondo to the grave.

"Is he too heavy?" I ask. "Should I get the wheelbarrow?"

"I can carry him," Mark answers, determined to do this one last thing.

Mark stoops and maneuvers his arms beneath Hondo's body. He stands, straining for balance. Hondo, even in death, is a heavy, muscular dog. The muscles in Mark's arms bulge. He grits his teeth. I straighten Hondo's legs and the angle of his head and, shovel in tow, we follow Mark. The early-morning sun has been replaced by low-hanging clouds. A dense foggy mist envelops the mountains. After walking a fair distance, past the barn and up the path toward the stackyard, I ask Mark, "Do you need to put him down for a minute?"

He shakes his head. "I'm okay."

We finally arrive at the grave site. Placing Hondo in the deep hole is awkward, but Mark manages. Cool dirt surrounds Hondo on all sides.

"Mom, I want to pick some flowers for him," Sarah says, "wait for me." She scoots away in search of anything wild and pretty. Matt wants to find a stick to bury with Hondo. "Would that be a good thing to bury with him?" he asks.

"Yes, Matt," Mark answers with a quavering voice, "a very good thing." Freckles runs after Matt, and together they search for just the right stick.

Mark and I stand by the open grave, left alone for a few minutes. We put our arms around each other, but we do not talk. We do not trust our voices. I cannot speak to his grief, for mine is too great. He cannot speak to my grief, for his is too great. We lean quietly on each other—the thing we do best.

Sarah returns with wild dandelions, a few long purple asters, lots of white yarrow, two bluebell stalks, and red clover blossoms.

"How are these, Mom? They're the prettiest I could find."

"They're beautiful, Sarah."

Matt and Freckles return with a smooth weathered stick about twelve inches long.

"It's perfect," Mark nods his head.

Matt places the stick in the grave, near Hondo's muzzle. Sarah lays half of the flowers on Hondo's chest and saves the rest for the top of the grave.

"Come over here for a minute," Mark says.

The four of us circle Hondo and hold hands. Freckles, sitting behind, pushes her way into the circle and quietly sits with us. Out loud, we take turns saying a short prayer.

"Dear God," Matt asks simply, "please take Hondo to heaven and make him young again."

"Will Hondo be able to chase sticks in heaven, Mom?" Sarah asks, turning her gaze from Hondo to me. My answer is automatic. I do not contemplate the question scientifically or theologically.

"Yes." I am confident of the answer, confident that Sarah's question falls into the realm of mystery, of *Taku Skanskan*, the sacred energy that molds all movement within time and space. I am confident that there exists, within God's realm, a new place for Hondo. I am confident that dried, lifeless flowers can indeed turn to silver sage, just as I am confident that my grandmother Effie listens once again to the sound of the wind.

Tuffy and Simon trot up from the barn to watch. Finally, the time has come. We cover Hondo with a burlap sack and Mark begins shoveling the dirt on top. Matt wants to help. We all take turns. Freckles stands close to the edge of the hole and peers in, a slight whine escaping her throat. Mark and I look at each other, humbled by what we do not understand. Mark finishes the job of covering the grave. The rain holds off, but the fog drops even lower. We place a large heavy stone on top of the mound of dirt, and Sarah tucks her remaining flowers under the rim of the rock.

It is done.

We gather the shovels and turn to go, walking shoulder to shoulder, lost in our own memories. As we pass the corner of the stackyard, Mark slows his pace and turns away. I hear a gut-deep, heartrending sob escape his tough exterior, and Matt, who has never before seen his father cry, asks "What's wrong with Daddy, Mom?"

"Nothing is wrong," I say lamely, Mark's lonely sobs quietly defying my answer.

I herd the kids on, urging them to follow Freckles and the cats, who trot down the path in front of us. I turn and look back. Mark is leaning on the corner post of the fence that surrounds the stackyard, great sobs shaking his manly frame, and though I have seen tears discreetly spill from Mark's eyes before, this is only the second time I have ever seen such anguish escape him. Coming from the depths of his soul, the shudder wells forth from the earth itself.

Hondo—loyal to each of us, answering every call, every whistle— but his true master was the land, the earth, whence he was born, where he lies buried, ashes to ashes, dust to dust. He is, and always will be, a creature of the earth. It is there that I will find his memory, in the solace of the wildness beyond the four walls of our home.

The mist becomes drizzle, turning the trees and the wooden sides of the barn black. The rain soaks the dirt and drips from the leaves of the oaks, washing the tears from my face—again and again.

The earth, too, is weeping. I know this to be a fact, not a sentimental cliché or a convenient bit of symbolism, but a fact—as irrefutable as a breaking heart, as full of solace as the breath of God.

Northeastern fog eased into the saddle of the Bear Lodge. Sundance Mountain, and Inyan Kara to the south, rose from the valley floor, suspended between layers of mist while the ground and sky disappeared into whiteness.

By 4:30 the encroaching fog enveloped the ranch. Mark and the kids were gone, so it was my night to do chores—it was also the first time I had been totally alone on the ranch since Hondo's death.

The snowcapped horizon had disappeared, withheld from view by the ethereal haze of moisture. Gone, too, were the roads, the ridges, the distant peaks. The fog claimed them all. The world grew small, its edges within reach—like a childhood shoebox diorama with a mirror pond, moss bushes, and cotton-ball clouds. My universe became, suddenly, very private.

The sheep were lost to me. I followed the fence line walking the perimeter of the hay field, hoping to eventually come up on the far side of where they grazed. A wisp of fog cleared and the buck appeared, standing rear guard, only to vanish like an apparition. Then Square Ears materialized momentarily in front of me. I called out to her, and with my voice guiding her from behind, she led the others toward the barn. Dozens of quick, cloven hoofsteps moved forward, then hesitated and stopped. Like a shepherd's staff, my voice reached through the fog and urged them onward again, until finally the grayness of the barn emerged—a port in the storm.

Once the sheep were safely corralled, I eased my way up the snowy path, then detoured until I stood beneath the ice-lined oak trees overlooking the draw. Beyond the draw, hidden by the fog, stretched the hay field where the sheep had been grazing. And rising from the field was the invisible ridge where the two old trees stood side by side.

Hondo had walked with me many times to that far ridge and had sat with me many times beneath these oaks. He had, in fact, *died* beneath these great burred oaks that now hid their crowns in the mist. I searched the fog, wanting him to glide through it and stand by my side. My hand reached out instinctively to pet his glossy blackness but found nothing to cling to—only the snow, the whiteness, and my grief.

Then, very quietly at first, a thin, high-pitched, lonely wail floated across the draw, lengthening and thickening in the fog.

Hondoooo ...

The sheep recognized my keening even before I did.

The ridge caught my anguish, held it for a moment, then returned it to me—softer, partly absorbed, not totally mine any longer. And from somewhere in the white, colorless distance, a coyote answered.

35

Call of Duty

BIRTHING SEASON ON THE RANCH, and elsewhere, had arrived. Early Wyoming wildflowers—the minuscule white-lined spring beauties, star-shaped sand lilies, and velveteen pasque flowers—braved the late freezes and April snows to begin their eager upward thrusts.

Last night the temperature dropped to eighteen degrees. Frost covered the ground, the wooden fences, the tractor's metal—even the frozen imprints of the sheeps' muddy hooves. Then dawn came, the sun yawned and stretched, and the temperature warmed to forty degrees.

Five ewes had lambed so far—five sets of twins born. The testosterone-scented bucks, with the thick folds of wool hanging from their necks, had tended to their fathering duties well.

Half giddy with the promise of spring, I opened the barn door to the lambing area while Freckles, who knew she shouldn't enter, crouched just outside the corral. A dead lamb lay sprawled on the hay-strewn dirt. Square Ear, with a second, healthy lamb at her side, stood guard over the stillborn lamb. I herded the other sheep out into the corral, then walked slowly over to the ewe and picked up the dead twin.

The lamb, a ewe lamb, looked flawless: well fleshed, well wooled, and well birthed. I put her back down and picked up the twin (a smaller male), poured iodine on his umbilical cord, and placed him in a pen. Square Ear, torn between two conflicting urges, followed the live lamb but would not go in the pen. She pivoted on her hind feet, then walked to a point halfway between the two lambs. I picked the dead lamb back up and placed her in the pen next to the bleating male. This time Square Ear went all the way in. She sniffed both lambs, then began licking their ears and throats.

I left her alone, allowing her to come to terms, in her own animal way, with the lamb's death. I did not expect her to grieve or feel sorrowful. Nor did I want to interfere, at least not yet.

A few hours later, I cradled the dead lamb in my arms, looking for an appropriate place to leave her. Freckles followed me to the chokecherry bushes by the old cabin, then wandered with me down into the draw. Still undecided, I made Freckles stay in the main barn, away from what I feared would be the temptation of dead flesh.

Alone now, I carried the lamb, still cradled in my tired arms, past the house and deep into the oak trees. Patches of snow and deep drifts clung to the shaded draws. Putting the lamb down, I covered her with dried leaves, piled dead tree limbs and branches on top of her, then returned to let Freckles out of the barn before going inside the house.

An hour later I looked out the half-circle window. Freckles has lugged the dead lamb, still intact, into the yard. They lay side by side, napping in the morning sun.

This time, still afraid Freckles would gnaw on the carcass, I locked her in the granary before taking the lamb back into the woods. I buried the still-limp body beneath a deep drift, digging three feet into the snow and thinking, naively, that by doing so I was obliterating her scent.

I kept Freckles locked in the granary for over an hour, enough time (I hoped) for my own scented trail to dissipate. Five minutes later, the lamb and Freckles once again rested together on the lawn.

Freckles, a border collie, had strong herding instincts. When helping to get the sheep in at night, she would keep the ewes tightly bunched, herding the stragglers by crouching in the grass, then nipping at their heels. While lugging the dead lamb around, I had been thinking only of Freckles's instinct to kill and devour, without realizing that she possessed other equally dominant instincts. I had assumed that she would want to eat the dead lamb, as she and Hondo had gnawed on the dead fawn and on Redy's aborted foal. I was wrong.

Spring rain began to splatter against the bay window and onto the wooden deck. Freckles picked the lamb up gently by one hind hoof and pulled her across the wet grass to Sassy's tree, where it was dry. She began slowly and deliberately to clean her, licking the dirt from the lamb's soft pink mouth and the rainwater from her nappy woolen coat. As the day wore on, she alternated between grooming the lifeless form and napping nervously beside it. Her duty was to protect, but *for how long?*

"Freckles," I enticed, "let's go for a hike." She had never before resisted this invitation. She rose, thumped her tail, looked at the dead lamb, then took a deep breath and lay back down, resting her head on her outstretched paws. She would not leave. I headed up the mountain and into the secluded woods without her.

In an old-growth area where ponderosa pines tower overhead and the dried red leaves of wild grapes crumble beneath, the call of a great horned owl filled the woods.

Hoo! Hu-hu!

Expecting the bird to be above, I looked up before realizing the call came from below the hill on which I stood. An underground spring trickled from the south face of a small, steeply wooded canyon. The resulting creek meandered through the bottom of this narrow draw. Pine trees grew like angled spikes, their tenacious roots clinging to the steep sides, their green-needled crowns cresting the canyon's upper rim.

A *swoop, swooping* sound echoed up the trunks of the canyon trees. It was here the great horned owl made her home. I watched as she lifted herself from the uppermost branch of one pine, traversed over the narrow creek, and landed with a swishing noise on the top of an opposite tree. Sunlight struck her white Y-shaped throat, while the rest of her—tufted ears and brown-barred feathers—receded into the shadows of the pines.

Hoo! Hu-hu! she whistled out again. Then her white throat disappeared from view and a faster *swoop, swooping* noise could be heard skirting the tops of the ponderosas that lined the canyon walls. A cool breeze ruffled my hair.

I have heard the great horned owl many times.

I have seen her only once.

Freckles greeted me with desperate enthusiasm upon my return, then went and stood over the cold, stiff lamb, looking as if she had somehow failed in her duties to protect the flock. I took the bull by the horns (as Mark would say) and locked the lamb in the granary. Maybe Mark would know what to do.

Freckles watched protectively as I carried the lamb to the wooden storage shed and placed her inside. She peered through the narrowing crack as I shut the granary door, then sat guard for more than a hour, rain soaking her long-haired coat. After two hours she lay down, resting her head on her paws without ever taking her eyes from the closed granary door.

When Mark got home, he put the dead lamb in the truck and drove down the road, where Hondo and Freckles had never been allowed to follow. She whined as she watched him disappear. Finally, when not even the rumbling sound of the old Ford engine lingered, she walked slowly down to the corral and stood outside, watching the ewes chew their cud and the healthy lambs gambol on the manure pile.

In the pasture below where the great horned owl lives among the old-growth ponderosas are thick stands of hawthorn, willow, scrub oak, and an occasional red dogwood. Here also the rib cage of a wild turkey hangs tangled in the branches. It has been suspended there all winter.

Near the turkey skeleton, hidden in the bushes, are the bones and hide of a whitetail deer. It was here, near the weathered bones of a whitetail and the scattered remains of a wild tom, that Mark placed the dead lamb.

An owl is believed to be a symbol or harbinger of death. Some Lakota also believe that the *Nagi*, or restless part of the soul, occasionally will take the form of an owl to warn of impending death or illness. The owl is rarely someone's *power animal*. And if she were, one would not speak of it. For to speak of another's power animal is to run the risk of robbing that person of his or her power. A person's spirit power, or guardian spirit, often takes the form of a four-legged or winged-one and is sometimes revealed when one "cries for a vision."[1]

At times I have wondered about my own judgment. Is it wise to tell (let alone write about) the great horned owl, or the fox that appeared like an apparition, or the two trees that stand like sacred sentinels upon the ridge? Do I dare speak of the people who once roamed this land? And roam it still?

The stories exist, whether or not I write about them. Mark, and most male ranchers I know, are reluctant to tell their stories. They inter them beneath layers of denim and leather, like strata of sedimentary rock hidden beneath the skin of the earth. These hidden stories can empower by serving as intimate guides and mentors, or they can weaken the person within whom they reside, as does a painful injury left untended.

Mark's strength of character is born of layered stories, some of which are his own, some of which were bequeathed him. Yet only *he* knows the stories that weaken because they are *not* being told, or that strengthen because they remain sequestered.

Power animals. Power stories. This time I do not mention the dead lamb's body to anyone. I wait for the flesh to decay, for the earth to cover her with a dusting of ash. I wait for the lamb's body to become a carcass, for her story to join the continuum of stories—animal and human—that enrich this land.

Perhaps a century from now paleontologists will wonder how the skeletons of a turkey, a deer, and a lamb all came to be found in this same stand of willows. Their theories may touch upon part of the truth, but they will never unearth the mystical call of the great horned owl. Her call will echo, unfettered, through this silver-sage valley forever.

36

The Act of Healing

MY ONLY SISTER, WHO LIVES thousands of miles away in Hawaii, has given me an incredible gift for my fortieth birthday. She has offered me (because of generous spirit, not abundant wealth) the equivalent of one year's salary from my job at the bank to enable me to quit work, stay home, finish my book, and be with Matt and Sarah during summer vacation. I don't know if I have the courage—to give up the steady income, the profit-sharing plan, the pension plan, the well-mapped road of my future. This predictable and secure road, however, leads me farther away from where I *really* want to be.

I want to be here, on the land. Where the breeze carries the occasional smell of skunk and the sound of falling acorns through my open window. Here, where Romie listens for my footstep, where the cows laze in deep draws and coyotes howl from red-topped ridges. I want to stand with loose dark soil beneath my feet and gnarled, aged oaks above me. I want to seek the high places—where sage-scented voices from the past whisper timeless and sometimes painful truths. I want to hear my children's laughter filter through the cracked walls of an old barn and see the horse-mounted shadow of my husband riding the horizon.

My sister offers me a chance at life—a year to pivot inward, a year to radiate outward. She is offering me a chance to walk the sacred path; she is offering me *kinship*.

Far more stories escape my attention than capture it. Though stories swirl around me like whirlwinds upon the plains, I am able to grasp only the most obvious. I am too used to listening solely with my ears and watching only with my eyes. I walk the sacred path without realizing it—searching always to the left or right, forgetting to look within.

The animals with whom I share this land lead me gently down the story-path. They allow me to minister to them so that they can in turn minister to me. And in so doing, I become not the healer but the healed.

"We've got a lame horse," Mark said, coming back up to the house after doing the morning chores. I immediately thought of Romie, who, despite her frailness, had endured a winter of heavy snows and subzero temperatures.

"Redy's got a pretty bad cut on her back leg. It's gonna need some doctoring." I breathed a guilty sigh of relief.

I had noticed Redy lying down by the old cabin yesterday but dismissed it as unimportant. Nothing like ignoring the obvious, I thought, irritated with myself.

A jagged puncture wound marred her hock, which was swollen to twice its normal size. The swelling continued up and down the length of her leg, and a dry yellow crust had formed where the abscess had begun to drain, creating a frozen streak of pus and blood.

Matt and Sarah watched as I haltered her and tried to lead her a hundred feet through the snow to the corral. She wouldn't, or couldn't, move her stiff, unbendable leg.

"Matt, you try leading, and I'll get behind and push."

I applied my shoulder to her rear and heaved but she stood firm, her feet planted in the deep snow. I swatted her fleshy buttocks with a stick. "Come on, Redy!" I said with authority, as if a stern voice would accomplish what gentle prodding could not. She swayed forward, lifted a front hoof, then set it down and went no farther. I swatted her again with the stick.

"Don't hurt her, Mom," Matt pleaded, "she's already hurt." He pulled gently on the lead rope, but she didn't budge.

"We can't doctor her here in this deep snow. We've got to get her to the corral where she'll have fresh water." Though I didn't tell the children, Redy seemed feverish and dehydrated.

We pushed and pulled, and I carefully applied the stick a few more times. She swayed and stomped her front feet but wouldn't walk. Her ears were pricked forward, not laid back against her head, as they would have been if she were stubbornly resisting. Was it fear rather than obstinacy that kept her anchored?

"Come on, girl." Sarah moved closer and patted her neck encouragingly. "You can do it."

I stroked her nose and rubbed her ears, ran my hand down her neck and across her ribs, then over her hip and down the stiff, injured hock. She flinched as I put pressure on the inside of her leg, where the frozen bloody pus had formed the small rivulet.

"Let's try again, Matt. If this doesn't work, we'll go get Dad off the tractor."

Matt pulled hard this time, while Sarah and I pushed again from behind. Redy took one faltering step forward in the deep snow, moving the injured leg only an inch or two. Then she began pawing at the snow impatiently, finally irritated, I thought, by our harassment. But she continued to paw beyond the point of irritation. The snow on the path flew as she pawed frantically, until she had managed at last to expose bare ground. She stopped pawing, shivered, took another tentative step forward, then began pawing the snow out of her way again.

"She's making a path!" Matt yelled.

"It's the deep snow she's afraid of," I said, smiling at the simple realization. "Sarah, run up to the house and get the snow shovel."

Once we cleared a partial path for her to walk in, her fear diminished. I could not blame her for not trusting her injured leg on the snow-covered ground, in which jagged rocks and splintered tree branches hid. Perhaps that is how she injured herself initially— slipping on the ice and puncturing her hock on an unseen hazard.

Once we got Redy in the corral, Sarah got a bucket from the barn and we filled it with water from the thawed section of the horse tank. I began the hard task of chipping the six-inch-thick ice from the rest of the tank with a thirty-pound solid-metal rod. A few minutes later, Mark shut off the tractor, quit plowing the snow, and threw some hay over the fence to Redy. He took over the chipping job while Matt and I used pitchforks to lift the chunks of ice out of the tank. Sarah helped by shoveling a circular path in the corral on which Redy could easily walk.

The abscess had not infected the joint itself. A diuretic drug allowed the tissues to absorb the fluids, and antibiotics and sulfectants attacked the infection. I ground up sulfur pills and fed them to Redy in her grain for two days, and Mark followed up with a combiotic shot (penicillin and streptomycin) in the evenings. Three days later the leg, back to normal size, moved without stiffness, though the abscess continued to drain, staining the back of Redy's leg a blood-tinged yellow.

This accounting is the obvious external shell in which the story of Redy's injured leg is encased. The story ends happily: Redy's leg is healed with no permanent injury—just a scar where the hair grows in tiny swirls. The story not told, the story of the *healer* and not the *healed*, remains hidden. It is the story of a woman who spends her first days away from the security of a full-time job tending to an injured horse. Her Mondays lose themselves in Tuesdays, Fridays in Saturdays. Her days revolve around a wound that begins to heal not from the outside in, but from the inside out.

She learns that sorrow born of death and illness need not be a permanent sorrow, one that permeates life and robs it of its joys. It can be a temporary, enriching sadness, one that imparts wisdom and clarity.

With this healing also comes the realization that no path is free from danger, yet all paths can be walked in a sacred manner—as long as one is willing to take that first frightened step of faith.

37

A Crippled Legacy

M

Y ABILITY TO FULLY ENJOY my time at home is hampered by knowing that Mark is spending even longer hours working for the forest service. To compensate, I increase my share of the outdoor chores, knowing all the while that these very chores are what keep Mark sane.

For a while I begin doing the evening chores as well as half of the morning chores. As a result, the cows and I finally become friends. Big Red and the Reisland bellow when they see me come as they used to bellow to Lois, and as they have grown used to bawling for Mark. I do not kid myself that I am much more than a food provider, yet sometimes they will lift their heads from the pile of hay, stare at me with clear eyes, and utter companionable mooing sounds. They are patient with me when I throw only a half a bale of hay at a time instead of the heavier whole bale that Mark would throw.

Our small herd of cows has grown to eleven, not counting Bright Eyes and the Longhorn heifer. It is a number that allows for intimate exchanges. It is a number with promise.

Friday night the temperature, which reached only to zero during the day, dropped to ten below.

"Mark, one of the new cows didn't come in to feed tonight," I told him as he came in the door, stomping snow from his boots.

"I'll go check it out," he said almost eagerly, changing from his work coat to his coveralls.

He found her deep in a snow-covered draw with a newborn calf, wet and half-frozen, wedged beneath some scrub oak. From the looks of the skid marks, the calf had been born on the upper edge of the draw but had slipped down a steep crevice. Her tail was broken and her left ear frostbitten.

The cow eyed Mark suspiciously as he cautiously climbed down the draw and, in order to pick up the calf, stepped between her and the calf. She followed him as he lugged the newborn calf up the slick-sided draw, stopping every fifty feet to catch his breath and let the cow smell her offspring. She followed nervously, not wanting to be shut in the barn yet not wanting to leave her calf, either. Despite the cold and subzero wind, Mark arrived back at the house damp with sweat.

The calf, soon named Broken Tail, was too weak to suck. We also suspected brain damage, perhaps from the fall, perhaps from a breech birth. She lay on the cold ground, listless. Her tail jutted off to the right and, when assisted, she could barely stand on weak, slightly misshapen hips. If she was in pain, she suffered quietly, as do most animals.

Though Mark and I discuss the politics of ranching on a daily basis at least in theory, we do not often allow ourselves to personalize the depressing and dire media predictions. "A mass exodus of young people from rural communities continues to occur," the newspapers say. "Small Towns Across Rural America Close Up Shop" the headlines predict. *Not our town. Not our children.* We console ourselves with optimism, wondering all the while if we are indeed foolishly searching for the future in the shadows of the past.

As I stared at Broken Tail—crippled, unable to stand on her own feet—I could not help but wonder if she embodied the future of traditional rural life in America. If I removed the romance from our life, was this what remained? A young family struggling in vain against the anti-ranching politics of the day? Should we give up the struggle, move to the city, admit the disability?

It did not make economic sense to try and keep Broken Tail alive. Yet there was something immediate about new life, something urgent, so we put the mother cow in the chute and Mark milked two pints of milk from her. Broken Tail, with one single burst of survival instinct, sucked a full pint from the bottle, then would drink no more. Not from the bottle. Not from the cow. As a last resort, we tube-fed her the rest of the milk mixed with mineral oil, electrolyte water, a protein pill, and a raw egg. She surprised us by surviving the night.

Mark gave me milking lessons before he left for work in the morning, which I failed miserably, managing only to squirt minuscule amounts of milk into the bottle. When he came home that night, he milked the cow again, giving me a supply for the next day. But in the morning, the cow wouldn't let me near her calf.

"Out, Freckles!" I ordered, realizing that she was following closely on my heels. She slunk to the fence, disappointed, then crouched and watched, ready to spring at the slightest command.

The cow, less nervous now, allowed me to tube-feed the milk and another raw egg to Broken Tail. I lifted the crippled calf and prodded her into walking, into taking one faltering step after another. Her hips moved stiffly and awkwardly. I rubbed her spine and massaged her muscles, stimulating her circulation. I thought of bulldozers tearing up native ranchland to make way for subdivisions and rubbed all the harder. She flinched and twitched, just as Bright Eyes had, seeming to enjoy the sensation. I spend several hours with her, basking in the knowledge that it wasn't my lunch hour and I didn't have to hurry back to town.

The next day I switched from the stomach tube to a lamb's bottle (an empty Seven-Up bottle with a rubber nipple attached). The calf tested the new, smaller nipple, rolling it over her tongue while I squeezed milk into her mouth. She began to suck, finishing almost two ounces. Ecstatic with the small victory, I refilled the bottle. She sucked on my finger and, in a little less than an hour, managed to drink another ounce. Achingly slow progress, but progress nonetheless.

I still had not mastered the technique of milking out the cow. But I was determined that, where I had failed, the calf would succeed. The cow (used to very little handling) now allowed me to kneel next to her while she stood in the open corral. I lifted Broken Tail, helping her to gather her unsteady legs beneath her, and pushed her uncooperative nose into the cow's udder, squeezing a wimpy stream of milk onto her face. I tried again, this time squeezing it into her mouth while rubbing her throat to stimulate a swallowing reflex. Broken Tail made a few feeble sucking noises.

I squeezed the slippery teat while the cow stood patiently, allowing me this unusual intimacy—she was, after all, a range cow. My legs soon ached from squatting, and my neck from tilting my head, but I continued the tedious feeding for another half an hour, and then every two hours after that for the rest of the day.

A touch of pneumonia added a new complication. But despite the infection, the calf rallied, her will to survive strengthening. Again I knelt next to the cow, breathing in her warm, milky smell, but once again, Broken Tail would not take the teat on her own. I forced her mouth open and began the process anew. My hands grew stiff with cold even though steam rose from the cow's moist udder. Half an hour later I stood, slowly unbending my creaky knees. The cow turned and licked her calf, alternating between roughness and gentleness, patience and impatience. I returned to the house defeated.

Two hours later, warm sunlight cast bands of brightness across the corral while two robins, early-spring birds, picked their way through patches of snow looking for kernels of grain. Broken Tail, standing unaided, waited hungrily next to her mother.

"Hey, girls," I greeted them, loosening the chain around the metal gate while telling Freckles to stay. The cow lifted her head and swiveled it in my direction. "Easy now, Mom." Her eyes cut through the corral to where Freckles crouched, then followed me until I knelt next to her, scooting Broken Tail beneath her. I pushed down on the calf's neck and gently aimed her mouth at the udder. A teat brushed against her mouth and, miraculously, she grasped it, butting the cow's udder with her nose.

I eased my hand away, not wanting to disturb the tenuous connection—both of calf to udder and calf to instinct. Broken Tail pulled and pushed on the teat, contracting the thin muscles in her neck as the liquid ran down her throat.

Slowly, I inched my way over to the feed bunk and sat down, feeling a ray of sunlight upon my cheek. The calf's deformed tail began to twitch back and forth, and the cow, with lowered head, began the relaxed, ancient motion of chewing her cud.

As Broken Tail grew, her deformity became even more obvious. Her mother learned to slow her pace to that of her slower daughter.

They were easy to spot out in the pasture, for they were always the last to water, the last to feed. They trailed down the path in single file behind the others, and only rarely did Broken Tail ever try to kick up her heels with the rest of the calves. At branding time I had to help her stand and regain her footing, returning her to her mother's side smelling of smoke and singed hair.

Her future, like ours, is as insecure as her stance, for her death will come sooner than the other calves. Does she live her life in vain, I wonder? For naught? When I ask her this in private moments, with no one else around, she answers me by pushing her slow-moving head beneath my arm and then waits patiently for me to massage her crooked spine.

38

Raising Meat

Buffalo, the staff of life, was plentiful, and a good hunter could produce enough meat in a few hours to feed his family for months.
—Anthony McGinnis[1]

COUNTY FAIR IS LESS THAN two weeks away. Bright Eyes has been such a big part of our lives that it will be hard to look out in the corral and not see him standing there. Matt is doing a better job of facing the fact that he will be sold—and butchered—than am I. Perhaps if we butchered him ourselves, if we came full circle with the experience … ? Instead, he will be loaded into a truck full of 4-H beef, headed for a dank, blood-damp meat-locker plant. I wish, instead, that he could meet his death upon the prairie beneath the sun, amid stalks of scented sage and purple coneflowers.

Matt asked if he could keep Bright Eyes's hide to remember him by. I understood the question, the need behind the question. For I, too, wanted something by which to remember him—our first bucket calf, our first bovine friend.

Bright Eyes comes eagerly when he hears my voice, comes even more eagerly—running and bucking—when he hears Matt's voice. He butts him, half-gently, with his broad, hornless forehead. He likes it when I rub the thick ridge of bone between his ears and the raised scarred remnants of dehorning.

Bright Eyes is friend to all. Tuffy rubs against his legs. Freckles still licks his muzzle and buries her head in the grain bucket with his, sharing his daily ration of corn, oats, and barley.

There will always be a little bit of Bright Eyes in every calf we have, in every Hereford steer I see standing knee-deep in pasture grass, in every T-bone and every hamburger.

He will be there, looking over my shoulder, breathing green breath in my face, when I hear the echoes of such radical slogans as "No Moo by '92," or "Cow Free by '93." I like the slogan our local university extension agent recently heard at a wool growers' convention much better: "Co-exist by '96"—a philosophy more beneficial to the earth than to politics.

Why is it that so many self-proclaimed environmental activists (not the sincere conservationists) neglect to include the calves, cows, and bulls in their picture of the perfect world? Cows are permissible if they're elk; calves are okay if they're walrus; bulls are fine if they're moose. But bovine? The beast who unceasingly feeds us and clothes us somehow no longer charms the news media. The extremists in both camps expect Bright Eyes to carry a heavy burden.

Radical environmentalists have placed a yellow star upon his hornless grass-eating head, and he is forbidden equal status with wild animals; his domesticated bloodline is considered inferior. Those who husband domestic cattle take the blame for poor rangeland, high levels of methane gas in the atmosphere, and clogged arteries.

Radical ranchers (like the frustrated Nevada rancher who chose to bulldoze his way through federal regulations with a D-7 Caterpillar) in turn make so much noise that the public hears only their cries of indignation. The rancher viewed his desperate act as civil disobedience, and it received front-page media coverage, leading a misguided public, once again, to make erroneous assumptions about the nature and stature of America's ranchers.

Rarely do the praiseworthy joint efforts of conservation-minded ranchers and environmentalists make front-page news. The government range technician and the cattleman who kneel, side by side, examining the growth points of a field of bluegrass to decide if the time has come to rest the pasture, do so alone. Their cooperative efforts do not make for sensational reporting. All this places a very heavy burden upon the unsuspecting calf who frolics in the meadow with our son.

Bright Eyes, like Big Red, the Reisland, the Longhorn, and Broken Tail, is destined to die. "But he's had a really good life, better than most, huh Mom?" Matt consoles himself. I find more consolation in the metaphysical, in knowing—or hoping at least—that the essence of Bright Eyes, the good stewardship and love lavished on him since his birth, pays homage to this land. He is our offering to Father Sky and Mother Earth and the Four Directions. He is our offering to God, the one Grandfather of all creation.

Hope can be found in the circle that she, our earth, provides us—the encouraging cycles of death and renewal, the never-ending relationship that exists between us all—bovine, range, and human alike.

I hope I will remember this cycle two weeks from now, when I sit on the wooden bleachers in the sale barn and listen to the auctioneer bellow out, "Now, here we have a good example of a Hereford steer. Maybe not as showy as an expensive club calf—says on the papers he's an orphan calf—but he's slick and shiny as a penny. Long-backed, needs a little finishing, but there's a lot of good beef on the hoof there. Who'll start the bidding? Do I hear fifty cents a pound?"

39

Incarnate

MIST HUNG OVER THE CORRALS, hovering among the gnarled oak trees and dripping from their dark green leaves much as it had a year ago, when Hondo died. Inside the old wooden barn the wind blew through the splintered cracks and knotholes. Although the traditionally hot days of Fair were almost upon us, our Wyoming summer continued to be cool and wet.

I held on tightly to the orange nylon lead rope, part of Matt's homemade calf halter. The self-adjusting halter hung loosely about Bright Eyes's drooping head. There really was no need to hold on tightly while Warren, the veterinarian, probed and prodded. Bright Eyes, too tame for unruly steer behavior, posed no danger. His bloated, distended stomach displaced any thoughts of mischief.

Freckles stood protectively next to Matt, watching the veterinarian's every move. Bright Eyes's left side, where the rumen is located (the first and largest of a cow's four stomachs), protruded like an overinflated balloon. Even the right side, which this morning had been only slightly swollen, now swelled above the spinal column. Warren continued to poke and prod, thumping on Bright Eyes as if he were a ripe watermelon.

This was Warren's second visit of the day. When he responded promptly to our panicked call this morning, the situation had not yet become critical.

"Well, we've definitely got a bloat here. But not a dangerous one. Looks like a dry bloat, too much grain maybe. The frothy bloat's what you don't want. I've seen animals bloat and die within an hour from a frothy bloat—usually from being put out on a fresh alfalfa field."

Matt had led Bright Eyes into the head-catch chute, immobilizing him. Warren had gone to work, pouring half a gallon of mineral oil into a bucket. He inserted a twenty-inch-long stainless steel pipe down Bright Eyes's throat. Then he inserted flexible tubing into the pipe and snaked the tubing into the digestive tract. The gurgling sound of gas escaping up the tube lasted only a few moments.

"Still looks like a dry bloat to me. I hate to do anything drastic. How long until Fair?"

"A little over a week."

"Well, Matt sure can't show his steer if I shave and cut him. Sometimes that's the only thing you can do, though—cut right through the abdomen and clean out the rumen."

Warren fished around with the tube again, hoping to release more gas. Then he sucked on the free end of the hose and quickly put it in the mineral oil. "Here, I'll need you to hold the stomach tube and steel pipe together, so they don't slip apart."

I held tightly to the stainless steel pipe and the tubing. The suction siphoned the oil up the hose and into Bright Eyes. The oil would coat the grain, lubricating the stomach's contents and intestinal tract.

Warren got a ten-gauge needle out of his vet bag and, thumping again on Bright Eyes's side, suddenly jabbed the six-inch-long needle into the rumen. Air escaped, sounding like a deflating bicycle tire. Warren had hoped for the sound of a deflating *tractor* tire.

"Usually tap into a big pocket of air," he said, perplexed. He manipulated the direction of the needle several times, and more air hissed through the opening. "Well, let's hope that helps. You'll have to back him off the grain for a couple days, then ease him back on it. Start with some rolled oats. It'll slow his rate of gain up some, but Matt still ought to be able to show him."

We thanked Warren, waving as his truck pulled up the driveway onto the county road. Matt led Bright Eyes over to the weedless corral by the water tank. Before Warren was even out of sight, Bright Eyes lay down by the fence, groaned, and put his head in the dirt.

"Mom, he doesn't look any better."

"No, he doesn't. Warren said that oil takes three to four hours before it does much good. We'll just have to wait."

As I left to go back to the house, Matt wormed between the corral fence and the steer, then pulled Bright Eyes's heavy head onto his lap. He stroked Bright Eyes's throat while Freckles licked droplets of blood from the punctured left side.

I checked them every half hour. Four hours later he still had not improved but in fact had worsened. I phoned Warren.

"The distention on the left side is worse, and his right side is bloated now too."

Warren sounded discouraged. The oil should have helped with a secondary, dry bloat. "How's the steer acting?"

"Not good. He won't get up and his breathing is labored. His rectum is distended too—a couple of inches."

"Can you bring him in? I'm having office problems—no one's here but me."

"I'll try—if we can get him up."

"Call me back if you can't get him loaded in the trailer. And Page? If it gets desperate ... you saw where I poked him with that needle?"

"Yes, high on his left side."

"Right. Well, if it gets desperate, use a sharp knife—kitchen or pocket, whatever—and jab it into him. You can't hurt him, there's nothing vital there."

Just jab it into him? Only a few days ago, when I had taken Matt to the 4-H office to reserve a stall for Bright Eyes, Matt and I had both fought back tears. That night Matt had confided in me, "If we hadn't found him when his mom left him, the coyotes would have eaten him. I just keep telling myself that that would've been a lot worse than this."

We tried to cajole, then force Bright Eyes to stand. Forcing seven hundred pounds of unwilling animal is not easy. His belly distended grotesquely. The tired, labored moans of his arduous breathing filled the air. His eyes rolled halfway back, his head stretched out in the dirt. Finally, when Warren arrived the second time, we got Bright Eyes to stand and walk stiffly through the cold mist into the old barn, where he was now.

Warren's instruments—bucket, stainless steel pipe, flexible hose, six-inch-long ten-gauge needle—and various bottles of medicine lay within easy reach.

This time, rust-colored bubbles of air hissed from the needle stuck in Bright Eyes's rumen. "I shouldn't be getting any fluid.

Maybe there's more going on here than I thought," Warren mumbled to himself. He pulled the needle out and, thumping again, jabbed it forcefully back into the rumen. More air hissed, more frothy bubbles escaped. "We might have a frothy bloat here, after all."

The frothy bloat medicine didn't work. The belly filled with gas, Bright Eyes became weaker, his condition critical. Mark came home from work early. We loaded the steer in the trailer and took him to the clinic. Warren rolled up his sleeves and filled a stainless steel bucket with warm water and disinfectant. Bright Eyes stood immobilized in the operating chute. Matt stood motionless by his side.

With quick, confident strokes, Warren shaved the hair from an area eighteen inches square—a stroke for each month Matt had nurtured his calf, a stroke for each month leading closer to the show ring.

Injections along the incision site numbed the skin, a spinal injection for pain kept Bright Eyes from straining. A sharp knife cut through the hide, through the muscle, and into the rumen. Rank fermented gas bellowed into the air.

"Mark," Warren asked, "I might need your help." While he reached his hand inside the incision, Mark washed up. "I need you to hold on to the rumen soon as I get it out of here." With one hand Warren pulled open the incision, with the other he fished around for a good grip on Bright Eyes's stomach.

Blood seeped from the wound and trickled onto the cement floor of the clinic. Bright Eyes flinched but stood quietly while Matt rubbed his head. Sarah spoke reassuringly to him, an attempt to reassure herself as well.

"Usually the rumen just pulls up out of there. Has he ever been cut on before?"

"No," answered Mark.

"Ever been injured there, or had an infection?"

"No," answered Mark again.

"The dang thing's adhered to the abdominal wall—lesions or something. Don't understand it. Might account for part of the bloat, though. Rumen can't move around like it ought to."

Bright Eyes tried to move away as Warren forced his hand between the muscle wall and the rumen, severing the connection. Little by little Warren worked his way around, pulling more and more of the rumen free.

"Mark, you hold on to this side—yeah, like that. Just hold on to that so it doesn't slip back inside." Warren splashed water on the rumen, and diluted blood sloshed down Bright Eyes's belly, then ran into the floor drain.

"Page, get me another bucket of warm water, would you? Just put a squirt of that Nolvasan in."

I poured the remaining water, which by now was red, down the drain, rinsed the bucket, then filled it with warm water and disinfectant. Warren had his hand deep inside the rumen, bringing out handfuls of frothy green roughage. He repeated the process again and again until a mound, knee-high, piled up at his feet. Very little grain was interspersed among the chewed hay. Removing his hand from the rumen, he rinsed it in the bucket. Then he plunged his arm elbow-deep back into Bright Eyes, this time groping about for a possible intestinal blockage. Bright Eyes's knees threatened to buckle from stress, but no blockage was found.

The stitching needle moved rapidly and precisely, closing the rumen, the muscle, then the hide. The internal catgut stitches would dissolve; we would remove the external stitches in two weeks. Warren sloshed the last of the disinfectant on Bright Eyes. It ran over the stitches, down his side, and onto the pile of green roughage—washing away the surgical debris, washing away Matt's hopes.

Disappointment at not showing Bright Eyes at Fair and not selling him at the 4-H livestock sale was balanced out by the consoling thought of having him home for another month. When Fair arrived, it became obvious that Bright Eyes never would have stood a chance with the heavy-boned steers who competed for the purple grand champion ribbon. Born a twin, orphaned, forced to rely on our attempts at mothering—Bright Eyes, like Broken Tail, entered the world handicapped.

"Dad," Matt asked, "are we still gonna sell him?"

"Yeah, we can still sell him. Maybe private-treaty. We're bound to know someone who needs some beef this winter."

"Don't we need some beef this winter?"

The question surprised me. Would Matt rather that we butcher him ourselves than sell him to someone else?

"You don't think it would bother you to eat Bright Eyes?" I asked Matt, wondering what my own answer would be, wondering if I could cook Bright Eyes all winter.

"No," he answered. "It would be lots better if *we* butchered him. 'Cause if someone else was eating him, how would we know if they were saying a prayer each time—you know, to say thanks and everything?"

We wouldn't know, of course. So it was decided. Bright Eyes would be staying with us a little longer than we had anticipated. A lot longer, in fact.

40

Big Red and the Reisland

BIG RED, WHO HAD BEEN STRUGGLING to get around in the heavy snows all winter, had become severely lame. She was due to calve within a few weeks, but we were not sure she would make it.

"Guess we should have culled her last fall," I admitted to Mark.

"Yeah, we probably should have—she was an old cow when we got her from J. W. and Lois, and she's not getting any younger. I was hoping we'd get one more calf out of her." Mark smoothed his mustache with his fingers, twisting the ends into a curl.

"Well, if we can get her loaded in the trailer," he continued, "I think we should try to sell her while she can still walk."

It was a business decision, one we both loathed; her belly was full and round with calf. But if she got any more crippled up she wouldn't be able to walk, let alone give birth.

The following Saturday we pushed the cows slowly past the stackyard and down the ice-covered path to the barn, sorting off Big Red before turning the other cows out. She stood alone in the corral, bellowing at the others as they headed back up the slick path. The Reisland stopped, turned her head, answered Big Red with a single bawl, and then trudged on.

Big Red had her own opinion about the situation. She would not allow herself to be loaded into the trailer. We tried cajoling her with hay, we tried tempting her with grain, we roped her and tried pulling her. We even tried whipping her until I saw her belly undulate with movement as the calf inside turned in protest.

"Mark, the calf's moving!" I threw down the rope in disgust. "I can't do this anymore. And it's not working anyway."

"Nothing's working," he snapped in frustration. "She sure as heck won't load. And there's no way we can take her to the sale barn if we can't even get her in the dang trailer."

"Maybe we're not supposed to sell her," I suggested, lowering my voice. "Maybe we're supposed to keep her."

The decision to sell her had been motivated by logical, unemotional business acumen. What I called a money decision. The fact that we couldn't load her made the decision to keep her an easy one—and one we both welcomed—despite the fact that we ran the risk of losing nearly five hundred dollars.

"Should we keep her in the corral 'til she calves, then she wouldn't have to travel so far for food and water?"

"Couldn't hurt to try," Mark answered. "Don't know if we have much choice anyway."

Separated from the others, Big Red stood aimlessly, showing little interest in the hay she shared with the sheep or the cake we tried to feed her. Spring moisture continued to fall, covering the corral with layers of snow. Occasionally the temperature would warm, allowing the snow to melt slightly, then would drop down into the teens, freezing the softened snow into hardened sheets. The corral became a treacherous rink of ice.

One morning, Big Red's lame back legs slipped out from beneath her and sent her sprawling on the ground. Once down, she could not get up. Using ropes tied to her back hooves, we managed to pull her legs under her, but she was still unable to rise.

"We could try hoisting her up, I suppose, but I don't think that would do the calf any good, if it's even still alive."

"The calf's alive," I said stubbornly. "I felt him turning."

"Well, hoisting isn't an option, anyway. There's no way I could get the tractor in here with all this snow. I guess all we can do is carry feed to her and hope she makes it."

We began the ritual of feeding the sheep, then turning them out and shutting the gate so that Big Red could eat. I carried a five-gallon bucket of water to her twice a day, placing a salt block within her reach. She tried a few times to get up but seemed to have no strength in her hips. Discouraged, I thought of Broken Tail. Why another crippled animal?

Big Red was vulnerable, and she knew it. She allowed me to brush her and stroke her head and didn't even seem to mind when I placed my ear against her belly and listened to the calf's heartbeat, which, despite the cow's paralysis, grew stronger each day.

As her heavy bulk settled into the snow, her body heat melted the ice beneath her until she had essentially created a cave around herself with twelve-inch walls of ice. Added to the twice-daily feeding was now the chore of chipping away at the ice to level the ground so that I could shovel her manure out of the hole and keep the birthing area clean.

"Do you think she'll be able to calve?" I asked Mark one day as he chipped the ice away from her hips while I raked the area. The temperature was unseasonably warm, forty-nine degrees, sunny, with enough snow melting that water was running down the draw.

"It'll be a miracle," he said. "She can't even turn herself around. If we're not here when it happens, we'll probably lose 'em both."

One way or the other, we were going to lose Big Red. Even if she survived the calving, then what?

Monday morning, when the other cows showed up at the stackyard for feed, I noticed that the Reisland's udder was bagged up. Her time was near; I had been so concerned about Big Red that I hadn't given her much thought.

"You miss your buddy, old girl?" I asked, expecting no answer. She lifted her head from the hay, mooed once, then buried her nose again, eating in a nervous frenzy despite the balmy weather.

By evening, the storm had hit. Blizzard winds gusted at forty miles an hour, hurling six inches of new snow across the field. The Reisland didn't come in to feed that night. On Tuesday morning six more inches fell, and she still didn't come in with the other cows. She showed up Tuesday night with a flattened belly but no calf at her side. She ate quickly and sparingly, then headed back out into the trees at the west end of the pasture. We hoped the calf was safely sequestered away from the storm.

But when the Reisland came in Wednesday morning alone and with a full udder of milk, ate only a few hurried bites and then left, Mark decided it was time to check on the calf. He headed out across the deep snow that covered the west hay field and found her—a beautiful big heifer. But she was dead, a victim of the ferocious spring blizzard.

The Reisland continued to come in for feed but would stay only long enough to grab a few mouthfuls of hay before passing by Big Red on her way to water, then returning to the snow-covered field where she would stand faithfully by her dead calf for the remainder of the day. What instinct, I wondered, caused her to stand guard by her dead calf? Was she guarding the body from coyotes? Did she still harbor some forlorn hope that her calf would rise?

She hovered over the frozen body for five full days before accepting the calf's death. Her acceptance came sooner than mine.

It was impossible to tell how close Big Red was to giving birth: her bag was buried beneath her and her hips already protruded unnaturally. All pertinent parts were hidden from view. But when her behavior noticeably changed, Mark got up at 2:30 A.M. to check on her. Still no calf.

A second storm hit that night. The next morning, Big Red, who had no shelter, shivered uncontrollably. I covered her with a large blue tarp, weighing it down with a mineral block on one corner and a round log on the other. I tied two corners of the tarp around her neck, like a cape. She looked ridiculous—a cross between a tent and a beached whale. But she appreciated my efforts, and the shivering soon abated. I went out into the blizzard every few hours to readjust the tarp, which, despite being anchored, was dislodged continually by the howling winds. Finally, as evening approached, the storm subsided.

"I think I'll get the Reisland in tomorrow," Mark said at supper. "She still has lots of milk."

"You think she'd take Big Red's calf?"

"She might. If it's born alive."

Two nights later, with the Reisland waiting in the next corral, Big Red started having contractions. I pulled on my coveralls, warm boots, gloves, and Scotch cap and met Mark down at the barn. He was chiseling the walls of ice away from Big Red, trying to make room for the calf that we both hoped was coming.

"Should I open the gate and let the Reisland in?" I asked, scattering some clean hay around Big Red.

"Couldn't hurt. Might as well have her in here from the beginning."

The Reisland approached Big Red and mooed softly. They touched noses for a brief second, then another contraction grabbed Big Red and she tried desperately to roll over onto her side. The Reisland moved to the end of the corral and stood staring off into the distance, her nose lifted to the breeze that blew in from the west hay field.

Mark put the shovel down, lifted Big Red's tail out of the way, and shone the flashlight on her. Two soft hooves and a blue tongue protruded. I ran back to the house to get the disinfectant and the chain calf-pullers, just in case. But we didn't need them. Despite her paralysis, despite the crippled hips, she moaned and pushed and heaved, then out slipped a wet, steaming calf onto the hay-covered snow. A wet, steaming bull calf—warm and alive.

Big Red righted herself and strained her head around, trying desperately to reach her newborn calf. Mark quickly pulled him up to her so that she could begin the task of drying him off. Her long rough tongue wiped the broken sack from his face, clearing the mucus from his nostrils and mouth.

Mark and I leaned against each other, touching for the first time in twenty-four hours. He put his arm around me and we stood quietly, watching the crippled cow with her calf, and I realized that the breeze that fanned my cheek no longer felt piercing but was warm and dry like a Chinook.

Low maternal rumbles filled the night air as Big Red talked to her calf, teaching him to know her scent and recognize her sound. The Reisland heard the noise, turned her gaze away from the west field, and came back over to where her old friend lay helpless in the snow. She sniffed Big Red—their noses touching as they exchanged breath. Then, in what seemed a hopeful gesture, she sniffed the calf, her large nostrils taking in his scent.

His smell was familiar, but not familiar in the way she hoped. He smelled of Big Red's birthing fluids, not her own. *The calf was not hers.* We held our breaths, daring to hope that she would lick him anyway, make some sort of mothering gesture, but she did not. She turned away slowly and wandered back to the far end of the corral, lifting her nose again to take in the scents the breeze brought to her from the west hay field—the field where her dead calf lay.

Big Red's dedication was heartbreaking. The calf stood on gangly legs and moved a few awkward steps away from his mother. She bawled but could not rise and follow. He collapsed in a newborn heap. She bellowed, her message clear. *Come back*. The calf answered. *Come to me*.

The calf's cry stirred the Reisland. She turned away, once more, from the corral's west end and trudged through the snow to the calf. She sniffed him again, smelling his head, his still-wet torso, his damp legs. Then she turned away from the calf and approached her old companion.

Mark and I watched, startled, as she squared herself up, head to head, with Big Red. The Reisland lowered her huge bony Hereford skull and placed it against Big Red's. She dug her feet into the ice and began pushing against Big Red, her massive frame like a bulldozer straining to move a mound of earth. She pushed her shoulders and head into Big Red, butting and grunting, digging her hooves deeper into the frozen snow.

"Are they fighting?" I whispered.

"I don't think so," Mark answered, as amazed as I.

Finally, the Reisland's bulk and strength, coupled with determination, forced the upper half of Big Red's body into a sitting position. The Reisland backed off, and Big Red, for the first time in two weeks, was able to straighten her front legs. She sat back on her haunches and inhaled deeply, her lungs momentarily relieved of the weight of her own mass. Then, with a shudder, she fell forward. From a few feet away, the calf bawled.

The Reisland walked over to the calf, sniffed him, then returned to Big Red. Once again she lowered her head, dug in her hooves, and laid into Big Red.

"She's trying to make her get up," I whispered, aware of the fact that we were being blessed with a rare glimpse into another world. Mark nodded his head and squeezed my shoulder.

Again the Reisland forced Big Red back on her haunches, and again Big Red collapsed forward, unable to support her weight. Three times the drama unfolded. Finally, after the third try, when Big Red was still unable to rise on her crippled back legs, the Reisland turned away.

Mark walked up to the calf, pulled him over next to Big Red, then returned to my side. Big Red mooed to her offspring, and finally able to attend to him, began diligently licking the frozen birth fluids from his coat. The calf answered with insistent cries—the sounds of a fighter determined to survive.

I leaned my head against Mark's shoulder, still afraid that if we spoke about what we had witnessed we would somehow steal the incredible magic from the experience—not only the drama of one old cow trying to help another old cow, but the drama of the crippled giving birth to the young and strong.

Finally, after a few moments of silence, with the warm Chinook caressing our faces, I spoke in a whisper.

"I had it all wrong."

"Had what wrong?"

"Broken Tail. I thought Broken Tail somehow symbolized the futility of our ranch, our future."

"What do you mean?"

"I thought she was a bad omen. Sort of like broken dreams. A sign that the ranch was a dying thing of the past—a sign that we could never pass on to Matt and Sarah what your grandparents passed on to you."

"We can't. It'll never be the same for them. Too many things have changed, too many people don't understand."

"I know it'll never be exactly the same. The old-time ranches are dying off, crippled and beaten, just like Big Red. But look," I said, pointing at the two old cows and the newborn calf, "look at the three of them. They've proven it—proven that no matter how threatened this way of life may be, no matter how fractured and disabled, there is still hope."

"Well, Big Red did manage to have one hell of a good calf," Mark smiled, "despite the odds. Kinda reminds me of you and me—we're managing to raise two pretty good kids, despite the odds. But that calf's not out of the woods yet."

"I know. He may never be out of the woods. Neither are Matt and Sarah—their future's as uncertain as his. But if Big Red and the Reisland are willing to try that hard, so am I."

"I never doubted it," Mark said, turning to look at me. The breeze ruffled his black neckerchief, and the moonlight flashed in his dark, slightly roguish eyes. "I knew when I first met you that you weren't a quitter. That's why I asked you to marry me," the hint of a grin softened the hard line of his mustache, "even if you couldn't dance."

41

Stone Stories

Old Sinaska had said that none among the songs reaches the spirit-realm more quickly than the stone songs. ...

—Ruth Beebe Hill[1]

A T THE TIME OF CREATION, the Cherokee say, the white man was given a stone and the Indian a piece of silver. Despising the stone, the white man threw it away. Finding the silver equally worthless, the Indian discarded it. Later, the white man pocketed the silver as a source of material power; the Indian revered the stone as a source of sacred power.

Peter Nabokov writes of this myth in *Native American Testimony*.[2] I find the myth significant not only because of the wisdom within it, but because there will always be a part of me that reaches out to my Cherokee ancestors—no matter how far back they may be, no matter how diluted their blood in me has become. *All* the blood of my ancestors has been diluted: French, English, Scotch-Irish, Dutch. I am a compilation of peoples—a compilation of diverse stories. And from these compilations emerge new stories, new blood.

Stone symbolism is an ancient expression of man's search for his own origins, and for assurance of his own immortality. In the Brule Sioux creation story "Stone Boy," a young girl swallows a pebble hoping it will end her life only to discover that the pebble grows within her like a child, and she soon gives birth to a boy with great powers. The Stone Boy is later instructed by a group of round gray stones (whose language he is able to understand) to conduct a ceremony using heated rocks and combining fire, water, and air to bring about the resurrection of his dead uncles. Through this experience, the boy learns that there is a sacredness within all stones. *Tunka*, the sacred stone, becomes symbolic of *Tunkashila*, the Grandfather Spirit.[3]

"*Yuwipi wasicun*," says Lame Deer, holy man of the Lakota, "is also another name for *Tunka*, our oldest god. ... The ancient ones worshipped this god in the form of a huge stone painted red. The old word for god and the old word for stone are the same— *Tunkashila*, grandfather—but it is also a name for the Great Spirit."[4]

According to Lame Deer, the Lakota name for Moses (of the Old Testament) is the Holy White Stone Man. He is respected among the Lakota because he worships in the Indian way; he went alone to the top of a mountain to seek his God, and a vision, and he returned with the words of his God carved in stone.

References to stones and rocks abound in the Bible, both in the Old Testament and the New Testament. From Psalm 19:14, "O Lord, my rock and my redeemer," and from Isaiah 26:4, "Trust in the Lord forever, for in God the Lord, we have an everlasting Rock." From 1 Corinthians 10:4, "... and all drank the same spiritual drink, for they were drinking from a spiritual rock which followed them; and the rock was Christ." And from Revelation 2:2, "To him who overcomes, to him I will give some of the hidden manna, and I will give him a white stone ... ."

There is always symbolism within symbolism: "Listen to me, you who pursue righteousness, who seek the Lord. Look to the rock from which you were hewn, and to the quarry from which you were dug. ..." (Isaiah 51:1)

It was not until recently that I began searching for symbolic "rocks" in my own life. But other than the fact that my children's great-great-great-grandfather was a stonecutter from Maine, a hewer of marble and carver of rock, I could remember few significant events. Yet at the same time, I was desperately seeking to know more about "the rock from which I was hewn ... the quarry from which I was dug." Was that not what my quest for ancestral ties and traditional roots was all about? And did not this quest at the same time lead me back not only to my physical origins but to my spiritual origins as well?

Oftentimes, the truths that are the most difficult for me to grasp are the truths most obvious to my children. While I struggle with philosophical complexities, they accept life's simplicity.

At a writer's conference in Jackson Hole a few years ago, I purchased two small arrowheads as souvenirs for Matt and Sarah, paying twenty-five cents apiece for the factory-chiseled arrowheads. Sarah and Matt both enjoyed hunting for artifacts—signs of others who have lived on this same land—and they enjoyed collecting interesting stones; especially Sarah, who has had an affinity for stones since she was first able to toddle around outside. When I brought the replicas home and gave Sarah hers, she was ecstatic.

"A real arrowhead, Mom!" she said, caressing the smooth rock between her fingers.

"Honey, it's not special like a *real* arrowhead," I corrected her. "It's only a rock carved to *look* like an old arrowhead."

"But, Mommy," she insisted, "the stone isn't new, is it? It's old, isn't it?"

"Yes, honey, it's old. Very old. All stones are very old."

"Then it is special, Mom," she said simply. "*It is special.*"

Stories have a way of weaving themselves into our lives, becoming more meaningful, more colorful, more all-encompassing. At another workshop, this one in Riverton, Wyoming, I was able to hear Simon Ortiz, an American Indian poet and storyteller from Acoma Pueblo, New Mexico.

"My sense of self goes clear back to the creation of dawn, and forward to the present," he said. "There is a sense of continuity of consciousness. ... I have been a poet for thirty thousand years." There are probably stone lyrics hidden within all his poems.

He went on to tell about his family, their histories, and their stories, explaining (among other things) Acoma naming traditions. He too has a daughter named Sarah, who shares the same middle name, Marie, as our Sarah.

"Her Indian name means, well, the closest I can come is to say it means *Crushed Stones.*"

I jotted down the story of the factory arrowhead and of the lesson Sarah had taught me about the sacredness of all stones and gave it to Mr. Ortiz following the workshop. Later, after he had read it, he smiled warmly and said, "It is a beautiful story. Do you mind if I tell my daughter?"

And so the story is shared, as most stories are meant to be. Given time, Sarah's story may even take on the sacredness of myth, as did the Cherokee creation story about the stone and the piece of silver. But in this new story of Sarah's and mine, this embryonic myth, the white man does not throw away the stone. Instead, in this new, female, version, the white child caresses it between *her* fingers, teaching her elder a long-forgotten ancient truth—passed down from long-forgotten ancestors.

42

The Barn Bequeathed

O Great Spirit, bring to our white brothers the wisdom of Nature and the knowledge that if her laws are obeyed this land will again flourish and grasses and trees will grow as before. ... Bring to all the knowledge that great cities live only through the bounty of the good earth beyond their paved streets and towers of stone and steel.

—Jasper Saunkeah, Cherokee[1]

I STAND IN THE BARN, pitchfork in hand. Mark, outside, leans for a moment against the south side of the barn. One leg is bent—his cowboy boot braced against the gray wood. His hands rest in the front pockets of his Wranglers. His black hat shades his eyes, his mustache, and the stem of hay on which he chews.

I jab at an old pile of hay with the pitchfork and toss it into a stall for bedding. The tines of the fork scrape the wooden floor where the hay, our hay, has accumulated.

A few short years ago Mark swept dusty, moldy hay from the floor of this orphaned barn, sweeping away the signs of other owners, other lives. Now our lives are ingrained in the weathered wood, our children's voices ring from the rafters. Romie's halter hangs by the door, sage grows among the marigolds that bloom on Hondo's nearby grave.

It is the barn back in Colorado that now stands orphaned, abandoned—an anachronism amid subdivisions. Only a few apple trees still produce fruit; the stone applehouse is scheduled to be torn down. The shadow of Wildcat Mountain falls upon the shrinking alfalfa fields, upon the graves of Mark's ancestors, upon the scattered bones of the Ute and Arapaho, and upon even *their* predecessors.

Does anyone still know Chief Colorow once rode these hills? Does anyone care? Does anyone still listen for the echo of drums, or the sound of a thousand black-horned buffalo? Even the hoofbeats of the white-horned cattle are fading from our nation's memory.

In the pasture beyond Hondo's grave, Matt and Sarah walk with heads bent. They are in search of wild onions—they claim they will eat a dozen, but I know it will only take one to satisfy their craving.

A breeze blows against the shaded north side of the barn. The south side, where Mark stands, is bright with sun. He straightens, lowering his bent leg. With the toe of his cowboy boot he begins digging small holes in the dirt, as his father did a quarter of a century ago when searching for his lost wedding ring.

Instead, Mark finds the sprouts of young plants pushing up from the old gnarled roots of the oak trees. His father's ring, lost in Colorado soil, may never be found, but his family's roots—generations deep—grow strong once again in new, fertile soil.

Perhaps the vision Black Elk had when standing on Harney Peak *is* large enough to encompass even us. He saw that his people's sacred hoop was only one of many sacred hoops belonging to many peoples living together as one spiritual being. "In the center grew one mighty flowering tree to shelter all the children of one mother and one father. And I saw that it was holy."[2]

If we are to learn the wisdom of traditional truths inheritant within all cultures, then we must begin to incorporate these truths into our own lives in very intimate, personal ways. We must, as Jasper Saunkeah says, be taught anew that if the laws of nature are obeyed, the earth and her people will once again flourish. And to whom does Jasper Saunkeah go with this plea? To the Great Spirit, the supreme lawmaker, God.

Ancient whispers abound. They swirl among us, filling the barn as the breeze filters in through the splintered walls. We begin to hear the ancient voices, see the ancient trails. Slowly, like the snow-covered path Redy pawed and the worn trail down which Broken Tail limped, a well-trod path emerges, marked with timeless yet sometimes faltering footsteps. New stories landscape the edges of the path, built upon layers of stories that have been silent for generations, perhaps centuries.

I am tempted to press my ear to the path and listen for the echo of a Baine Thimbleskane wagon rumbling across the plains, with an asthmatic boy eagerly looking westward. I am tempted to seek out the heat of the Mojave Desert, to listen for the sounds my grandmother Effie was unable to hear. Or perhaps I will walk the shores of the Potato River in the old Choctaw nation, for I have just learned that it was on the shores of this river that my grandmother Helen was born. "*Mahala*," my great-aunt writes, "was your great-great-great grandmother's name. It means 'Indian Maiden.' " I press her letter to my heart and whisper, "*Mahala, Mahala*," as if it were an ancient sacred prayer.

The temptation is strong.

But perhaps, for the moment, I will listen to the sound of my children, who are here and now, whose voices call out to the future in expectant songs of hope. I will try to see the world through their wondrous eyes—a world worthy of celebration and laughter.

High in the loft a pigeon coos and a feather drifts down, settling onto the hay layered upon the wooden floor. Sunlight spills through the open door of the barn and, suspended in this beam of light, the hay dust glimmers like stars in the night sky of a new moon.

Epilogue

The Song of Songs
Which Is Wyoming's

But now ask the beasts, and let them teach you; And the birds of the heavens, and let them tell you. Or speak to the earth, and let it teach you. ...

—Job 12:7, 8

ROMIE, AFTER TWO DECADES of being together, I watch you walk away from me, led by my young daughter. You stumble. Your brittle legs betray you, and I see you as others must—an old horse whose prime has long since passed. I have been asked by others why we don't shoot you.

Are you miserable? Do your old bones ache in the cold? Is it, indeed, time to put you *out of your misery?* Your almond-shaped eyes, still brown with the black widening slit of a pupil, do not look pained. They look weary, but full of memories.

You and I grew up together. You a skittish four-year-old, I a young girl of fifteen. You gave me freedom, and I gave you free rein. Together we had courage enough to conquer the world, to try anything. We swam in the forbidden pond, and I held on to your tail while your strong legs and hooves pumped furiously only inches from my bare limbs. I rode you, wet and dripping, my cutoff jeans rubbing against the roan hairs and horse-stall dust of your back.

Our first summer together I rode you passionately, with abandon. Each evening, while you rested in the shadows of the stables, I soaked my bruised thighs in tepid bath water. I held palmfuls of crystal bubbles to my breasts and closed my eyes, on the brink of womanhood. I contemplated the swirls of petrified wood gleaned from the shores of the Platte, wondering whether—and later knowing—that our wild bareback rides through green, wet canals and over fields of ripening mustard had robbed my first lover of his rightful badge of conquest.

And now I watch the other horses run you off. They bare their teeth and you retreat with ears laid flat in defiance. You walk away, and I see how like an old woman you have become. Your bent and crooked legs would seem almost spindly were it not for the fine-boned Arabian petiteness that has always made you beautiful.

What will I do when you die? I am barely surviving Hondo's death. But you, Romie, you are my youth, my link to times of daring excitement, my doorway from the magical world of Black Beauty to the vestibule of the boudoir.

You weaned me from the lap of my father to the arms of a man. A girl and a horse—that first sense of knowing that my body could link up exquisitely with the strong, dominant body of another. But now, this symbol of my yearning, my exploration, stumbles down a slight hill as if it were a mountain.

Redy carries on. Sarah stretches up and away. Memories cloak and comfort. Time has, for each of us, a different measure. Your decline in many ways frees me to become a new woman whose past is just beginning to catch up with the future.

Actually, it is *you*, Wyoming, and not Redy, who has taken over Romie's role in my life. *Our* affair began despite my grudging nature, despite my loyalty to Colorado—land of my youth. At first, these gentle black hills hid their power from me. I compared your eastern edges to the Rockies of my childhood and thought them not worthy of my devotion.

I recoiled from your red-slashed buttes, scoffed at those who called them mountains; these mere places where your face wrinkled with age. I was, at first, deaf to the ancient whispers of those who had found shelter within your arms. I trod the ancient paths but saw only my own footsteps.

How is it, then, that you crept like Romie and, yes, especially like Mark, into my being—so quietly that I did not notice? Was it when I mistook your eagle for a black-baldy calf—watching as he rose from the prairie and, ever wary of my scrutiny, circled and soared away? Was that when the deed was done?

I, who never thought I would love any place as I had loved the cottonwood-forested banks of the Platte, found myself succumbing to your subtle charms. I learned your history, learned the stories of your Lakota and of my own pioneering relatives. You taught me that the land is the only tangible connection to the past that I really need. *You* are my ancestor primeval.

You demanded new loyalty. You did not tolerate lack of commitment, ambivalence, the kiss of death that threatens to sour the winds that are your breath. I must either love you totally or leave you. There is no in-between. One cannot practice sacred ecology halfheartedly.

Sitting in cool shade, sheltered from your summer sun, I dreamt of faraway places, forgetting that we had wed, for better or for worse. Your winter snapped me out of my contentment, this fickle reverie, and drew me to you like a jealous lover.

No, it was not the eagle who soared above your trees. Our consummation happened long before that. It was easy for you to slip unnoticed into my realm. And so you did. With wild and unpredictable temperament and too-brief flirtations, I let you touch those private places, afraid that I would be given only one chance to sleep, invited, in the protected crevices of your red-eroded loins.

I did not realize the rains that ran down your sinewy ridges would wash from me all desire for the bright, fickle city lights of my younger days. I peered into coyote dens tucked into washouts and saw only darkness. When I heard, under a full moon, the passionate howls, it was too late. There was no returning to a state of indifference.

It was not fair of you to tease me with your elusive antelope, to flaunt your whitetail deer before my modern human eyes. You seduced me with the perfume of your summer sage, kindled memories of other women, dark-skinned and light.

But then, when I dreamt of home, of innocent days unburdened by painful truths, of running like the wind upon Romie's back in pursuit of the mythical buffalo, you pulled tight your sovereign rein and let loose the fury of your winter. You taught me that the true mythology of the buffalo, like the words of the Bible, must not be taken lightly. "Ask the beasts," it is written in Job. "Speak to the earth, and let it teach you."

Your storm raged around me, the vibration of your anger reaching deep chords. When I dared to open my eyes, you offered me a crystalline world, frosted brilliance glittering from every branch, a chance to start anew.

Like a reprimanded child, I pushed thoughts of former places from my consciousness and let you stake your claim on my no-longer-innocent soul.

It would have been easier had I not sifted your red earth through my fingers—had I not breathed in the musky odor of your mountain asters. I should have turned away from your hideless tipi rings, from your bouquets of dried weeds turned to silver sage, and from the shadows of your buffalo bones before it was too late. But I did not.

And now you will not let me go. You demand an enlightened future—whose very hope lies in the lessons of the past—a past that *all* our ancestors bequeath to *all* of us.

Notes

Preface: The Dawning of Connection

1. Peter Nabokov, ed., *Native American Testimony* (New York: Viking, 1991), 50.

2. Barbara Means Adams, *Prayers of Smoke* (Berkeley, Calif.: Celestial Arts, 1990), 33, 157.

3. Fred Dubray, quoted in Jacqueline W. Sletto, "Prairie Tribes and the Buffalo," *Native Peoples Magazine* (Winter 1993): 38.

Prologue: The Barn Inherited

1. Josephine Lowell Marr, *Douglas County: A Historical Journey* (Gunnison, Colo.: B & B Printers), 113.

2. Ibid.

3. Ibid., 10.

4. Ibid., 117, 184. For further reading on the families of Douglas County, see Douglas County Historical Society, *Our Heritage: People of Douglas County* (Shawnee Mission, Kans.: Inter-Collegiate Press).

Chapter 2: The Forked Path

1. Clyde A. Milner II, Carole A. O'Connor, and Martha A. Sandweiss, eds., *The Oxford History of the American West* (New York: Oxford University Press, 1994), 177; Robert L. Perkin, *The First Hundred Years* (New York: Doubleday, 1959), 261.

2. John C. Neihardt, *Black Elk Speaks* (New York: Pocket Books, 1972), 233.

3. Perkin, *First Hundred Years*, 27.

4. Ibid., 27–28.

Chapter 3: Planting Roots, Raising Logs

1. Neihardt, *Black Elk Speaks,* 230.

2. Ibid., 212–213.

Chapter 5: Old Shadows, New Stories

1. Robert Bly, quoted in Bill Moyers, *A World of Ideas II* (New York: Doubleday, 1990), 267.

2. "The Black Hills, Once Hunting Grounds of the Red Men," *National*

Geographic, vol. 52 (July/December 1927). For further reading, see: Anthony McGinnis, *Counting Coup and Cutting Horses: Intertribal Warfare on the Northern Plains* (Evergreen, Colo.: Cordillera Press, 1990); George Hyde, *Red Cloud's Folk: A History of the Oglala Sioux* (Norman: University of Oklahoma Press, 1937).

3. Adams, *Prayers of Smoke,* 52–54.

Chapter 6: Simon

1. Paula Gunn Allen, *Grandmothers of the Light: A Medicine Woman's Sourcebook* (Boston: Beacon Press, 1991), 5.

Chapter 7: Eagle Feathers and Wounded Spirits

1. Adams, *Prayers of Smoke,* 65.
2. Ibid., 66–68.
3. Ibid., 68.
4. Willa Cather, *O Pioneers!* (Boston: Houghton Mifflin, 1913), 71.

Chapter 8: If Trees Could Talk

1. Lauren Brown, *Grasslands: The Audubon Society Nature Guides* (New York: Alfred A. Knopf, 1985), 520.
2. Perkin, *First Hundred Years,* 262.
3. Ibid., 281–284.
4. Wallace Stegner, *The American West as Living Space* (Ann Arbor: University of Michigan Press, 1987), 47.
5. Ibid., 46.
6. Ibid., 60.
7. Ibid.
8. M. E. Ensminger, *Animal Science,* 7th ed. (Danville, Ill.: Interstate Printers and Publishers, 1977), 312, 321.

Chapter 9: Deerstalking

1. Arthur Amiotte, quoted in *Parabola: The Magazine of Myth and Tradition* XVII, no. 3 (Fall 1992): 30.

Chapter 10: Forced to Trade

1. Standing Bear of the Poncas, quoted in Thomas Tibbles, *Buckskin and Blanket Days* (New York: Doubleday, 1957), 201.
2. John (Fire) Lame Deer and Richard Erdoes, *Lame Deer: Seeker of Visions* (New York: Washington Square Press, 1972), 197, 199–200.
3. Ibid., 200.

Chapter 11: Elusive Prey

1. Wallace Black Elk and William S. Lyon, *Black Elk: The Sacred Ways of a Lakota* (San Francisco: HarperSanFrancisco, 1990), 3.

Chapter 12: Turkey Tracks
1. Joyce Sequichie Hifler, *A Cherokee Feast of Days* (Tulsa, Okla.: Council Oak Books, 1992), 7.

Chapter 14: The Dance Goes On
1. Mari Sandoz, *These Were the Sioux* (Lincoln: University of Nebraska Press, 1961), 99.
2. Ibid.

Chapter 15: Growing Velvet
1. Dallas Chief Eagle, quoted in Brad Steiger, *Indian Medicine Power* (West Chester, Pa.: Para Research, a division of Schiffer Publishing, 1984), 140.

Chapter 17: Purring
1. Dhyani Ywahoo, Priestcraft Holder of the Ani Gadoah Clan, Tsalagi (Cherokee) Nation, quoted in Bobette Perrone, H. Henrietta Stockel, and Victoria Krueger, *Medicine Women, Curanderas, and Women Doctors* (Norman: University of Oklahoma Press, 1989), 69–72.
2. Wilma Mankiller and Michael Wallis, *Mankiller: A Chief and Her People* (New York: St. Martin's, 1993), 20.
3. Ywahoo, in Perrone, Stockel, and Krueger, *Medicine Women,* 80, 82.

Chapter 19: Black Jack
1. Brooke Medicine Eagle, *Buffalo Woman Comes Singing* (New York: Ballantine, 1991), 363.
2. *The Merck Veterinary Manual,* 6th ed. (Rahway, N.J.: Merck & Co., 1986), 604–605.

Chapter 20: The Red Shirt
1. John (Fire) Lame Deer, quoted in Allen, *Grandmothers of the Light,* 23.

Chapter 23: Renewals
1. Evelyn Eaton, *Snowy Earth Comes Gliding* (Independence, Calif.: Draco Foundation and Bear Tribe Publishing), 25.
2. Lansing Christman, quoted in *Ideals Magazine* (Ideals Publishing, Nashville, Tenn., vol. 47, no. 2, March), 50, 51.
3. Anonymous Indian prayer.
4. Christman, quoted in *Ideals Magazine.*

Chapter 24: Lambing
1. Black Elk and Lyon, *Black Elk,* 4.

Chapter 25: Layers of Time
1. Dhyani Ywahoo, quoted in Perrone, Stockel, and Krueger, *Medicine Women,* 58.

Chapter 28: Gifts

1. William Willoya and Vinson Brown, *Warriors of the Rainbow* (Happy Camp, Calif.: Naturegraph Publishers, 1962), 9.

Chapter 29: Gathering Bones

1. Willoya and Brown, *Warriors of the Rainbow*, 23.

Chapter 31: Our Own Cows

1. Trebbe Johnson, quoted in *Parabola: The Magazine of Myth and Tradition* XVI, no. 2 (Summer 1991): 83.

2. Ibid., 82–83.

3. Ibid., 83.

Chapter 32: The Longhorn Calf

1. Ed McGaa, Eagle Man, *Mother Earth Spirituality* (San Francisco: HarperSanFrancisco, 1990), xvii.

Chapter 33: Rites

1. Joseph Epes Brown, *Animals of the Soul* (Rockport, Mass.: Element Books, 1992), 13–14.

2. Laurens van der Post, quoted in *Parabola: The Magazine of Myth and Tradition* XVI, no. 2 (Summer 1991): 16.

Chapter 35: Call of Duty

1. Brown, *Animals of the Soul*, 2–3.

Chapter 38: Raising Meat

1. McGinnis, *Counting Coup*, 51.

Chapter 41: Stone Stories

1. Ruth Beebe Hill, *Hanta Yo* (New York: Doubleday, 1979), 28.

2. Nabokov, *Native American Testimony*, 33.

3. Richard Erdoes and Alfonso Ortiz, eds., *American Indian Myths and Legends* (New York: Pantheon, 1984), 15–19.

4. Lame Deer and Erdoes, *Lame Deer*, 174.

Chapter 42: The Barn Bequeathed

1. Jasper Saunkeah, quoted in Steiger, *Indian Medicine Power*, 201.

2. Neihardt, *Black Elk Speaks*, 36.